The Republic of Choice

The Republic of Choice

Law, Authority, and Culture

Lawrence M. Friedman

Harvard University Press
Cambridge, Massachusetts
London, England

To Leah

First Harvard University Press paperback edition, 1994

Library of Congress Cataloging-in-Publication Data
Friedman, Lawrence Meir, 1930-
  The republic of choice : law, authority, and culture / Lawrence M.
  Friedman.
    p.   cm.
  Bibliography: p.
  Includes index.
  ISBN 0-674-76260-6 (alk. paper) (cloth)
  ISBN 0-674-76261-4 (pbk.)
  1. Law—Philosophy. 2. Sociological jurisprudence. 3. Culture
  and law. 4. Civil rights. 5. Individualism. I. Title.
K230.F75R47 1990   89-34329
340'.1—dc20   CIP

Acknowledgments

I want to thank Marc Galanter, Robert Gordon, Thomas Grey, Robert Kagan, Robert Post, David Rosenhan, Deborah Rhode, Joyce Sterling, Gunther Teubner, and Stanton Wheeler for valuable comments; and Thomas Russell and Benjamin Quinones for research assistance. Thanks too to Joy St. John for her enormous patience and help. I also owe a great debt to the staff of the Stanford Law Library for their wonderful and courteous assistance.

Contents

tinct but are in fact organically linked. First, Western societies are societies of *rights*, which means, among other things, that they are held together by a tough, pervasive skeleton of *laws*—especially laws which grant, define, and protect a network of entitlements. Second, their citizens think of themselves as free, unique individuals, each possessing his or her zone of privacy, his or her precious realm of free choice. Rights, laws, free choice: these are crucial terms and ideas in modern Western society. They are crucial in ways that were not true in the past and may not be true in other parts of the world.

The central argument of this book is quite simple. The starting point is the modern concept of the *individual*, at least as Western societies frame it. In these societies, in the twentieth century, people firmly believe in the value of individual rights and individual freedom. "People" is of course a vague word; I mean to say that the belief is widely diffused among various publics. Admittedly, different people have different ideas on the subject—rich and poor; black and white; men and women; young and old. Our Rip Van Winkle is not entirely wrong to be surprised; individuals trapped in misery and failure are probably much less likely to hold up the banner of rights than well-off and well-positioned people. But the well-positioned are a vast and powerful group; and, in some ways, the same current seems to flow through all strata and levels of society, essentially in a single direction. The behavior and language of people in Western societies could be said to disclose certain underlying premises and notions: first, the *individual* is the starting point and ending point of life; second, a wide zone of free *choice* is what makes an individual. *Choice* is therefore vital, fundamental: the right to develop oneself, to build up a life suited to oneself uniquely, to realize and aggrandize the self, through free, open selection among forms, models, and ways of living.

This concept of individualism is sharply different from the individualism of the nineteenth century, which placed a much higher value on self-control and discipline, on traditional values, and on the norms of the group. It is often said that the nineteenth century was an age of individualism, while the twentieth century is an age of collectivism and conformity. "Individualism" is therefore said to be in crisis today; in our urban, industrial anthills the individual disappears, and mass society takes over. In a similar vein, some critics argue that in comparison to the nineteenth century, modern Western societies severely restrict choice, consent, and freedom; that there is

Contents

ONE

Introduction

A S WINTER drew near, in 1985, the weather in New York City turned ugly. Temperature dropped below freezing; street people were faced with nights of intense cold and bitter suffering. The city responded by issuing an order to pick up the homeless, the drifters, the derelicts, and bring them into municipal shelters—by force, if necessary. The intentions were perhaps good, but some among the homeless resisted; they did not want to go, either because they were afraid of the horrors of municipal shelters, or because they were confused and befuddled, or for other reasons. A white man who wore a green knit cap and lived in a "coffinlike cardboard box," talked to a reporter about "freedom" and said, "They can't take me, unless I do something wrong."[1] And on the evening news Americans could watch a remarkable dialogue between a homeless black man and a reporter. The black man complained with great vigor about the city's plan. "They can't do that to us," he said. He climaxed his argument with this simple point: "We've got rights."

The television audience, arguably, saw nothing astonishing here. A modern Rip Van Winkle, however, coming back to consciousness after a century of sleep, might have reacted with utter amazement. That the city would try to help the homeless would not be, in itself, so startling; that some of them might resist—well, those things happen. But for a person so down and out to advance so strong a claim of right—for him to argue in so legalistic a way—this would be a source of paradox and wonder. Yet the voices of the two men are in some ways deeply characteristic of our society; they are authentic, and, to a degree, they represent the distinctive core, the very marrow, of contemporary American civilization. They do so in ways that seem distinct but are in fact organically linked. First, Western societies are societies of *rights*, which means, among other things, that they are held together by a tough, pervasive skeleton of *laws*—especially laws which grant, define, and protect a network of entitlements. Second, their citizens think of themselves as free, unique individuals, each possessing his or her zone of privacy, his or her precious realm of free choice. Rights, laws, free choice: these are crucial terms and ideas in modern Western society. They are crucial in ways that were not true in the past and may not be true in other parts of the world.

The central argument of this book is quite simple. The starting point is the modern concept of the *individual,* at least as Western societies frame it. In these societies, in the twentieth century, people firmly believe in the value of individual rights and individual freedom. "People" is of course a vague word; I mean to say that the belief is widely diffused among various publics. Admittedly, different people have different ideas on the subject—rich and poor; black and white; men and women; young and old. Our Rip Van Winkle is not entirely wrong to be surprised; individuals trapped in misery and failure are probably much less likely to hold up the banner of rights than well-off and well-positioned people. But the well-positioned are a vast and powerful group; and, in some ways, the same current seems to flow through all strata and levels of society, essentially in a single direction. The behavior and language of people in Western societies could be said to disclose certain underlying premises and notions: first, the *individual* is the starting point and ending point of life; second, a wide zone of free *choice* is what makes an individual. *Choice* is therefore vital, fundamental: the right to develop oneself, to build up a life suited to oneself uniquely, to realize and aggrandize the self, through free, open selection among forms, models, and ways of living.

This concept of individualism is sharply different from the individualism of the nineteenth century, which placed a much higher value on self-control and discipline, on traditional values, and on the norms of the group. It is often said that the nineteenth century was an age of individualism, while the twentieth century is an age of collectivism and conformity. "Individualism" is therefore said to be in crisis today; in our urban, industrial anthills the individual disappears, and mass society takes over. In a similar vein, some critics argue that in comparison to the nineteenth century, modern Western societies severely restrict choice, consent, and freedom; that there is less liberty in societies today than in the past; and that liberty is and probably always was a mirage. Statements along these lines, I believe, seriously distort important aspects of contemporary reality. They misapprehend what present-day "individualism" is all about. Modern individuals are, if anything, more individualistic than their nineteenth-century forebears. This is because we live in what I call the "republic of choice." It is a world in which the right to "be oneself," to *choose* oneself, is placed in a special and privileged position; in which *expression* is favored over *self-control*; in which *achievement* is valued over inborn or inherited traits and in which *achievement* is defined in subjective, personal terms, rather than in objective, social terms. All this, of course, is a matter of more or less. Society is complex, and individuals are, well, individual. This hardly needs to be said. This is a book about trends and directions, not about immutable physical laws.

At any rate, the concept of the individual, in its peculiar modern form, is the starting point of our analysis. What follows is an exploration of causes and consequences in two key areas of social life: the legal system, and the structure of authority more generally. These are important sectors, though their importance (especially as regards the legal system) is easy to overlook. What kind of legal system, and what types of authority structures, does a society create when the Western idea of individualism, the glorification of free, open *choice*, comes to dominate the culture or at least to extend its domain in a radical way? The rest of these pages will be devoted to sketching out an answer.

Thus this book is about *law* and *authority* in the modern West. More precisely, it is about the distinctiveness of law and authority in the modern West. I assume, as a governing principle, that essential structures and features of law are not autonomous; that is, that legal systems are not self-contained, closed entities, responding entirely to their own logic, traditions, and imperatives. The autonomy of law is a much discussed issue these days among legal scholars.[2] It seems to be making something of a comeback among sociolegal theorists. Scholars think they see evidence of a tough and durable independence; they picture the legal world as a powerful cultural entity; they look on lawyers and judges as a kind of tribe with its own tight, imperial customs, which change slowly, if at all, and resist the encroachments of the outside world.

No one seriously asserts, of course, that law and legal systems are *totally* autonomous. In my view, even the case for partial autonomy has not been well established.[3] In any event, it is not necessary to resolve this dispute. It is clear enough to every legal scholar that the structures and substance of law depend, at least to *some* degree, on events and movements in society at large. The argument starts, then, from the (plausible) assumption that social structure, technology, and political arrangements have an impact on the way people think and act; and that these thoughts and actions in turn create (I use the word deliberately) configurations of law specific to a given time and place. The legal system is an elaborate working machine, but the members of the society in which the machine is placed are responsible for programing it; they plug it in and turn it on; they can turn it off as well. Law is a form of authority, but there are other modes and manners of exerting authority in society; and these are among the factors that decisively shape the law.

To tell a meaningful story about modern law, one cannot talk only about law itself, that is, law as it is lived and felt within the world of the jurists. Nor is the story best told in the language of law and in the categories that are peculiar to law. One has to start the story somewhere else, that is, outside the law itself. No doubt this very distinction—between "law" and "society"—is in an important sense artificial; the legal system is part of society in the same way that muscles and the circulation system are part of the body; the legal system does not and cannot exist as a viable, independent entity.[4] But we must separate law from society for the purpose of analysis, just as we distinguish muscles from nerves and bones, in order to describe and explain legal phenomena. In so doing we necessarily assume an "inside" and an "outside." (This does not imply "autonomy" of systems, any more than would the distinction between body and heart.) Popular culture also assumes an inside ("law") and an outside ("society"). And popular culture is where we start—more specifically popular *legal culture*, by which we mean people's ideas, attitudes, and expectations about law and legal process. Out of the legal culture flow lines of force, pressures, and demands that envelop legal institutions and ultimately determine their shape.[5]

This book is centrally concerned with law, secondarily with authority; but before I can focus on these subjects, two prior questions need to be answered, at least in a tentative way. I began with the premise that what is "out there" in society shapes the law. But infinite numbers of events, structures, and instructions are "out there." Which characteristics of modern Western society can be singled out as crucial or central, in shaping legal arrangements? What aspects of personality, habits of thought, and attitudes toward law most accurately explain how and why legal arrangements took their present form?

The second question is inseparable from the first. Where did these crucial characteristics come from? How did we get these characteristics, and why? Obviously, these questions are so broad that no precise answer is possible; but we can at least sketch out the rough outline of an answer. If we can grasp a few fundamental traits of modern society, we can then go a step further and ask what regimes of authority and what legal structures such a society is likely to develop. Of course, the *actual* legal structures of Western societies, and the *actual* regimes of authority, which are all around us, act in a rough way as a check on our conclusions. In addition, a subsidiary question hums lightly but persistently throughout: who counts as the "we" that appears in these various questions and propositions? If our statements and conclusions are correct at all, are they correct only for Americans, for the whole modern West, or for the wider world? And within societies, are the conclusions true of everybody, or only some people; and if only some people, who?

The general line of argument has already been hinted at. *What are we like?* We are rights-conscious and individualistic, at least as compared to people in the past. There is a central concern with the development of the self and the molding of unique individuals. The core mechanism for constituting the self, according to the prevailing point of view, is through free and unrestrained choice, exercised with regard to many and competitive options. *How did we get this way?* Through a complex historical process; no simple answer is possible. But in a word; through modernization. What "modernity" is, and how it evolved, are themselves vexed questions. Obviously, it would go beyond the scope of this book to deal with the long-term development of Western society. The basic argument, in fact, only takes account of a fairly short span of time—the last century and a half, give or take a decade or two; that is, the period beginning with the early nineteenth century. This time-span, short as it is, is crowded with events and innovations. It has been a time of rampant change. "Modernization" is a convenient name for many of these changes. The process has obvious relevance to law and authority, and to social structure in general.

My key concepts, individualism and choice, are of course familiar terms. At the same time, they have complex meanings—meanings that shift and vary over time and from culture to culture; they are slippery, kaleidoscopic terms. Part of the story is about how the meanings of concepts have changed in the course of the last century or so.

The way a society actually governs itself, the way it keeps its control system moving, requires us to think about four other factors: law, authority, personality, and culture and how they interact, working with or against each other. (On the social meaning of these terms, see the Appendix.) In fact, any attempt to describe an actual society, to grasp its nature *as* a society, is bound to involve these four elements (among others). If we look at society from the top down—as an entity that is ruled—the tendency is to stress law and authority. If we look at it from the bottom up, as the behavior of citizens or subjects, there will be more emphasis on personality and culture.

Of course, even if we could describe these elements fully, in cross-section, as it were, the description would be too static to account for history and behavior. Behavior is strongly situational; people behave otherwise in good times than in bad; one way in peacetime, another way in time of war. New technology is another powerful source of situational change. In modern times science and technology have totally transformed society; they have altered every element of the social equation, and the rate of change from this source is steadily increasing. Technology must get major credit or blame for the revolution in the way we live today. A society brought up on television and accustomed to computers is bound to be different from societies without these modern miracles. The transforming effect of technology on authority systems and on legal culture is one of the main themes we intend to pursue.

TWO

Legalism and Individualism

THIS BOOK can be described as a modest attempt to explain one or two pieces of a gigantic jigsaw puzzle. Nobody, of course, can possibly understand human society as a whole. Nobody can grasp the full meaning of events taking place in his own century. But I want to come to grips with two oddly discordant features of Western society; more precisely, I hope to show how these features interact. Much of my material is drawn from the United States, and perhaps these features are most pronounced in this counfry, but I intend my argument to apply more generally, that is, to all of the modern West, at least to a certain degree.

The first feature is our modern involvement with, indeed obsession with, processes of *law*. The second is the incredible flowering—at least as an ideal—of a radical form of individualism, a kind of intense *personalism* that manifests itself in a rainbow of styles and ways of life; an efflorescence of habits, customs, fashions, practices, ways of eating, drinking, dressing, worshiping, making love, carving out a life. There is nothing new in the fact of human diversity, but it is striking to see so many patterns coexisting in a single country or society and to realize how much the dominant ideology, as reflected in popular culture, supports this diversity. Moreover, followers of many of these styles and ways of life—including some once outlawed and despised—demand and sometimes get recognition, acceptance, and legitimacy.

Indeed, this last-mentioned aspect of our culture is perhaps the most distinctive: not that there are heretics, lost sheep, and black sheep—but that so many of them reject all negative labels, and insist on a place of honor and dignity, as members of the flock in good standing. Again, this is hardly a modern invention. But the underlying ideology, causes, and scale of the development do seem to be quite unprecedented. The most obvious manifestation is the revolt of various minorities, who assert strong claims of right and search for a handhold on the levers of power; as a minimum, they elbow through the crowd, fighting the majority for a place in the sun, for a view of the parade, for a social niche as respectable as anybody else's. In the United States, and in other countries, racial minorities spearheaded this movement. The American paradigm was the civil rights crusade in the 1950s and the 1960s. Other groups followed quickly: very notably, the women's movements. This too was hardly the first sign of protest from "the second sex"; but the new feminism has been stronger, firmer, more broadly based, and deeper than prior movements. Moreover, it got results. The outbreak of so many "liberation" movements has been coupled with, and appears connected to, an apparent decline in traditional authority, that is, religious authority, political authority, the authority of parents, husbands, and fathers, teachers, prison wardens, bureaucrats—leaders and elites of every stamp.[1]

How much real change these movements have brought about is another question. Women have invaded the occupational world of men, but most wives still cook and sew and raise the children. There have also been countertrends and backlash. For example, traditional religion is making a comeback, if indeed it ever lost its grip. There is an astonishing increase in religious fervor in the United States and in a number of other countries. The countertrends are important and must be taken into account—as countertrends. They do not deny the main lines of development: they react against it. I will argue that some aspects of the countertrend are in fact features of the trend itself in disguise. For instance, the religiosity of the 1980s is, in large part, not the same as the religiosity of the nineteenth century. The mass of the faithful are no longer really *faithful*; people see religion in strikingly personalistic terms, that is, as a matter of *choice*, of individual will, rather than (as before) a question largely of birth and ascription; and they value religion mainly for what it can do for them, rather than as an expression of their place in a fixed cosmic order.[2] Religion, in other words, is at bottom another form of self-help; the highest and truest mode of personal therapy.

In our *individualistic* age the state, the legal system, and organized society in general thus seem more and more dedicated to one fundamental goal: to permit, foster, and protect the self, the person, the individual. A basic social creed justifies this aim: each person is unique, each person is or ought to be free, each one of us has or ought to have the right to create or build up a way of life for ourselves, and to do it through free, open, and untrammeled choice. These are the unspoken premises of popular culture. They find their way into policy not because of some direct, conscious command or decision of the rulers, but because of deep, global, powerful forces—forces that flow upward or sideways, out of broad segments of society, out of "the public"—forces set loose or stimulated by long-term historical trends and by the technological revolution in society.

"Public" of course does not mean everyone. Pressure comes from those who can and do exert pressure. In the societies of the modern West this means primarily the middle-class mass and those above it in the stratification system. In other societies the strata that matter may be broader or (more usually) narrower. But in Europe and North America we assume a deep, fundamental social demand directed toward the one basic goal. We leave to one side, for now, whether any such goal is attainable or even desirable. For purposes of the argument here those questions are irrelevant. The aim is to describe legal culture. The goal or attitude described is an important factor in modern politics and law. It is implied in what people (middle-class and up) say and do, whether they are aware of their attitudes or not.

There is an astonishing increase in the first feature of modern society: law. The number of lawyers is growing rapidly—catastrophically, some would say—in many countries; but this is not the central point. Rather, it is the growth of law itself, the burgeoning of rules and regulations, the blurring of the border between what is amenable to legal process and what is immune, together with the triumph of "due process"—the spreading of court-like procedures and forms to areas of life which were once beyond the pale. In certain corners of American law—products liability is a notable example—many people see utter disaster. Litigation has gone totally out of control, reaching the point where, under this view, it threatens the economy itself.[3] Mighty companies, towering oaks of Wall Street, have been struck down by lawsuits. In a number of fields use of law seems positively epidemic.

The "law explosion," or what appears to be an explosion of law, has been sometimes described as if it were quintessentially American. In some aspects this may be so. It is hard to think of another court quite as powerful as the United States Supreme Court. Judicial review—the power of courts to monitor, control, and supervise the work of the legislatures and the executive branch—is less highly developed in most other Western countries, including England and France. Yet in some ways the trends are common to the whole Western world. The number of lawyers has increased in other countries as well as in the United States—often quite rapidly. The Belgian bar grew 5.5 per cent a year between 1970 and 1982; in Norway admissions doubled in roughly the same period; in England and Wales the annual harvest of law degrees almost tripled.[4] Judicial review has had an astonishing upsurge in a number of countries, for example, West Germany.[5] Canada has adopted an "entrenched" Bill of Rights;[6] countries as dissimilar as Cyprus and Japan have embraced a form of judicial review.[7] Similar forces are at work in every Western country, though bent by specific configurations of history, tradition, and social structure.

The expansion of law implies as well the proliferation of entitlements—rights, in short, and the consciousness of right. The very term "right" implies law. But the law that the consciousness of right implies is law with a strong formal element—in the sense of precision, objectivity, enforceability. The formal element, moreover, contributes to the legitimacy of rules and institutions. Form and procedure seem to be key elements in legitimating modern law. And legitimacy is presumed to be indispensable to the success of authority—a vital substance without which authority is dead, inert, a statue of stone.

In modern society one hears a lot about the revolt against formalism, and formalism tends to be a derogatory word. It is no compliment to describe a system as "formalistic." ("Legalistic" is as bad or worse.) Yet there is a movement *toward* legal formalism in at least one important sense. The rights that people want and demand are meant to be firm and enforceable; and this they cannot be if rights depend on the discretion of some functionary or the goodwill of some bureaucrat. Indeed, complete discretion is flatly inconsistent with the concept of right as popularly understood. People want rights in black and white; incised in stone, as it were; they want them to have formal reality. Of course, rights enshrined in codes and constitutions are nothing without enforcement; formal reality is nothing without informal reality as well; but rights that are real in practice, yet formally unrecognized, seem unnecessarily precarious and indeed often *are* precarious. Moreover, they tend to lack the precious fluid of legitimacy. In the modern world, then, the demand for rights is a demand for law as well, that is, for formal recognition of right.

The two processes—the growth of law and the growth of personalism—seem at first glance to be in conflict or contradiction. Yet they coexist. And one key to this coexistence has just been mentioned: the strong development of rights, and hence an increase in a certain kind of law. There are two linked phenomena here, but their exact contours, meanings, and dimensions remain to be explored.

The Problem of Authority

Systems of authority and law are probably always in flux. There is never any solution to the problem of authority; there is no single, correct mix of authority, law, and personal freedom. The problem of freedom and authority may be an eternal riddle of human existence. No arrangement will ever satisfy on a permanent basis. The very criteria for what is satisfactory change from period to period, from culture to culture; moreover, the personality of the measurers or their station in life affects what even counts as successful or good.

But in any given period the authority system can be thought of as very problematic, as somewhat problematic, or as not problematic at all. Authority is successful when it imposes order or persuades people to act in conformity with order. At this time (1989) the government of Switzerland, for example, has society nicely under control. There are controversies about authority, politics, and policy in that country, of course; but on the whole public administration works, the legal system functions, and the population is not in a state of anarchy or riot. To the outside world Swiss society may appear boring or even contemptible, but the trains run on time; law and order prevail. At the other extreme are countries like Uganda or Lebanon; in these unfortunate lands public order has collapsed, authority is in shambles, and there is murder and anarchy on the streets and in the countryside.

In the West today, as far as authority, order, and law are concerned, Switzerland stands at one extreme, Northern Ireland perhaps at another; yet on the whole, Western countries are paragons of stability. Administrations and parties rise and fall, come and go; parties assume power and are later voted out, but all in an orderly way. The machinery of justice, the police, institutions of public order all function; the wheels turn, the jobs get done. An occasional riot erupts and is repressed. The societies all have underclasses, large or small; but on the whole these do not roil the waters, at least not beyond middle-class toleration.

Despite this relative stability, both authority and law are commonly said to be in difficulty in the West; many scholars even talk about a crisis. Of course, every country faces serious political, economic, and social problems; whether these amount to a crisis or not is a question of definition or of political ideology.[8] In any event, the problem of authority and the problem of law are in a curious way inverses of each other. Authority is a problem insofar as it is diminishing; law is a problem in that it is expanding.

In most Western countries there is nothing at present that could be described as organized rebellion or even much serious unrest. Nonetheless, critics and social observers often seem pessimistic about the health of the social order. Traditional institutions—the churches, the family, national leaders—seem to be losing their authority. Traditional values—piety, the work ethic, clean living—are also said to have gone into decline. These are common complaints, usually unexamined. Yet scholars and intellectuals assume that the complaints capture a reality, a genuine social process; that more is involved here than ordinary grumbling about the good old days.

The decline of authority is dangerous—so the argument goes—because a culture cannot survive without authority; it cannot survive without legitimate rule; it cannot survive without shared norms, which are the heart and mind of the social body. When authority degenerates, society will tend to disintegrate too. First, a kind of vague anomie will suffuse the social order, a faint decay, followed by boneless passivity and social narcissism; then vicious depravity and a war of all against all. Staggering rates of crime and drug use; family dissolution; heedless consumerism and materialism; the general neuroses of modern society—all these are taken as signs and indicators of impending catastrophe.

There are indeed serious problems and issues in modern society; but the question is whether an absolute decline in authority (whatever that would mean) has occurred, or whether authority is shifting forms and directions as society changes. Moreover, the very ideas of democracy, individualism, and self-government imply a certain disrespect for traditional authority. Modern Western society and modern democracy grew out of the ruins of older orders, which they undermined and then destroyed: the more hierarchical, more stratified, more authoritarian forms of goverment. But the kings were deposed or stripped of their strength long ago; the churches were disestablished and lost their power to bind and loose; the autocracy of the patriarchal father dissolved in the acid of family equality. For many people in many societies the process has gone far enough, and it is time to call a halt. Their strong impulse is toward a religious revival, and to support a conservative reaction against the welfare state.

The Problem of Law

The law problem seems to be the opposite of the authority problem: there is too much of it. Law and legal process—perhaps *because* of the decline of authority, the erosion of tradition—are growing like weeds. There is the familiar charge of a litigation explosion, a massive increase in lawsuits, which rips apart the fabric of society. We are also (it is said) dangerously overlawyered. There is something on the order of 700,000 practicing lawyers in the United States; and the numbers are growing much faster than population. There is explosive growth in some European countries too; the baseline numbers are smaller, but the trend is similar. The President of Harvard, among other people, has sounded a note of alarm. The lawyers are a parasite class; they do not produce. A massive diversion of exceptional talent has gone into the profession of law, and this is disruptive and dangerous.[9] Japan is held up as the model on the other side. In proportion to population, that country has about a tenth as many lawyers as the United States. Some people jump to the conclusion that this shortage of lawyers helps explain the phenomenal success of Japanese industry. Japan, said Bok, with half the population of the United States, "boasts a total of less than 15,000 lawyers, while American universities graduate 35,000 every year. It would be hard to claim that these differences have no practical consequences."[10]

No doubt these differences *do* have practical consequences, but it is far from clear what they are. There is good reason to be skeptical and cautious about the case against lawyers, law, and lawyering. For example, it is not at all clear that a litigation explosion is really taking place.[11] There is certainly a great deal of litigation in the United States and elsewhere, but quality and quantity of litigation are hard to measure; wild charges printed in the newspapers hardly capture the complexities of social reality. In any case, if such an explosion occurred, it occurred only recently, that is, after 1970 or perhaps even after 1980.[12] And the *scale* and *type* of lawsuits have probably changed much more than the numbers of cases per thousand population. Whether lawyers are parasitic and counterproductive is another debatable issue; and whether the nation is committing suicide through litigation—suing itself to death—is still another, and perhaps the most dubious claim of all.

It does seem true that law is ubiquitous in modern society, and that legal institutions have a major place in the structure of Western societies. But it is not easy to convert law into a quantitative term, let alone measure it accurately. (Perhaps the total money spent on lawyers is the closest we can come to some concrete yardstick.) In the United States today, compared to a century ago, Congress, state legislatures, administrative agencies, executive offices, city councils, county boards, school districts, port authorities, zoning boards, and the like certainly churn out an incredible number of pages of legal matter; law libraries are bursting at the seams with reported cases, statutes, rules and regulations, and local ordinances, not to mention treatises, digests, and guides for the legally perplexed. In other countries, too, there is talk about "floods" of legal matter. The facts are elusive, probably everywhere. Most likely, legal activity has increased relative to population in each of these countries, measured against whatever baseline in the past one might choose; whether it has increased relative to the number of possible transactions, incidents, and occasions for invoking law is a question nobody can answer—but if one had to guess, the answer here too would be yes.

But law is ubiquitous in important ways that crude numbers cannot possibly capture. Many rules of law, after all, are general commands intended or supposed to serve as long-term guides to behavior. Thus they cannot be measured or counted as if they were one-shot events, puffs of smoke that vanish in the wind. Measuring lines and pages, weighing volumes, and counting laws, rules, cases, and so on does not give a true sense of the import and impact of legal words and structures; one must look for other ways to assess the consequences of legal institutions and their parts—to grasp the process that rules set into motion or influence in some way. A decision of the United States Supreme Court on school desegregation, or on abortion—an act of Parliament creating a National Health Service—these are general commands whose effects ripple out in society and have institutional consequences. Counting the words tells us nothing.

Over the last century, I believe, law has increased its scope and scale in at least one very important regard: there are fewer zones of immunity from law—fewer areas of life which are totally unregulated, totally beyond the *potential* reach of law. This is the phenomenon of legalization, and it has been detected, often with cries of alarm, in France, Germany, and throughout the West. Legalization takes at least three distinct forms. The first, which is related to the "liability explosion," rests on the postulate that organizations—businesses, governmental agencies—should not enjoy immunity with regard to harm they may cause other people. The second, which is related to the "due process revolution," rests on the postulate that large organizations (and especially governmental ones) cannot legitimately take actions that affect peoples' lives unless those people have a chance to argue or fight back. The third is the notion that no instance of claimed injustice is beyond the reach of law solely because of its subject matter; nothing, in other words, is inherently nonlegal—whether because it is personal or occurs within the family, or because the claim is not the sort of thing courts or agencies could, should, or customarily hear. In connection with this, Jürgen Habermas coined a vivid and much repeated phrase: the "colonization" of personal life by the law.[13]

A single example, from the United States, illustrates all three aspects of legalization—indeed, the three are tightly linked. Suppose that Stanford University dismisses a professor, on whatever grounds. The professor, today, has the right to some sort of formal review within the University. In an extreme case (this has occasionally happened), the professor goes through the steps and stages at Stanford, loses, and then continues the struggle in court by filing a lawsuit. In earlier times—in fact, as late as the first part of the twentieth century—all this was unthinkable. First of all, the discretion of the University was nearly unlimited; it enjoyed both practical and legal immunity. That immunity has now almost vanished. Modern law—and modern legal culture—do not define the dispute over a job at the University as inherently nonlegal or private. The organization is expected to do justice, to live up to the standards of justice. And it should do so both in terms of the *procedures* it follows, and in terms of the rules and norms it applies.

Several legal theorists have tried to define what types of dispute are or are not inherently justiciable. Lon Fuller, for example, argues that courts do not do a good job of resolving polycentric disputes. He does not really define "polycentric," but he gives examples; they are disputes that have "complex repercussions," that are made up of many strands, like a "spider web," so that a "pull on one strand" produces a ripple effect "throughout the web as a whole."[14] But neither popular culture nor the courts themselves have paid the slightest attention to his strictures. Immensely complex and interwoven problems have gravitated to the courts in the United States and have been duly adjudicated. A federal court, for example, declared the whole prison system of Arkansas unconstitutional; the court ordered the state to reform its prisons root and branch.[15] It would be hard to imagine anything more polycentric, especially since reforms of this kind are expensive and to carry them out means pulling strand after strand of the spider's web.

In fact, virtually everything is potential fodder for courts in modern society. Nothing is nonjusticiable. Nothing is too big or too small. American newspapers often report, and sneer at, examples of litigation gone wild. In one notable instance, a man sued a former girlfriend, trying to "force her to pay for his time and expenses on a date she did not keep."[16] Nothing came of this threat. What is significant, however, is that a case of this sort is not unthinkable; most courts would dismiss the claim with a snort of derision, but perhaps not all courts. In fact, this story, extreme as it is, points up the dramatic erosion of zones of legal immunity. Everything today is subject to the reign of law. This was by no means true in the past.

This example was drawn from the United States; foreign readers may thus relax in their easy chairs, soothed by the notion that American law is both peculiar and pathological. But is this the case? To be sure, a due process revolution is not to be found, in the same strict form, in strongly centralized countries like France, whose legal culture retains a strong element of *dirigisme*.[17] Yet signs of creeping "Americanism" are everywhere. Can a restaurant sue a customer who made a reservation and then, without canceling, simply failed to show up for dinner? An editorial in the *London Times*[18] spoke approvingly of the possibility. This attitude matches anything in American legal culture.

Of course, "potentially justiciable" is not the same as "actually adjudicated." Stanford and other universities dismiss hundreds of professors every year, most of whom accept their fate. Only a handful invoke the procedures for review; almost none go to court. Thus lawsuits over dismissals at universities make no contribution whatsoever to the so-called "litigation explosion." But, undeniably, such lawsuits are possible. The administrators at Stanford know it; the professors know it; heads of departments know it. The University is thus "legalized;" and perhaps life inside the institution is permanently altered. It might be more accurate to say that *legal culture* has altered; the climate of life within the institution reflects legal culture, and the procedures set up internally are reflections of reflections.

In any event, it is the ubiquity of law which, I believe, has grown so dramatically over the last century or so. The disappearance of zones of immunity is at the core of the expansion of law; and though we can treat this or that fact or figure as an indicator, at bottom quantitative measurement does not easily capture what has occurred. Our examples stressed the expansion of the role of courts, but the phenomenon is clearly more general; it extends to all institutions of law. That poses the central paradox quite vividly. Traditional forms of authority seem to be in decline; moreover, a radical form of individualism seems to be on the rise. How does that individualism coexist with so much law?

The paradox, I will argue, is no paradox at all. The shrinking zone of authority is remarkably similar to the shrinking zone of immunity to law. Thus law appears to be a kind of replacement, a substitute for traditional authority. This emerges clearly when we think about the dispute over tenure at Stanford. The authority of University officials is no longer absolute. Another authority, the court, has picked up some of the slack, and can now issue binding orders to the University. Of course, this is only a partial explanation. To answer the question more fully, we have to take a closer look at the "law explosion."

In addition, we will have to explore legal culture. Is our description of the ideas underlying law and authority essentially correct? If so, what brought about these changes in legal culture? Is modern legal culture fundamentally new, or has it been, in essence, rattling about in the attic of society for decades, or centuries? To answer these questions, we have to look to the concept of individualism and the ways it is understood in the modern West.

THREE

Modernity and the Rise of the Individual

EVERYONE probably thinks the society he lives in is distinctive, and in some sense all societies do differ from each other. Most of us who live in the 1980s, in the developed world, tend to believe that life in our societies is unique, unprecedented, unlike anything that came before. One unique aspect, surely, is the feeling that we live in the midst of swift, breath-taking, constant change. The planet seems to revolve much faster than ever before. People are acutely conscious of the fact of change. They feel swept along on some immense, mysterious journey rushing from the dim past onward like a space-ship into the darkness and void of the future. Awareness of the future implies awareness of the past. People know that things have been different. They have some notions about history, even though these ideas may be terribly inaccurate; they realize that society is changing, and rapidly, and that a great gulf separates them from their fathers and mothers, not to speak of more remote ancestors. By the same token, people may suspect that they will be cut off from their own children and their children's children, who will inhabit a world of undreamt-of marvels (or horrors). We live in the shadow of an unknown and unknowable future. It is natural for many of us to wonder about the nature and meaning of historical experience, to think about trends and evolutions, and to ask ourselves where we are going. This awareness is part of the essence of the modern. Medieval and tribal people had no concept of news, no sense of revolution—or of the banality of revolution.

The twentieth century has experienced catastrophic alterations— the fall of the great colonial empires, the revolution of rising expectations, exploding population growth, colossal wars and massacres of populations, global upheavals, frantic gyrations among systems of government, massive changes in the ecosystem. There have been deep-seated changes in religion, the family, sexual behavior and patterns of living. Authority structures have also changed; the permutations of life were bound to affect law and legal systems profoundly, and affect them they did.

Modernity

Modern society is extraordinarily self-conscious. The citizens at large are self-conscious; the intellectuals among them even more so. Dozens of scholars have written about, considered, defined, and disputed what modernity and modernization mean.[1] What constellation of factors makes our present society distinctive? Of course, "modern society" is a slippery term. It is not easy to distill the essence of what is "modern" in society, law, or authority. In any society, modern or not, structures of authority, governance, law, and legal culture can be extremely complicated; they are not to be summed up in a few lapidary, gnomic formulas. Moreover, in no two countries are these structures exactly the same. The legal systems of France and Belgium are supposed to be closely related, yet they differ in many large and small details. Each Western country has its own peculiar form of government. Legal culture and general consciousness are elusive concepts. Legal culture—the ultimate source and shaper of law—is for the most part unexplored territory; research on the subject is thin and tenuous.[2] But it surely differs from society to society and from group to group.

This does not mean that it is hopeless to make general statements about Western legal culture. There is a larger picture, beyond the details. A number of traits seem basic to the countries of the West. Two in particular are pertinent to our general theme. First, each country in the West is in some degree what we will call an *open society*. Second, in each country the functioning of authority and law to a large degree depends on (or is thought to depend on) *choice* or *consent*—free, voluntary acts of those subject to authority and law. The two traits, moreover, are closely linked.

By an *open* society I mean nothing more than a society whose organs of law, authority, and government are constructed so as to expose them to some degree of public opinion or public pressure, and in which these organs in fact respond, to some degree, to such pressure. The public exerts pressure in various ways: by voting in elections, by writing letters to congressmen or members of Parliament, by lobbying for passage of laws, by marching in the streets with banners or signs, by exercising legal rights, by bringing lawsuits, by directing complaints to administrative bodies, by calling the police, or by consulting lawyers. This is merely another way of saying that these are relatively free societies: not totalitarian, not under the tight control of dictators, not dominated by oligarchies. They have independent court systems, and they have legislatures, which periodically face the ordeal and testing-ground of elections.

In politics, the movement away from autocracy and toward some sort of representative government has been realized, unfortunately, only in a select club of countries. These are clustered mostly in North America and Western Europe, along with a rather scattered group of outliers that includes Australia, New Zealand, Israel, Costa Rica, Barbados, and Japan. Many people in the West no doubt think of the trend toward democracy as some sort of natural historical progression. In fact, it has often been reversed (Chile, for example), or has gone through various oscillations (Greece, Uruguay, Turkey, Spain). Moreover, the twentieth century has been cursed with some of the most vicious and evil regimes ever devised (Nazi Germany, Pol Pot's Cambodia, Amin's Uganda). It is worth mentioning, perhaps, that even the most bloodthirsty and cynical regimes seem to feel the need to mimic democratic forms—to run some trumpery sort of election, to pretend to some kind of popular ratification. These empty rituals—the Moscow purge trials were an example, and various plebiscites in totalitarian countries—are supposed to confer legitimacy on the ruling regime and wrap a mantle of approval around its oppressions. Whether anyone is taken in is another question.

It is possible to dismiss the open systems of Western countries as sham, false consciousness, mystification, mirage. The more bitter voices of the left clearly do so. But I prefer not to blur the line between an open and closed society. The important point is the widespread *perception* of openness, and the structures that promote that impression. In an open society, the state allows and fosters public participation in politics. Clean, frequent voting takes place. It is a little less clear whether the legal systems in these countries are open in any meaningful way. To be sure, they are open at the level of lawmaking—at the parliamentary level. The public elects representatives and through them exerts some control over lawmaking, in theory and in practice. In many countries, jurists—law professors, legal scholars, or civil servants—draft many of the laws and devise the codes, but nothing can become *law* without the approval of an elected assembly. In many countries, too, certain basic principles or rights have been given special status. They are fixed in some more or less immutable form, as part of a written constitution or a fundamental law, or are otherwise entrenched. The American Bill of Rights is one example; the German *Grundgesetz* another. The legislature has no power to alter these basic rights, at least not in the manner of ordinary law. But the theory of (ordinary) law insists on public control—over law and the organs of law.

This is even true of that part of the law the courts themselves develop. Here theory (and practice) are rather complex. Judges and high courts constantly influence, alter, modify, and invent doctrines and applications of law. No serious scholar treats the lawmaking power of judges as anything but an established fact. Legal theory in the strict sense is more circumspect and ambivalent, especially on the Continent and in Latin America. There the classic view, in the nineteenth century, insisted that legislation made up the whole of the law;[3] the judge had no independent role to play; he merely interpreted. The general public still shies away from, or rejects outright, the idea that courts do and should make law; yet litigants push them to do exactly that. The judges themselves are not entirely candid. Some of the most blatant lawmaking, in common-law countries too, gets covered by the fig leaf of "interpretation."

No doubt popular opinions about law and courts are somewhat hazy and muddled. Clearly, no one approaches a court with a demand so blatant and bald as the appeal of lobbyists in the legislative halls. Nonetheless, the judicial system is open in at least one crucial sense: the right to go to court is in theory totally unlimited—everybody who has a claim, or a claim to a claim, can try his luck. (As we shall see, the judicial system is becoming open in other ways, too.) To be sure, there are barriers of cost and culture. It is not easy for an ordinary citizen to bring a claim. But the official line in the West is that these barriers are pathologies, flaws, problems, evils to be corrected, proper subjects for legal reform. They are not defined as legitimate limits on rights that would be otherwise unlimited; or as a sensible way to ration justice; or as valid adjuncts of dominion.

Another complex issue is that of the responsiveness of the bureaucracy to the general public. Modern government is bureaucratic government; it cannot get along without an army of hired experts and general civil servants. Bureaucracy is rule-bound, yet at the same time vested with a great deal of discretion, and deliberately so, as far as the public is concerned. Nonetheless, in no Western society is the civil service totally beyond the reach of legal process. The sharpest limit on bureaucratic discretion is judicial review, which embodies at some level a notion of *public* accountability. Judicial review is an old and powerful weapon in the courts of the United States. In recent years, it has leaped across traditional legal barriers and gained surprising strength in unexpected countries.[4] The idea and institution of the *ombudsman* have also spread widely, bearing witness to a similar idea: that the practices and decisions of bureaucrats must be open to scrutiny and control.

In sum, in all of the Western societies theory and a struggling practice treat the structures of the legal system as if they were ultimately subject to control by the population at large. That is, the law is defined instrumentally, at least in part: as a tool, an artifact, which the constituent parts of society can manipulate deliberately and openly for personal or social ends. Law is, therefore, open to the public and its representatives; it is, ultimately, *their* instrument. This is in marked contrast to the basic conception of law in other and earlier societies. Each society, no doubt, has its own dominant theory of law, but instrumental theories of law were alien and unthinkable in premodern societies. In these societies, theories of law emphasized the sacral, magic, meta-human. Law was tinged with the quality of the miraculous. God had delivered the laws from the realm of the heavens; or laws were extruded from oracles, encrusted with sacred tradition, and treated as a precious treasure, within the circle of power of the sages or special, charismatic personalities who alone had the right to elaborate law or expound it. In any event, laws were at their core timeless and immutable; they had their origin in time beyond memory, beyond the meaning and experience of men; or they appeared in a flash of revelation; at the very least, the whims and wishes of ordinary human beings had no power over the laws; they were fixed, definite, inexorable, part of the very order of being.[5] Some of the magic of immutable rightness still clings to modern law, in pockets and corners, very markedly in charters of basic right, but the rest of the codex, the main body of laws, is frankly and prosaically instrumental. God, the natural order, or pure reason may have ordained freedom of speech and the fundamental rights, but none of these can be credited with the Internal Revenue Code.

A second modern trait, closely connected to the open society, is the centrality of individual *choice* or *consent* in the structure of legitimacy. An open, representative government is by definition a freely chosen government. Somewhat less obviously, an instrumental legal system is a chosen legal system—not inherited, imposed, or immanent, but produced by the actions and behaviors of individuals moving and planning and conniving in society. The Italian legal system, if it does not come from God or nature, must come from the choices and wishes of the Italian population, mediated to be sure by officials and deputies. At least so the theory goes. Of course, this notion of a chosen system is not new; it is implicit or explicit in the very idea of representative government. What is newer, I shall argue, is the *kind* of choices which the system embodies and gives high rank to— personal, expressive choices—to a degree unheard of a century ago.

Individualism and individual choice, in some senses, are central themes in the work of most theorists who have tried to distil the essence of modernization. Of special importance is Max Weber's classic approach to what is distinctive in modern society—his notion that rationality (or rational-legal authority) has replaced traditional and charismatic authority. There are of course many other insightful and provocative theories and explanations, differing from each other in large and small ways. For our purposes, we will omit most of their subtleties and concentrate on what they have in common: until recently, at least, they all tended to put heavy stress on *individualism*. A modern society, in contrast to a nonmodern society, is one that emphasizes the individual rather than the group; modern society allows free-wheeling choice among options; it structures relationships contractually, rather than through time-honored customs and mores; it does not force people into fixed social roles, decreed by sacred tradition and inexorable at the moment of birth, or at set stages of life; it turns its back on inheritance and ascription, and opens the door to freedom, mobility and choice.[6]

On the whole, social theorists and thinkers tend to draw a picture of primitive or ancient man as a prisoner of status, locked in the iron cage of custom, and unable, except in rare instances, to break free of this cage. What you are born to, that you remain: you *are* your family, your tribal connection, your status as Brahmin or untouchable. Modern society, on the other hand, is a society of looser connections, a society of rubber cages; in it, the citizen makes rational choices, she is freer, there is more play for voluntary decisions. Society is an aggregate of *individuals*, men and women.

In this spirit, Sir Henry Maine, in a famous passage from his classic *Ancient Law* (1861), described the evolution of "progressive" societies as the movement from status to contract. In ancient society, he said, the unit of legal empowerment was the family headed by a patriarch; over the long run, however, "family dependency" dissolved, and the single naked individual became the unit of legal rights.[7] Ferdinand Toennies drew an equally famous distinction between *Gemeinschaft*, the old-fashioned status community, and *Gesellschaft*, the society of modern times, in which ascriptive status loses its dominance.[8] Emile Durkheim described two kinds of social solidarity or bonding, "mechanical" and "organic." According to Durkheim, in older societies (societies of "mechanical solidarity") shared, universal social norms were the source of social bonds. Modern society, with its complexities, generated a new form of social cohesion, characterized by extensive use of free voluntary agreements or contracts.[9] Such a society is of course more individualistic. Durkheim stressed *social* rather than individual roots of behavior, and the level of analysis was societal. Nonetheless, to Durkheim too modern society places more weight on individual choice than the extinct societies of the human past.

Nineteenth-century theorists were on the whole optimistic men; they believed in human progress and considered progress inevitable. This was even true of Marx. Social theorists in this century tend to have a gloomier outlook; the confident exuberance is gone. Perhaps this is only natural. Maine, Durkheim, and Marx could hardly foresee a day in which human beings had power literally to blow up the human race; in which people ran a real risk of choking to death on their own poisonous byproducts. And the political and social catastrophies of the twentieth century could shake the faith of the most deep-dyed optimist. Victorian smugness is hard to sustain in the era of Auschwitz.

Yet modern theorists do tend to agree with older ones in some essential regards. They see the same fundamental designs, historical progressions, and basic patterns of development. They differ in the labels they pin on these patterns; they are less convinced that "progress" is always benign; they see dangerous countertrends: mass societies, totalitarian states, conformity, herd-like behavior, overpopulation, failures of nerve, environmental destruction, and exhaustion of resources. These problems and jeopardies, however, are regarded as somehow abnormal; they are unfortunate detours, pathologies, or perversions; they are not taken as historically inevitable. Modern theorists, on the whole, share with their forerunners the celebration of human freedom as a goal and as an ideal. But freedom for them implies individual choice. The history of humanity is a history that moves, or ought to move, from choicelessness to choice.

Choicelessness and choice, of course, are terms that refer to aspects of governance or authority. Where there is authority, true choice is largely absent; yet the matter of choice is necessarily guaranteed by or assumed by law. A number of major social theorists in the nineteenth century were trained as lawyers, or wrote explicitly about law—Sir Henry Maine, for example. Max Weber, too, had legal training; he devoted a major section of his masterwork, *Economy and Society*, to the sociology of law.[10] The transformation of legal norms is an important social event in its own right and an important indicator of changes in society; but clearly, social norms of a more general nature underlie, support, and give meaning to whatever legal norms exist in society. What is true of law is probably true of social theory itself: great minds filter and refine it, but it reflects, at some level, the raw, yeasty stuff of popular thought, the ideas rattling about in the heads of some broader public. Social thought always presupposes its own context. A Max Weber would have been unthinkable in the Middle Ages; or even in the eighteenth century. Insight and intellect can and do exist in any period; but different problems attract these minds—and they use different approaches—depending on the period and on the world around them.

In the modern period, general social norms and popular culture assume an ever-widening sphere of individual choice, as an ideal and as a part of working reality, at least in the West. The conceptions of what the individual is and ought to be, as we described them in the last chapter, run parallel to the way social theory looks at freedom and choice, though with important exceptions. It is likely that social theory simply stumbles along behind changes in human consciousness, which are themselves the product of profound changes in the social and physical environment of human beings. For example, the emphasis on choice, consent, and contractual behavior will immediately remind readers of thinkers and writers from Rousseau and

Locke through John Rawls and beyond. But the thread of political theory or philosophy is not the issue here; it is interesting only insofar as it influences or affects "pop" theory or philosophy; and in most regards perhaps it follows rather than leads. In any event, whatever their intellectual source, concepts of choice, consent of the governed, and open contractual behavior seem central to modern democracies. Each generation, to be sure, reinterprets the meaning of these concepts, implicitly or explicitly; reinterpretation may come subtly and gradually, or (at times) in a more radical and abrupt way. Changing circumstances and changing technology force these new interpretations on society. Words like freedom, choice, law, justice, are not replaced, but their subtle nuances alter—the emotions they evoke, the pictures they call to mind. Examining the slow, delicate shift in the meanings of concepts, like the slow fading of colors at a sunset, is an essential part of social history.

Briefly speaking, we can distinguish *three* phases in the history of the social meaning of the concept of choice or individual autonomy. Of course meanings do not shift abruptly. They blend and blur and turn like a color wheel. We pass quickly over the first phase, in the age of status, only to remark that society allowed relatively little scope for individual choice. No doubt to say this does not do justice to the subject; in past societies ideas of individual choice and autonomy were surely richer, more subtle, and infinitely more various than most people imagine. Ancient Rome or Greece were very different from, say, ancient Babylonia, or from tribal societies, which have their own complexities. People were nowhere mere robots of custom.

But the legal cultures of antiquity, of the Middle Ages, and of pre-literate societies are not our concern. More important for our purposes is the second phase—the nineteenth-century phase—and its conception of the individual. In this period an expansive, universalistic view of human freedom and individual choice took a hold on Western thought, and we will have to pay some attention to this view. The third type, the twentieth-century notion of choice, is the widest, most pervasive of all. Thomas Jefferson was a great democrat and a great apostle of freedom, but if he came back from the dead today, the range of choices would amaze and no doubt horrify him—choices people are allowed and encouraged to make in every walk of life, all in the name of freedom: choices about sexual and family relationships, about religious identity, about ways of talking, dressing, acting, and so on.

Individualism in Its Nineteenth-Century Meaning

From our contemporary viewpoint, the scope of individualism was more limited in the nineteenth century. Theorists (and perhaps the majority of the population) certainly celebrated freedom, democracy, and popular sovereignty. And, of course, their concept of freedom necessarily implied individual choice, as a central value in social life. Personal autonomy was another value—freedom from outside interference, as well as the right of the individual to develop the self to the fullest, to pursue his or her own goals, to control the conditions of existence. All this sounds a great deal like the modern form; but the definition implied in actual practice was subtly different. Theory and practice defined freedom primarily in political or economic terms—in terms of markets and votes. Those who spoke about development of the self were thinking of a self quite unlike its twentieth-century descendant. It was a God-fearing, hard-working, disciplined, traditional self, as far as private life was concerned.

Nineteenth-century changes in economic and political life were, to be sure, important in their own right. Freedom of markets and votes made miraculous headway. Political democracy, so boastful and proud in its American version, won a foothold in country after country; the franchise was extended further down the economic scale. It was an age of fallen kings and decaying churches; likewise, of Adam Smith and economic liberalism. Sir Henry Maine, in the famous passage mentioned previously, proclaimed the movement from status to contract in "progressive" societies. The *idea* of contract was certainly one of the basic building blocks of nineteenth-century law; it had an important role in political theory as well. Contract was tied in closely with liberal economic theory. Contract was the transaction freely bargained in the market; it was the wedding of two separate minds, the union of two private and voluntary choices.[11]

Free choice thus was always associated with the individual and with individualism; but for many theorists in the nineteenth century free choice meant above all behavior in the economic realm, in the market. Property rights and markets were the core of free choice; freedom was defined "in terms of a legally assured measure of autonomy for private decision makers," as Willard Hurst puts it with regard to economic affairs.[12]

Whether ordinary people conceived of choice and freedom in these terms, even in the United States, is by no means clear. The high culture, the culture of theory, is shouted from the rooftops, published everywhere, and studied by later generations. Ordinary opinion is much less accessible. It is possible that the official line coincided with the views of ordinary farmers and small business people; possible, too, that the official line percolated down from the top to a broader public. In any event, dominant theory tended to equate individualism or individual liberty with economic liberalism. Thus individualism was essentially a political and economic creed; it put faith in the "invisible hand" and in democratic government; it was coupled with a (largely implicit) belief that people would and could govern and control themselves, without paternalism, without the authority of nobles and kings—that they could be trusted to manage on their own.

Individualism was therefore, in many regards, a reaction against past systems. It stood in contrast to older autocracies, to the mercantilist monarchies, and to the belief structures of traditional elites. In the nineteenth century, the nations of the West, or some of them, embarked on a radical experiment in self-rule. The United States was very much a leader; it was, in the eyes of contemporaries, the most radical of the democratic countries. It was a magnet for foreign visitors; it evoked curiosity because of its sharp break with the past, its egalitarianism, its extreme individualism. Alexis de Tocqueville, one of the most clear-eyed of all these observers, was convinced that America was the wave of the future. He "saw in America . . . the shape of democracy . . . its inclinations, character, prejudices, and passions." It prefigured, he felt, the future of France. Frances Trollope, a visitor less impressed with America, deplored American developments. Jefferson's "hollow and unsound" doctrines, she felt, would "make of mankind an unamalgamated mass of grating atoms." Americans, alas, were only too eager to embrace the faith of total equality—it was a country where "I'm as good as you" threatened to "take the place of the law and the Gospel," where the "assumption of equality" was "sufficient to tincture the manners of the poor with brutal insolence."[13] Whether they liked or disliked what they saw, foreign observers agreed on the phenomenon: radical egalitarianism. Yet even in the United States, the scope and scale of that aspect of individualism, that profound leveling of hierarchies, was narrow and restrictive compared to its twentieth-century descendant.

The idea of popular government, in 1800 or 1850, struck members of the old European elites—landed gentry, rich merchants, clergymen—as dubious and dangerous. Upper classes did not in general believe that "the people," that is, the bulk of society, or any stratum other than the small group that had traditionally run society, could be trusted to exercise political power. Popular government was a radical notion in that it imputed to ordinary people great powers of self-control and discipline. The people were, or could be, responsible adults—as responsible as their "betters," as responsible as those with money, family background, and education. If people "could learn to discipline themselves," as Patrick Atiyah put it, it would "obviate" the need for the state to "do the disciplining for them."[14] They had, or could have, enough intelligence, knowledge, and moral sense to run their lives, to choose a government, and even to run that government. Of course, even the most convinced democrat knew that self-control or self-government was beyond the power or will of some people. Those who failed to live up to the standards—who were deviant, or committed crimes—rudely shattered the compact of freedom. Democracies were capable of considerable savagery toward criminals and toward others who would not or could not follow the norms. American and British systems of penology are cases in point; this theme is taken up in Chapter 8.

To sum up, "freedom" and "individualism" in the nineteenth century meant zones of open choice for people with the strength and maturity to choose correctly for themselves and to control their darker impulses. Such people could be trusted to act intelligently and honestly in the political sphere. Restrictions on choice were not needed; in other words, people would elect voluntarily to walk down right roads. That these right roads were, as far as personal life was concerned, the old roads, the traditional roads, went essentially unquestioned.[15]

What sustained these traditional norms in an open society? Tocqueville implied a structural reason. "When the public governs," he wrote, "all men feel the value of public goodwill and all try to win it by gaining the esteem and affection of those among whom they must live." In local government, too, "the same people are always meeting, and they are forced, in a manner, to know and adapt themselves to one another."[16] Tocqueville's point may or may not be correct. But it does point up one feature of democracy in its nineteenth-century setting, a feature which encouraged moral behavior in public, if not in private. That is the small social and geographic scale within which people lived and worked. America was, for its time, an incredibly mobile society; certainly so in contrast to the older nations. People were not condemned to a life rooted in a single spot. Nonetheless, life meant predominantly small-town, village life; both politics and economics were narrow, local, face-to-face.

Whatever the causes, nineteenth-century democracy, outside the economic sphere, continued to assume a code of traditional *personal* values and to value moderate, respectable behavior which did not offend time-honored norms. People depended on each other, and not just physically; social disapproval could easily block success and personal development; equality implied a single code of conduct: the familiar code of the Western tradition. This code was, if anything, strengthened; the rules moved toward *greater* emphasis on moderation and self-control in personal life.

The pragmatic defense of democracy, ultimately, must be that people have the will and the skill to govern themselves and also their community. Authoritarian government is paternalistic. It regulates a great deal of primary conduct when it can, and it does not allow the governed to choose rules or rulers for themselves. It legitimates its power in a number of ways. Some regimes have insisted, explicitly or implicitly, that a stratified order is ordained by nature or by God; the top strata deserve to rule because of their inborn superiority, or because of some divine plan of hegemony. These kinds of legitimation were so common at one time they were basically taken for granted. God had set up the world as a place of rank and authority, with God himself at the apex and the lower animals at the bottom. The image of the "Great Chain of Being . . . stencilled in people's minds" the concept of a hierarchical political structure, "with power descending from the king and his court through different ranks marked off from one another by birthright and title."[17] Modern authoritarian regimes shy away from such old-fashioned modes of legitimation; but they invoke the same spirit of paternalism, justified on other grounds or through fictions. Even the tyrannies of Hitler and Stalin invoked "the people"; a language of legitimation that would have mystified Attila the Hun or Louis XIV. The end results are perhaps more authoritarian, however much the rhetoric and philosophies may differ.

Democratic societies, of course, reject these classic forms of legitimation and substitute others of their own. In the first phase of self-government, historically speaking, democratic theorists launched attacks on the methods and structures of authoritarian governments, and on such ideas as the divine right of kings. They did not necessarily attack the social values and behavioral norms of their communities. They argued for self-government as a better and more just way to run the social order, but they did not visualize a social order radically different from the social order under the old, authoritarian state in matters of family, leisure, moral norms, and ways of life. The theorists were neither anarchists, nor levelers, nor proponents of free love. The people, said the democrats, were not animals; they were intelligent, moderate, well-ordered, or they could be if given half a chance; in a free society it would be possible to put the people in the saddle (or at least white males) and trust them to behave. Indeed, according to one version of the gospel of Adam Smith, wealth and prosperity would flow in to the polity automatically if the economy were only let loose from its shackles.

The nineteenth-century brand of individualism, as it developed, rested firmly on this belief: the magic of those automatic markets. Let people act in the market place; let the invisible hand do its work, and society as a whole will benefit. The market was a social, aggregate concept. It guaranteed nothing to any particular individual, whose fate depended on his own exertions. *Individual* success was not automatic; the invisible hand did not guarantee prosperity. Skill and hard work produced success, with a bit of luck thrown in. It was also possible to fail through vice, laziness, misfortune, or sin. But all in all, discipline and hard work were crucial factors in individual advancement, and they paid off handsomely. There were no invincible barriers. Millions came to believe that they could and should find the ladder to success. Social strata in the United States, and later in other countries, became more fluid, porous, loose. In the old regime social strata were rigid; the upper class believed in its God-given right to rule and held tightly to power; the lower classes accepted, or had to accept, their place on the bottom. Law was the glue that bound society together, and it emphasized free markets and somewhat less free spirits: economic liberalism and moral purity. Discipline was a key *legal* element, too, as we shall see, though it was hidden behind a curtain of jargon and doctrinal disguise.

Thus the ideal of the nineteenth-century individual, as we deduce it from literature and other written records, was vastly different from the ideal of the individual today. It included a strong belief in massive self-control—temperance and moderation in all things. At the heart of it was the concept of the self-made man. (Women, of course, were not expected to make themselves, at least not in the same sense; they were certainly not expected to earn a living, to follow a career, or to create their own futures.) Exactly what was the self-made man expected to make of himself? Certainly not a rebel, a free spirit, or somebody who marched to his own drummer. He was expected to succeed in business or in public affairs if he could—but in all these efforts, he was to remain as he was trained to be in childhood, that is, a paragon of bourgeois morality: addicted to hard work, moderate in personal habits, adhering to traditional values as he lived his life outside the hours of work. This was the kind of person who could function and prosper in the free society, precisely because his inner controls were so firm, so powerful in governing behavior. These controls suppressed all deviant desires, idiosyncracies, and the thoughts and impulses that violated society's norms: that is, everything that made a man specific and unusual in his habits or personality, or that interfered with the pursuit of success. What was unique and remarkable about nineteenth-century individualism was precisely this model of man.

This image of the ideal individual presupposed a particular kind of society and generated a particular kind of legal order. In this society individuals (men at least) were set free from economic restraints, but remained bound to past values. The powerful socializing forces of a face-to-face society remained largely intact: the authority of family, neighbors, teachers, and preachers. In some regards nineteenth-century society tried to strengthen the influence of these private governors, turning their message even further toward sobriety, good order, and self-control—thus the ruthless suppression of old customs of frivolity and the war against popular amusements, carnivals, and fairs.[18] The work ethic and economic and social success in the Western world depended on *inner* norms that controlled behavior, that is, on self-control; and on *outer* norms of law and authority, which permitted freedom of movement and work but did not relax the restraints on life-style or personal habits. Middle-class morality was, or was felt to be, as vital as hard work to the social fabric. People generally expected to take care of themselves, to work hard on their own, to motivate themselves, to walk in traditional paths; and were also expected to accept democratic authority, the rule of law, and the decisions of the majority. People who had this kind of toughness, this strength of character, did not need coercion, policemen, laws, and jails; they conformed to right patterns without force, from inner conviction and habit.

In short, people did not *choose* a particular way of life; rather, they were trained to accept a preformed, preexisting model. They were inducted into a fixed pattern of behavior that controlled crucial aspects of their daily existence. The coercive parts of the law—criminal rules, primarily—were irrelevant to such people as coercion, but they were important in other ways. They protected the interests of the respectable majority from the weaknesses and crimes of people whose control systems were weak, defective, or altogether lacking. Control systems are necessarily imperfect, and thus society needs law to deal with people who deviate from the norm—tramps, thieves, paupers, moral delinquents. Legal coercion was needed when the norms governed ineffectively, and for people who could not internalize the norms and follow them. The law also had a vital *symbolic* function. It was a banner, a proclamation; it announced which norms were the right ones, the official ones, the preferred ones. This was no doubt important in itself, as a psychological support for correct behavior; presumably it also increased—to some unknown degree—the actual impact of the norms, their penetration in society.

Indeed, the nineteenth century bore down harshly on those whose control system did not measure up to legal and moral standards. This included the poor and those among the lower classes who were out of work, sick, or unfortunate. The poor laws were notoriously cruel—and, to modern eyes, amazingly unfair. But poverty *had* to remain degrading and unpleasant; otherwise people would be tempted to choose life on the dole rather than a life of hard work. At least this is what many people believed.[19] American prison regimes were also unusually harsh—Beaumont and Tocqueville called them "despotic."[20] These sharp-eyed visitors from France were not criticizing the American penitentiary system; on the contrary, they admired it greatly. It was, in their view, an efficient and effective instrument of crime-control and reformation. Compared to the old jails of Europe and America, nineteenth-century penitentiaries were models of stern but salutary order. The penitentiary was, in a way, a caricature of normal family socialization, an exaggerated form of one version of childhood life: regimented, paternal, rigidly disciplined (see Chapter 8). Good morals had their source in close-knit families, in surrounding institutions such as the church, and in the cohesion and solidarity found in village life. Bad morals came from peers, from "society," from horizontal, transient groupings.

General and legal culture agreed, too, that *excess* had to be curbed, and that institutions in society which fostered discipline and self-control had to be strengthened. The law codes and popular literature sent messages strongly disapproving of vice—of drunkenness, gambling, debauchery. Authority proclaimed the value of self-control and moderation; sexual exuberance was subject to special disapproval. Medical texts began to warn the public about the dangers of too much sex and its harm to body and soul. Masturbation and sexual excess were of course immoral in themselves, but they also led to bodily destruction—weakness, poor health, even insanity and death.

Strong warnings about sex appeared as early as the 1830s in America, in the writings of Sylvester Graham. Sexual excitement, according to Graham, "rapidly exhausts the vital properties of the tissues, and impairs the functional powers of the organs."[21] Nearly eighty years later, in a popular medical treatise, Dr. Richardson Parke claimed, on the basis of overwhelming evidence, that "artificial eroticism" did great damage, even to the "delicate mechanism of the eye"; thousands of men, he added, "fail in business because they are masturbators."[22] The royal road to health and virtue went by way of repression, thinly disguised as moderation. The human body was a "closed energy system," in "delicate balance."[23] The stress on self-control appears constantly in the literature of sexual advice in the days before Sigmund Freud. But it is also one way to read the message preached by Freud himself. Civilization, Freud believed, depends on repression and sublimation of crude, animal impulses. Civilization is "built up upon a renunciation of instinct;" it presupposes "precisely the non-satisfaction . . . of powerful instincts" by "suppression, regression, or some other means."[24]

A number of explanations exist for the nineteenth-century obsession with self-control. One plausible account, for example, links it to changes in the economic order. In a rural population, as Roger Lane has pointed out, "teamsters, farmers, or artisans . . . were all accustomed to setting their own schedules"; their work made them "physically independent of each other"; thus "fits of violence" or "bouts of drinking" did not disrupt any "vital patterns." But industrial capitalism, as it developed, had different needs and demands. The factory "demanded regularity of behavior, a life governed by obedience to the rhythms of clock and calendar." Industry needed workers who had regular habits—sober and moderate people, who would show up to work on time, ready and able to do the job; who understood industrial discipline, and were in tune with the rhythms of industrial life. Moreover, workers "in larger establishments" were "mutually dependent on their fellows." One man's business "was no longer his own." It follows that "violent or irregular behavior which had been tolerated in a casual, independent society was no longer acceptable."[25] Or, to put it another way, discipline at home, in bed, and on the streets influenced discipline in the workplace, practically and ideologically.

In the nineteenth century discipline became a vital part of the message social institutions imparted or implied. In fact, expansion of freedom—expansion of the zone of choice—*depended* on self-control. As Stephen Nissenbaum puts it, that era "inverted" the "long-held sense of the relationship between individuals and social institutions." Before then people saw society and its institutions as the source of "stability and order." Now "society itself and its institutions" became instead "the locus of instability"; the *individual* was the "one potential source of order." Instead of "scrutiny, control, and protection imposed . . . from without," a person "had to impose these things on himself."[26] And impose it he did. Political society removed the citizen's chains, so to speak; it set loose the citizen and allowed him to exploit his own furious energies; nonetheless, freedom depended on his personal self-control—on the faith that he would not run too far, too fast, or abuse the granted freedoms.

Individualism in Its Twentieth-Century Meaning

The contemporary understanding of choice and individualism—perhaps it would be more accurate to say the contemporary *feeling*—is significantly different from what it was in the past. These concepts have now come to include those areas of personal life summed up in that somewhat obnoxious phrase, "life-style." The new variety of individualism stresses self-expression, that is, cultivating the inner human being, expanding the self, developing the special qualities and uniqueness of each person. The idea naturally seeps into legal culture as well. The fundamental law of the German Federal Republic states boldly that each person has the right to the free development or unfolding (*Entfaltung*) of personality.[27] The phrasing, and the underlying idea, would never have occurred in this form to friends of freedom and civil liberties in the eighteenth and nineteenth centuries. Older constitutions—like that of the United States—do not contain this concept. But the Supreme Court, undaunted, reads it into the text. The central concepts of modern legal culture are choice, consent, freedom, and individual rights. These are old terms, but what they mean in the 1980s is startlingly different from what they meant to Jefferson or Locke.

The passion for sexual repression, to take one example, has passed into total oblivion. The old medical textbooks seem ludicrous today. Modern society stands the medical message completely on its head and reinterprets Freud to suit itself. Now it is not sexuality which leads to disease and decay; it is repression which has these dire effects. Sexuality is a good, a joy, a gift; it is an aspect of the richness of life, part of a person's irrepressible, essential self; it cannot and should not be denied. (The recent arrival of AIDS may, of course, make a difference in the future. As of now, AIDS is a warning to be careful and safe, not to abjure.)

This is only one example out of many. In every area of social life institutional behavior has been reconstituted, gradually or rapidly, to reflect the new culture, the new versions of choice and individualism. The history of public education is particularly rich in instances. Education has passed through various stages of growth and various ruling ideologies. In eighteenth-century England, for example, some elite opinion rejected the very idea of educating the lower orders. Why encourage people to rise above their station in life? Education would merely "render them fractious and refractory."[28] The nineteenth century, on the other hand, found general education a social necessity, which had to be extended to all classes. Education was a vital form of social control; it was essential for preparing free citizens and training them in responsibility and governance. Education reinforced and carried forward the established values of society—it was a mode of indoctrination or socialization and of job training as well. It was society's way to make little people think and behave the way big people did. Schooling was an extension and reinforcement of the parental role.

In the United States the schools had particularly important functions in regard to foreigners. Immigrants had to be trained in American ways; the job of the schools was to "inculcate the Protestant-republican ideology." Horace Mann claimed, too, that "educated workers were more productive. . . . Schooling made workers more industrious, obedient, and adaptive."[29] At the end of the nineteenth century, at a time when the older elites felt threatened, the spokesmen of orthodoxy were more insistent than ever that American schools must drill proper, accepted values into children's heads.[30] Modern educational theory downplays this role, and has added to it notions of quite a different character. Education has been reconceptualized; now it is a way of forming *individuals*, a way to awaken the latent selves of children, each of whom has potential for growth, each of whom is the bud of a separate flower.[31] Whether it succeeds at this goal or not—whether it even seriously tries—we leave to one side.

If my account of modern individualism is correct, at least in rough outline, then one would expect to have seen monumental change in society. Profound consequences for legal and authority systems would flow naturally from such a change, that is, from the transformation of individualism, and the glorification of autonomous individuals. Changes in fact are visible everywhere. The sphere or zone of *choice*, already great in the past, seems to have expanded even more in the twentieth century. This is most obviously true with regard to people's expectations, their notions of what is coming to them. Popular culture and opinion surveys suggest that people feel they should be able to select, out of a rich menu of possibilities, whatever patterns of living and behaving seem to suit them. They may be dissatisfied, of course, with the menu actually before them or with the arrangements for obtaining their choice, but that is another story.

The notion of a wide zone of choice alters authority systems almost by definition. It diminishes the power of older forms of authority, and it recasts the legal system as well. Changes in law cannot, however, be summed up in a single formula. There is a conventional idea that the nineteenth century was (legally) freer than the twentieth century; it was the age of the free market, of laissez-faire, of small government. This notion, however, is misleading in two ways: first, it underestimates the role of government in the economy and polity; and second, it ignores the fact that the extensive liberty of the citizen applied most notably to aspects of economy and polity, not the rest of life. Other domains—sex life, marriage, divorce, and family life— were fettered by custom and law, certainly in comparison with the world of the 1980s.

Law is the vehicle through which modern notions of choice are translated into living social arrangements. The issue, then, is not one of "more" law or "less" law, but rather of what kind of law, and what kind of arrangements. What is the relationship between modern individualism, on the one hand, and law, legal rules, and legal institutions, on the other? Our general thesis, as we noted, is that the "autonomy" of law is only apparent and only skin-deep. Thus modern legal arrangements *must* be congruent with modern legal culture and with modern individualism as well.

Rationality, Legitimacy, and Choice

Modern law, government, and authority, are also *rational*. This is one basic theme of Max Weber's work on the sociology of law.[32] His writings suggest a long-term drift from traditional forms of authority toward a form he called rational-legal.

A large literature of exegesis[33] asks exactly what Weber meant, and whether he was right. There is much to argue about, but many social thinkers would at least agree on the basic point: that the decline of traditional authority is a basic mark of modern society, and that rational-legal authority has taken over from tradition. Legal authority is distinctive in that it is not rooted in particular persons whose authority is derived from tradition or inheritance (for example, a tribal chief), or from personal magic or "charisma." Instead, authority is lodged in the office or position whose incumbents change by election or appointment, at regular or irregular intervals. There is a new American president every four or at most eight years; there is a fresh election for Parliament in England at least every five years; prime ministers of Italy or Belgium revolve in and out of office more often. These offices and the methods of filling them are what is stable in modern societies. Incumbents come and go.

Authority in modern governments is also overtly bound up with law and legal process; hence it is "rational-legal" in this literal sense, again as compared to older forms of government and to the governments of preliterate peoples. But why should this be so? What is it about authority grounded in law that makes it so suitable for contemporary life? In some ways the answer is obvious. Modern governments assume complex, technical tasks; these do not lend themselves to magic, charisma, or naked authority; they call for more regular and routine methods, for order and bureaucracy, and for modes of manipulation that follow definite rules. It would be impossible to run a National Health Service, an urban planning operation, or a system of old age pensions, on a charismatic or customary basis.

Nonetheless, there *is* something of a puzzle here. Legal process is a curiously bloodless phenomenon: dry, technical, formal. It is easy to understand why tradition should be tough and tenacious, encrusted as it is with historical experience and enforced by powerful bonds of culture; it is easy to see how the passion and magic of charismatic authority make it irresistible. But what sustains the *basic* rules of the modern state? What is the source of the power of law? No doubt it is possible to make a kind of religion out of following rules—this is a common stereotype about German culture, for example. And elements of ritual, magic, and ceremony do survive in modern law; there is an occasional glint of symbolism and enchantment. Yet these elements do not seem vital enough to capture and sustain the underlying power of modern authority.

Part of the answer surely lies in the very fact that rational-legal authority rejects the person in favor of the process. Legitimacy (and authority) rest on procedural norms, in contrast to the legitimacy of charisma and tradition. But what is so special about procedures? Procedures are nothing in themselves, but everything insofar as they are instruments for ascertaining, measuring, and aggregating *choice*. Procedures in modern societies are ways of arriving at decisions that will reflect, in some orderly way, what people choose; procedures can handle problems of adding or subtracting the choices of great numbers of choosers, or of conflicting choices. The paradigm case is voting. Elections are fundamental processes in modern states; voting is what many people think of as the ultimate legitimator, the ultimate base on which true government rests. At bottom, modern authority is *chosen* authority; or, more precisely, authority that either is or *looks* chosen. The modern state and modern authority structures are legitimate insofar as they have power to facilitate, channel, and realize individual choices. The legal procedures are methods of solving problems of conflict among or with regard to various kinds of choice. Voting is simply a way to register and objectify choice.

Reduced to its essential elements, the modern state rests on the authority of law, and law rests on the authority of personal choice. There are two kinds of public norm in the modern state, which correspond to two elements in the state's constitutional structure. There are, to begin with, "ordinary" norms. These are the laws that the legislatures enact, adopted by majority vote; or they are rules and regulations of agencies which were created by law and can be abolished in the same way—a planning board, a tax agency, a railroad commission. All such norms are said to reflect "the will of the people," as expressed through their elected representatives or by offi-

cials appointed by them. In addition, there are certain specially
sacred norms—fundamental rights, whether enshrined in a written
Constitution, or treated as basic elements of a just social order. These
rights are the building blocks of a system of personal freedom.

. None of this is new. But in contemporary society the meaning of
the fundamental rights has been subtly altered. They have come
more and more to refer to personal choice and private life—they are
interpreted more and more as creating zones of freedom and realms
of open option, which the state must not encroach upon. (Jefferson
and Locke would be amazed at the modern "right of privacy.")
Choice is the central idea that underpins many of these rights.

Later chapters of this book will expand on this point. For now, it is
worth emphasizing how the alteration of rights-theories alters types
of legitimacy as well. In classical political theory, voting and elections
were essential tools of a democratic polity; rights were visualized
mainly in economic or political terms. The American Constitution, to
be sure, never created a "pure" democracy. In particular, it protected
certain economic and political rights from the encroachment of the
majority. The Bill of Rights set up safeguards for criminal trials, to
avoid the despotic practices of Old World monarchies. Other provisions protected religion from the state, and property against appro-
priation. That was basically as far as the declarations went.   .

Nothing has been more surprising and dramatic than the explosion
of constitutionalism in the twentieth century; constitutional courts
have arrogated to themselves a vast infusion of power. Constitutional theorists, somewhat baffled and perplexed, find it hard to
explain exactly why judicial review should have become so high and
mighty and how to justify that power of courts, since it is, after all,
"countermajoritarian"—that is, undemocratic—a long word that is
applied only to courts, as far as I can tell.

But the ordinary person today does not think of democracy solely
in political terms of voting and elections. She tends to think in concrete, substantive terms: democracy is personal rights, personal
choices, style of life. Freedom means substantive claims, entitlements, and options, anchored in particular individuals. No majority
can and should touch the zone of rights. Thus there is nothing
undemocratic about an institution that declares, sustains, protects,
and supports these individual rights. Indeed, in the citizen's eyes the
court is profoundly and meaningfully democratic, even if this contra-
dicts political theory. And rational-legal legitimacy is not restricted to

voting or bureaucracy alone or in themselves, but only as controlled and chastened by institutions of fundamental law.

Models of Culture, Models of Man

The historical meanings of individualism, and the shift in meaning over time, have been themes in studies of many aspects of culture, especially those which contrast nineteenth- and twentieth-century culture, or urban and rural culture. The various studies, of course, emphasize disparate elements and have different centers of gravity, yet also striking symmetries that bear on the theme of this book. For example, in Edward L. Ayers's study of crime and punishment in the American South in the nineteenth century, the concept of "honor" plays a key role. An honor code implies an "overweening concern with the opinions of others." Ayers contrasts the honor code of the South with what he considers a key cultural trait of the northern states, the concept of personal dignity—"the conviction that each individual at birth possessed an intrinsic value at least theoretically equal to that of every other person."[34] White males of the South, the ruling elite of that region, tended to avoid the use of formal law. The code of honor frowned on litigation. The code called for violence, for physical reaction to insults. Personal dignity, the ruling concept in the northern states, rejected violence in favor of self-control. Legal coercion was an acceptable instrument of power. It was not shameful or dishonorable to sue, to use legal process; the state in turn did not hesitate to use law upon those too weak or sinful to comply with accepted standards. Law was a substitute, in short, for both violence and a failed self-control.

A code of honor is a male, peer-based code with a strongly traditional flavor; it is relentlessly rigid in subordinating personal choice or interest to the demands of norms shared in the peer group. Honor requires men to conduct themselves in patterned ways—toward women, for example—and they are not to accept personal insults meekly. Codes of honor have a distinct aristocratic flavor. As European literature makes clear (Theodor Fontane's *Effi Briest* is an excellent example out of Germany), honor cultures have been widespread in the West; they have also been prevalent in premodern warrior societies. In this sense, the "dignity" code of the American north, as Ayers defines it, has a much more modern flavor. It stressed the individual's duty to follow his conscience; to stick with principles learned

in childhood; to derive values from internalized standards rather than from the peer group. The norms and standards were those of self-control, hard work, and conventional morality: classic aspects of nineteenth-century individualism. The new individualism of the twentieth century has replaced both codes (honor and dignity); it differs from the older models in its insistence on personality and on the right of each person to choose among options and norms to create a free-standing self.[35]

The transition from an older to a newer form of individualism is also the theme of *Habits of the Heart,* by Robert Bellah and coauthors, a book which aroused great interest when it was published in 1985. The authors saw individualism as a core American value, but drew a distinction between two types of individualism, "utilitarian" and "expressive." Utilitarian individualism "sees human life as an effort by individuals to maximize their self-interest," conceived mostly in economic terms; expressive individualism "holds that each person has a unique core of feeling and intuition that should unfold or be expressed if individuality is to be realized."[36] For Bellah and his coauthors these two forms of individualism represent enduring aspects of American character. But expressive individualism is or has become the dominant form. Today, for most Americans, "the meaning of life" is "to become one's own person, almost to give birth to oneself."[37]

The distinction between these two forms of individualism can be compared with the distinctions drawn by David Riesman in his famous book, *The Lonely Crowd* (1950). Riesman was interested in the factors of personality that underlie conformity, obedience, and norm-following. He described three distinct personality types. In one category, found in older societies, individuals tended to be "tradition-directed," following norms that had "endured for centuries . . . modified but slightly, if at all, by successive generations."[38] A second personality type, characteristic of nineteenth-century America, was "inner-directed." An inner-directed person follows norms that are "implanted early in life by the elders and directed toward . . . inescapably destined goals."[39] This is the classic hard-working, God-fearing, norm-following Protestant. The third stage is "other-direction," in which the peer group constitutes the main source of the norms people conform to. At first glance, the "other-directed" conformist of Riesman's modern period does not closely resemble Bellah's expressive individualist, but as we shall see they are at bottom the same.

Riesman's categories are character or personality types, but character and personality are not independent of social structure, as Riesman of course clearly recognized. In each historical period there are modal personality types, as well as typical patterns of behavior. Riesman was looking for these patterns, and his book is an attempt to detect shifts in modality. On the surface, too, the Riesman scheme does not deal with law or government; it concerns authority in a more general social sense. In a complex society, however, authority inevitably rests on pillars of law. Authority patterns as aspects of culture (formal or informal, public or private) play a vital role in the dynamic processes that lead to the making and breaking of law.

Any number of studies of cultural change could be brought in to reinforce the general pattern. Thus Ronald Inglehart sees a shift among Western publics from "materialism" to "post-materialism," that is, from emphasis on needs for "sustenance and safety" to such needs as "esteem, self-expression and aesthetic satisfaction."[40] David Engel, studying "Sander County" in Illinois, distinguished between "rights-oriented individualism" and "individualism emphasizing self-sufficiency and personal responsibility." The question was why old-timers in this rural county were averse to suing for damages after an accident. The answer was that *their* individualism "emphasized self-sufficiency rather than rights and remedies"; it retained "values . . . [from] an earlier face-to-face community."[41] Warren Susman argues that the "modal type" of the self has evolved, in the last century or so, from "character" to "personality." The culture of character emphasized order and discipline; the culture of personality emphasizes the idiosyncratic self.[42] Daniel Bell sees a "striking disjunction" between the "techno-economic order," the world of "efficiency and functional rationality," and a "culture" in which the "self is taken as the touchstone of cultural judgment" and in which the old "bourgeois values" of the nineteenth century, "self-discipline, delayed gratification, and restraint," have been "completely rejected."[43] Sociologists, historians, and scholars of social thought in general all seem to agree on the basic lines of change in cultural meanings and forms of individualism. Current popular views about human nature and the goals and aims of society also run in a similar direction with regard to personality, individual rights, choice, and self-realization.

Evidence about popular culture and about legal culture hardly amounts to mathematical proof, to say the least. It is cobbled together from surveys and interviews, conversations, the testimony of newspapers, magazines, movies, and television programs; inspirational and how-to-do-it books, and books about how to raise children, make love, and improve oneself. The evidence is slippery but real. In any event, this evidence feeds the notions of the authors mentioned and quoted; as they see it, it converges on a single point. It attests to a new form of individualism, centered on the autonomous, idiosyncratic, self-making self. The new concept is a creature of the amorphous public mass, or at any rate, of the middle-class mass. The concept may or may not dribble down, but it certainly filters up, so that in the end it shapes political philosophy and other forms of higher thought. The "idea of personal autonomy," says Joseph Raz, is the "vision of people controlling, to some degree, their own destiny, fashioning it through successive decisions throughout all their lives." The "ruling idea" is to be "author" of one's own life.[44] It becomes, as well, the ruling idea of systematic thought, in Raz and others. Prescription recapitulates description.

Of course, this particular popular theory does not lack for rivals. It is not universal and unchallenged, either in high or low thought. There are other models of man in science and social science, some congruent with expressive individualism, others not. For example, the rational maximizer, a cold-blooded and unlikable creature who stalks the pages of economics textbooks, is reminiscent of Bellah's utilitarian type. The extreme maximizer is hardly a real or whole person; but economists assume and insist on the core of truth in their model. The maximizer was not an expressive individualist—not, at any rate, in his Adam Smith or utilitarian form. Yet today, even the maximizer has fallen in line. What the maximizer maximizes, after all, are her own tastes, wishes, and goals; to some economists, no taste is illegitimate, no want improper, so long as it has or can make a market.

Other images of man, from sociology, anthropology, and some strains of radical thought are less congruent with the assumptions of modern individualism. There is a conception of the human being as tricked and manipulated, his range of choice reduced to the trivial so that he merely enjoys, in the sneering phrase of Herbert Marcuse, "free choice between brands of gadgets."[45] There is Michel Foucault's nightmare vision of the "carceral society," a bleak and horrifying depiction of modern life in which fiendish experts, "the judges of normality," are "everywhere," and "each individual may find himself, his subjects . . . his body, his gestures, his behaviour, his aptitudes, his achievements" exposed and subjected to the pitiless discipline, the minute, detailed prescriptions of these invisible powers.[46] Foucault's picture is, in some ways, the very opposite of the one expressed here. But in a curious, unconscious way, it too pays tribute to the republic of choice. What makes the "carceral society" so horrifying is its inconsistency with modern individualism. Discipline and repression are so offensive and strike such a chord of horror in the reader precisely because of the assumption that free choice and expressive individualism are by rights the norm; the "carceral society" is not order and symmetry but a terrible perversion of the right sort of life.

The orthodox social sciences present less dour pictures of the human condition, but their images of man do not fit neatly in with the popular assumptions described above. The central message of the social sciences is that human beings are creatures of culture, dependent on the framework that surrounds them. These fields of learning *hint* at least that freedom of choice is often false consciousness or downright illusion. People are products of their environment; they swim in their culture like fish in the sea; they may think they are choosing freely, but their choices are brokered by context, though the process is submerged in the dim subconscious. At the very least, culture and individual mutually influence each other. The social scientist is keenly alive to the ways context boxes in the self; much more so than the selves are.[47] There is also a distinct form of psychological or psychoanalytic determinism at the individual level, pointing the finger at the primacy of preformed, unconscious motivations; this approach "offers a motivationally determined view of behavior," which seeks the explanations of conduct deep within the personality;[48] it tends to conceive of choice as essentially an illusion, a trick which the subconscious plays on the conscious mind.

All this may be correct, as social science, or politically or ideologically sound, yet rarefied and distant from popular culture. To be sure, some social science views and a large dose of diluted Freud, have filtered down to the mass magazines, or insinuated themselves into the plots of movies; but on the whole, deterministic views do not correspond to what people think as they go about their daily lives. In their lives people assume free choice. They consider most of their actions voluntary; they treat their tastes and habits as products of volition; they are unaware of or reject sociological determinism. They despise the very idea of psychological determinism, especially when used as an excuse for deviance and criminal behavior. Choice, consent, contract, and free will pervade both language and mentality; people are convinced that they behave, on the whole, in the way they have chosen. One cannot really fathom the structure of modern society without taking into account the primitive power of these popular concepts. Popular theories of personality and individualism have a deep impact on the legal order and on the governance of society. The process may also work the other way around: that is, new forms of law and governance may create an environment friendly to certain personality types and to radical forms of individualism. Modern democracy feeds on, and also fosters, expressive individualism.

What we are discussing, of course, is a general tendency. Social life cannot be summed up in simple formulas. I believe that the ideas of freedom and choice here described are dominant in modern society; that they are the popular, preferred notions of what individuals are and deserve in the way of right. But societies and their populations are dramatically heterogeneous. The public is certainly not of one mind. This is true not only at the level of groups but also at the level of individuals. The views that any given man or woman holds with regard to the real world and its ways can be thoroughly inconsistent, and frequently are.

As basic ideas about what is right and wrong, and what simply *is*, change, they elbow older meanings aside, but do not necessarily erase them. Many people are quite ambivalent about choice, obedience, authority, even in the United States and other Western countries. Some people like freedom but also want to be led; others want freedom of choice but believe in the old values; they like strict order, they like authority. They support compulsion, discipline, firmness in government, and strict morality in private life. Their attitudes may not be incompatible with the republic of choice. Democracy and freedom of choice themselves require a certain level of toughness, a certain solidity of structure. The legal framework must stand firm, to maximize liberty and choice; without it, society would be a booming chaos, and individuals would go hopelessly astray.

Choice, consent, and contract are not accepted, then, as absolute goods beyond all question, even in the modern world. As far as the nineteenth-century forms are concerned, such basic legal concepts as choice, consent, and contract were subjected to withering criticism by jurists on a variety of accounts: as stained by ideology, as incoherent, as false to the reality of people's lives. Powerful voices challenged the complacencies of the capitalist order. Choice in industrial society, these voices asserted, was and is forced or illusory; in particular, free contract has been a mirage, a shield for privilege. The criticisms have had their impact, notably on formal social thought and certainly on lawmaking and on legal doctrine. Perhaps, by osmosis, they influenced popular culture as well; indeed, many scholarly attacks began on the streets, in strikes and riots, in revolts against the excesses of unbridled markets.

Despite vast changes in the world, the classic ideas have retained enormous power. In law, the more naive (or ideological) versions of freedom of contract have long since been abandoned. The concept of freedom of contract itself is somewhat frayed about the edges; it no longer enjoys a tight and exclusive connection to the very idea of freedom. But freedom of contract—the essential core of it—remains alive as a *reality*, that is, contract in practice, rather than ideology. In many ways the regime of contract is stronger than it ever was. Markets exist; we buy and sell what we wish, as we wish, and our daily lives are full of those constant rhythms of binding and loosing which are the essence of contract. Choice and its passive form, consent, remain part of the *inner* definition of freedom, the subjective definition; they describe what it means to be a responsible human being. In the West, moreover, there is no cultural alternative to choice, that is, to the notion of the rational, independent human being who chooses her life. The popular ideal, unexamined, exalts the person who creates a way of living for himself. This popular ideal has its rivals, but none is a serious threat. As far as one can tell, enormous majorities reject the idea of a self that is programmed in advance, the self that birth and status establish, the fixed and immutable self, beyond the control of individual choices and will.

Individualism, National and International

The sphere of choice, and hence of individualism, has been expanding over the years in contemporary society. The aim of society must therefore be, above all, to foster individual growth, to maximize choices that are open to individuals. The centrality of choice should not, however, be exclusively or distinctively American; these traits should be common, in one way or another, to all the societies of the West.

The societies of the Western world seem to be traveling together, on a single master-journey, tracing a single line of evolution, despite glaring and obvious differences in their histories, traditions, and cultures. Complaints about the "law explosion" and the breakdown of old forms of authority are common to these societies. Both are frequently voiced in West Germany, for example.[49] Two generations ago that country was under the tight and tyrannical rule of one of the most savage dictators in history. Today it enjoys a constitution, a constitutional court, a code of fundamental rights, and these are not paper tigers. The German constitutional court is perhaps second only to the Supreme Court of the United States in judicial activism. German jurists and interest groups are preoccupied more and more with fundamental law and with the enforcement of individual rights.[50]

Moreover, in every country of Europe there is (compared to the past) tremendous mobility. The lines between classes and strata are more fluid than they used to be; people migrate from city to city and from job to job more rapidly and loosely than was ever the case. Under these circumstances, "expressive individualism" flourishes as it does in the United States, though with cultural variations. In short, authority and law in Western nations have been redefined in such a way as to reflect the primacy of choice and consent. Modern social structures are legitimate insofar as they rest on the assumed consent of the governed. Older modes of legitimation persist, but have lost most of their power to persuade. Hierarchy and stratification still exist, of course, but with diminished legitimacy and in revised forms. In some senses, they have gone underground. Political theory and popular sentiment have bored holes in all forms of privilege; established churches and aristocracies have all but vanished. Popular sovereignty is the crucial basis of governing structures; older forms of government have gone under, while the kings and queens that survive are figureheads.

In the United States these tendencies came to the fore early in the national experience, and in a particularly virulent form. This was only natural. The enthronement of individual choice proceeded rapidly in the United States because it was a new society, poorly and weakly linked to autocracy on the European model, with an abundance of land and vast empty spaces. The republic of choice grew more quickly and more emphatically in the North than in the South. In the South, of course, there was chattel slavery. The North abolished slavery, and many people came to condemn slavery as a monstrous evil. Yet there is little evidence that the masses of whites in the North believed in racial equality; on the contrary, the evidence of racism is overwhelming. Most people were at any rate convinced that blacks were inferior to whites, and indelibly so. Free blacks could not vote in many states. School segregation in fact began in the North, not the South.[51]

Why then was slavery so repugnant? It was an offense against the very core of Northern legitimacy, which was based on a theory of individualism—free choice, merit, individual consent. This was, to be sure, the nineteenth-century form of individualism. It did not stress (as yet) life-style, but it was the immediate precursor of that form of contemporary culture. Slavery was odious for a number of reasons, but surely one of them was that it offended against the ideal of free contract and free choice, so vital to dominant political theory and economic culture.

Sketched out here are, to be sure, only general trends in the Western countries; it is still worthwhile to draw distinctions between the (relative) rigidity of European society and the bumptious fluidity of American society; and between American legalism or litigiousness and the more restrained attitudes toward courts, claims, and rights in, say, France. Yet European countries seem to be moving in a definite American direction. It is, I think, wrong to think in terms of American influence, let alone cultural imperialism. One must even tread cautiously when speaking about cultural diffusion in the sense of influence exerted by an outside force. Such a notion can be profoundly misleading. Diffusion is not a process which makes tools and ideas flow from country A to country B, like water flowing downhill. It is a pull rather than a push or a flow: country B sucks in culture from country A. The Western countries share many features of political and social structure, of economic organization and levels of technology. Some of these features seem American because they first appeared in the United States, or developed there in their most powerful form. Coca-Cola, hamburgers, and judicial review have not been rammed down the throats of the Dutch or the Italians. As countries develop their own varieties of expressive individualism, they come to want these wondrous things for themselves.

Members of the "club" of democracies have on the whole evolved from tyrannical or authoritarian societies, whose authority structures lacked (modern) checks and balances, and whose ruling classes had untrammeled discretion, at least as far as the mass of the population was concerned. Thus it is no surprise that the "decay of authority" is common to all of them. In all these countries the divine right of kings has vanished; the established churches have been functionally if not legally disestablished; full religious tolerance is firmly anchored in law; the elites have lost at least some of their power; there is no longer much discussion of "natural" aristocracies, the importance of breeding, and the need for rigid lines between classes. On the contrary, their populations insist on popular sovereignty; governments are elected in and elected out; independent court systems and the rule of law are the ideal and the (more or less) real; and in most of these societies a peculiarly nonhierarchical, pluralistic, rights explosion has occurred or seems about to occur.

FOUR

Technology and Change

ONE CHARACTERISTIC of modern times is the rapidity of social change. Consciousness of that fact is perhaps no less important than the fact itself. The evolution of human societies seems to have gone from a crawl to a walk to a run—and then to flight in supersonic jets. Obviously, technology has made most of the difference. Technology is a crucial force in promoting social change; of course, it is not social change in itself. Writing home to mother is, in theory, the same act with the same cultural meaning whether the letter is written with a quill pen, on a typewriter, or transmitted electronically. But in practice, technological changes, when they are large enough and important enough, almost inevitably bring about changes in social arrangements. When the dust settles, so to speak, the electronic letter to mother is a different letter in many ways from the quill pen letter to mother, because mothers and sons and their relationships have changed in subtle details.

The point becomes clear if we try to imagine the ways in which we differ from people who lived in this country or in European countries a century ago or a century and a half. The world of our great-great-grandparents was profoundly different from our world, but why and how? There are, to be sure, elements of stability and continuity, especially in the United States, insulated as it is from European catastrophes. To begin with, the *political* system is still recognizable in certain basic features. The American Constitution is over two hundred years old; no living constitution is older. The framers, if they woke up from a sleep of two centuries, would recognize many aspects of government: the Presidency, the Congress, the Supreme Court, the federal system. The modern welfare and regulatory state would be foreign to them, but it is superimposed on a form of capitalism that is not totally different from the regime they knew in 1800. The free market has not by any means vanished; it is even making something of a comeback.

Formal, structural, and cultural features of society also show elements of continuity. The English language is essentially the same as it was in 1800, despite modern slang and thousands of new words. Scholars constantly write the obituary of the nuclear family, but it survives somehow; society is still organized and stratified into rich and poor, educated and uneducated; the basic design of cities, the very pattern of streets, is also recognizable. Other countries in the West, such as France and Germany, have been far less stable politically and have suffered periodic reversals, revolutions, and upheavals. But in other respects, the same point can be made about their social institutions—family, language, church, organization of life.

Yet surface continuity can be misleading; perhaps only outer forms have survived; perhaps the inner meaning has been bent out of shape, even for institutions that look much the same as they did two centuries ago. If we pursue *this* line of argument and look for the discontinuities, we cannot avoid beginning with the massive fact of technology. A person who went to sleep at the end of the eighteenth century and woke up in the nineteen-eighties would be amazed above all by machinery, equipment, gadgets, and scientific wonders. Men or women now blowing out the candles on their ninetieth birthday cakes were born before airplanes, automobiles (practically speaking), radio, movies, television, refrigerators, plastics, air conditioning, and computers, not to mention birth control pills and test-tube babies, satellites and the hydrogen bomb. This much is tangible. The twentieth-century machines, however, are more than ways to travel, add up columns of figures, or entertain oneself more quickly, better, and more efficiently. Their consequences go much deeper; they affect society root and branch.

Take the electronic letter to one's mother; or, for that matter, the long-distance telephone call. Family structure cannot stay exactly the same if family members can move great distances simply or quickly, even if it is simple and cheap to communicate across vast distances. New modes of communicating, in short, change family ties and, indeed, all personal relationships. Exactly how these relationships change is not easy to say with any precision; we will return to this point later. But—to repeat—an automobile is clearly more than a faster and better horse: it is a revolution. Any sustained, serious investigation into law and authority in modern society must reckon with social change, and this means placing technological revolutions at the center of the argument—they are volcanic waves of change that have swept over mankind and have by no means abated.

Legal Legitimacy and Its Forms

Two general phenomena have engaged our attention: first, the explosive growth in legal forms and structures; second, the decline of traditional forms of authority and the rise of expressive individualism. In Weberian terms, traditional authority slowly recedes; rational-legal authority climbs into the vacant throne. But it is a limited authority, and in the great spaces separating positive prescriptions, there reigns a world of options and choice. It is not difficult to connect this double process with the technological revolution. For one thing, the sheer rapidity of social change alters the way people think and behave. The new ways of thinking and behaving are inconsistent with thought and behavior natural to people who live in societies where the pace of change is slow and the grip of traditional authority is strong. In a period of rapid change, the older theories of legal legitimacy, the meta-human theories, cannot sustain themselves. These theories weaken and die, and are replaced, as we saw, by instrumental theories.

It is a natural process. Change necessarily undermines belief in changelessness—belief in timeless, sacred orders of being. The pace of change sets in motion reactions and responses in the domain of law. Legislatures act; courts decide new cases, which arise out of new situations; this legal activity strips away the outer covering of law and reveals the machinery inside the box—the political, human, instrumental elements in the process of making rules, norms, doctrines, and laws. How is it possible to insist that the laws are in their essence divinely inspired, when anyone with eyes to see and ears to hear observes ordinary men and women lobbying for laws, passing laws, and changing laws? How is it possible to believe that laws are the product of innate reason, when every fool knows and sees the way laws are made—that it was not the dictates of pure reason but the furious connivance of farmers, merchants, bankers, or the National Association of Apple Growers that accounts for this or that recent statute?

Of course, there is always a way to reconcile old beliefs with new situations, even in this gyrating, dizzy new world. Indeed, for many people it becomes more necessary than ever to have something of the past to cling to, some wreckage of old timbers to hold on to in the raging seas. This is one function of religions and religious beliefs: they provide a "haven in a heartless world,"[1], a world, moreover, that is shifting as well as heartless, a world in constant eruption. But the nature of religious belief alters in the process. Religion becomes a *chosen* haven. It is no longer ordained and established at birth, part of an unquestioned heritage; rather, it is an affiliation, a voluntary joining, a pattern of beliefs and an institutional membership freely elected on personal grounds.

New habits of mind emerge from the educational process of modernization. People are exposed to social institutions—factories, workplaces, schools—which create or reinforce modern ways of thinking, and modern ways of looking at the world. Out of these experiences, as Inkeles and Smith have argued, emerges a distinctively modern character or personality type. The new man or woman "has a marked sense of personal efficacy," is "highly independent and autonomous in his relations to traditional sources of influence, especially when . . . making basic decisions about . . . personal affairs;" and "is ready for new experiences and ideas."[2]

In this modernized world, law and authority are, as it were, horizontal rather than vertical. Traditional law and authority emanated from high to low, from past to present, from old to young, from the magical and the sacred to the everyday. Deference and obedience flowed in the opposite direction. Modern law and authority at least *appear* to function much more horizontally; tradition and vertical authority, in the course of time, have receded; the will and wishes of the present generation move to the center; legitimacy—and hence power—concentrate within the peer group and the general public. The new rather than the old is glorified; the secular rather than the sacred; the active young, rather than some revered clan of elders.[3] All this seems appropriate to a world in which social change takes place with startling rapidity, in which people are oriented more to the future than to the past, in which the future will be certainly different from the present—and people know this—and in which (they believe) personal sovereignty is and will continue to be king.

Technology is responsible for the invention and engineering of modes of traveling and communicating that vastly increase the sheer physical mobility of the millions. Mobility is perhaps the outstanding fact of modern life. But the individual, not the group, is the unit of modern mobility. Modern mobility is not the wandering of tribes and clans from one hunting ground to another, the migration of warrior peoples, or the patterned travel of nomads from habitat to habitat. Rather, it is the movement, in social and geographical space, of specific individuals, or, at most, of fragments of families. It can be described in aggregate terms, it can be measured statistically, but the inner reality is intensely personal: it is the decision of a young man to move to Philadelphia, of a young woman to leave a small town and get a job in Paris, of a Pakistani to join his cousin in London. Family ties are still important in determining individual mobility, but they are weaker and of a different order. Micro-mobility—moving down the block; or taking a ride in the country—is if anything more important in shaping the new world than mobility across thousands of miles. It opens up a world of new choice even to those who, in relative terms, stay put. But it is technology, of course, which makes modern mobility possible. The railroad, the steamship, the airplane, and above all, the automobile, have all been engines of migration; and, what is more significant, they provide means for an individual to detach herself from an environment of givens and move out to an environment of choice, a world of possibilities and unknowns.

There is no need to glorify this trend. Exposed to the play of impersonal, invisible market forces, many people fail the market test. Set loose, set adrift, individuals must sink or swim. Thousands sink. American society, a society of upstarts and migrants, has a long history of despising and oppressing its failures. These include the transient, the tramp, the hobo, along with a much more numerous group, the lonely, the disjointed, the friendless and anomic of all generations. The streets of American cities are full of the flotsam and jetsam of mobility—lost, detached souls. And many countries, though they welcome immigrants for their labor, despise and discriminate against "guest workers," who may sink to the bottom of the heap.

Modern society is mobile in many senses of the term—in the sheer physical sense, certainly, but also in the sense of fluidity between levels and classes of society. No fixed boundaries prevent a rise (or fall). This does not mean, to be sure, that great numbers of people *do* rise or fall, or that class and culture barriers have vanished. The social pyramid is strongly resistant to change. Indeed, evidence suggests that Western nations have not gone very far, in recent years, in reducing "inequalities in class life-chances"; in Britain (and other countries) the "main significance" of economic growth after the second World War was "not that it facilitated egalitarian reform but rather that it obscured its failure."[4] What failed here was mobility in one specific, measurable sense ("life-chances"). Britain and the rest of the West became much *more* mobile in other senses: in the whirling fluidity of physical position; in self-transportation; in vicarious mobility through mass media, with their bombardment of messages from and about other classes, strata, and cultures; in the availability of slots of opportunity, even if few people squeeze through them; in the decline of *theories* of fixity and authority; and in the proliferation of large and small escape hatches, as random as lotteries.

Countless aspects of modern law are responses to mobility, and to its discontents. The very fact of law—the pervasiveness of law—is a reflex of a society made up of strangers; a society in which the most rapidly growing "family" unit is the single person living utterly alone. Nineteenth-century individualism, as we remarked, was economic, political, and philosophical. Modern individualism is about *single* individuals, quite literally. People who live by themselves, in isolated rooms or apartments, are almost driven by necessity to become expressive individualists. In the nineteenth century (and earlier), detached people, whenever possible, were assimilated to families or other groups; they became hired hands, boarders, lodgers, forming fictive families. The unattached person—the tramp, the transient, the loner—was a figure of suspicion and dread. In the twentieth century the process is reversed: even families tend to become aggregations of individuals. Everybody needs his own "space." The idiom is revealing. Children must have a room of their own. Grandparents need a separate apartment. Mobility, space, individuality, isolation: these are the norm, even inside one's own home.

Of course, the transformation of the family is not *simply* a reflex of mobility but the result of a number of factors, links in a mighty chain: the changing nature of the economy, the rush to the cities, and the rise of the welfare state (with its old-age pensions, for example). The ambient wealth of society is also a critical factor: in the past, people who were rich enough to own their own carriages had a certain grade of mobility, after all. But however one thinks of the chain of consequences, mobility and its technology are part of it. The nineteenth-century picture of mobility was, of course, in some ways, quintessentially American. No one could describe European societies as made up of upstarts and immigrants. The scale of change and of movement was and still is somewhat different in Europe today. But Europe has begun to catch up. Massive migration from country to city is universal; it began long before this century, and it is no less important in its impact than overseas migration. London, Paris, Stockholm, Milan, Madrid are giant catchments of mobility. And today the big cities have become more heterogenous, cosmopolitan; London, Paris, and Amsterdam are filled with refugees from country life, along with population remnants of their shipwrecked empires. Regional customs vanish, and dialects wane; the metropolis swallows up local habits and levels them out horizontally.

The new forms of communication—telegraph, telephone, radio, movies, television—are themselves adjuncts of mobility in a crucial way. Through them, the outside world breaks in on the individual, bringing new messages and possibilities. The media leap across great distances. They put an end to traditional isolation. The new technology has also helped create an enormous stock of national wealth. As millions move up out of a subsistence economy, opportunities for leisure open up, and leisure itself expands beyond the traditional leisure class. Wealth may well be the most important contribution of technology to a changing world. Technology created possibilities for growth, movement, and choice that were completely impossible in the world before technology, a world of people tied to a farm or factory for sixty to eighty hours a week, who were barely able to earn enough to keep from starving and fell exhausted onto a bed or a pile of hay at night.

In the nineteenth century and earlier, life was precarious to a degree and in ways we can hardly imagine. Medicine was a crude half-science. Men, women, and children had to live their lives under the constant threat of plague, fever, and disease; death was a particular scourge for child-bearing women, and a deadly visitor among small children. The work-life too was full of uncertainty and risk. There were no loan guarantees, no subsidies, no public programs to cushion disaster. The insolvency system was rudimentary, the poor laws narrow and vicious. People lived out their lives in the shadow of possible disaster. Hunger was a constant companion of the poor. Thousands each year in cities like London and Paris were forced to steal to keep from starving.

This precariousness can be overstated; life in cities and towns in the nineteenth century was not so anomic as the passage above might suggest; webs of kinship and circles of cordiality and mutual help provided support and comfort for millions. But the situation of exposure to danger, as I have suggested,[5] was so basic a fact that it must have had a profound effect on consciousness, social and legal. Clearly, these facts of life acted as a brake on any possible outburst of claims-consciousness; in the economic sphere, the harshness of making a living gave men and women a powerful incentive to toe the line, to obey the dictates of society, to practice self-discipline. For most, there were no social "safety nets;" no one was guaranteed a job, a place in society, a safe foothold on the cliff; no one was assured serenity within the web of connections. The oddball, the deviant, the screw-up, the person who flouted convention, risked falling very far and very fast. In this regard, America and England in the raw days of adolescent capitalism were perhaps riskier and crueler places than more traditional societies, despite the increase in social opportunities and the relatively high standard of living.

Of course, families, churches, and community groups softened the blows of the outside world; the intimate group in which people lived moderated the callousness of the social order. But on the whole people had become looser, more like rolling stones, more detached from their villages and families, with all the attendant advantages and disadvantages. Economic insecurity was a powerful engine grinding down those who dared to be different; if you marched to your personal drummer, you marched very likely to destruction or the gallows. In short, although society allowed and even favored certain kinds of risk-taking, notably economic risks, it punished those who lost in the game rather severely. Other forms of risk-taking—in personal life, in patterns of behavior, in rebellious action or dress, or in sexual behavior—were proscribed altogether; violations of the norms were treated on the whole with terrible and conclusive severity.

Technology was at the heart of the Industrial Revolution and the displacement of traditions; it was also the source of some of the characteristic nineteenth-century insecurities, particularly the economic ones. Later, still newer technology fundamentally altered the situation which the old technology had in part created. It did so dramatically and directly, sweeping away the very conditions and situations that made life so precarious—conditions which had existed since the very morning of human time. The miracle of modern medicine is the clearest example: death in childbirth, infant mortality, plague and

infections no longer ravage the population and haunt the consciousness of the survivors in, say, Sweden or Holland; or even in the
United States.[6] AIDS, to be sure, is a horrific exception to the trium-
phal march of medicine. The full impact of this plague, psychological
and social, has not yet played itself out. But even here, the modern
mind asserts itself. Everyone expects some vaccine or cure, some way
out of the nightmare, in time. Such a hope was not possible with
regard to the Black Death, cholera, or yellow fever.

Other technological changes unleashed economic growth and set
in motion forces that led to a vast increase in wealth, comfort, security, and mobility for the populations of Western societies. These
interacted with social inventions, which technological change had
indeed made possible. The two processes together produced a new
form of polity, the modern welfare state. In the welfare state, physical
insecurity is even further reduced. The welfare state seeks to insure
the public against calamities and their consequences. It is the "safety
net" society. It guarantees basic human wants and needs—food,
clothing, shelter, health care, education. The welfare state is common
to all the Western countries; the differences among them, though
many and interesting, are perhaps less striking than the similarities.
Welfare in every Western country provides a floor, a minimum below
which the individual must not and should not fall. Gaps of course
appear; primitive forms of human suffering—hunger, thirst, home-
lessness—have not yet been abolished. Life is invincibly inventive of
new forms of misery, and invincibly stubborn about old ones. The
child survives measles, only to die of pancreatic cancer. The displaced
worker gets a weekly check, but rots away inside. Still, some specific
nineteenth-century dreads have been banished from earth, perhaps
permanently.

The point, of course, is not that Nirvana is upon us; that all human
problems have been solved or brought under control. The reduction
of uncertainty is a specific historic event; like all historic events, it
cannot be undone. History is irreversible. New forms of uncertainty,
however, are possible, even probable. We have mentioned AIDS as
one example; other plagues of unconquerable virulence may lie in the
unknown future. A world economy risks world economic disaster;
the banks of one country totter, and those of other countries feel the
seismic waves. Brazil defaults, and New York shudders. In the contemporary world, too, the risks of technology have become more terrible; the benefits of invention turn out to carry steep and unexpected

price tags. The nineteenth century, in contrast, saw few clouds in its crystal ball; the human story seemed to promise endless progress. Nobody worried about doomsday or the ozone layer.

Today, population growth is a runaway train; the sheer mass of people threatens the world with spreading squalor and eruptions of conflict. If the peoples of the world begin to fight over the last drop of water, the vanishing stocks of coal and oil, the thin soil, the poisoned air, then the fabric of civilization could easily rip apart. The clock of nuclear destruction ticks away in the background; overcrowded skies, polluted oceans, acid rain, erosion, forest depletion, sick air, creeping deserts, and weapons that can snuff out life on earth—these are products and innovations of the twentieth century. They may yet produce, at some point in the future, another stage of legal culture.[7] But at this juncture in Western history, this destiny still lies far ahead. The consequences of the dramatic reduction of uncertainty, the last turn of the wheel, are still unfolding.

A new legal culture arose alongside the formation of the welfare state. Its most salient characteristic is an attitude I have called the general expectation of justice.[8] It stands in contrast to the attitudes prevalent in the past: resigned fatalism, diffuse rage, sullen apathy, or passive contentment. The argument is that some significant portion of the population possesses a heightened sense of entitlement, an expectation of possible redress in the face of calamity or injustice. People may or may not *expect* calamity or injustice, but when these occur—as of course they do—they feel entitled to some sort of reaction, some compensation, *some* form of what is socially defined as justice. In this climate, new forms of individualism flourish. Today's individuals presuppose a degree of technological control over the forces of nature, and *awareness* of control. They presuppose leisure, money jingling in the pocket, hence goods and services beyond bread, rags, and a roof; they presuppose mobility and instruments of mobility; they presuppose the social safety net. The general expectation of justice is both a cause and a condition of the contemporary form of individualism. How this occurs is the theme of the following chapter.

FIVE

On Modern Legal Culture

THE MAIN argument here has pivoted about a particular concept of individualism, characteristic of our times. The concept stresses the right of each person to develop himself or herself as an individual; to choose as freely as possible a suitable and satisfying style of life. It is worth saying again that I am talking about general and legal culture—people's ideas and expectations—not necessarily about the truth and reality of the world.

The culture of individualism does not depend on whether people are actually free to choose, or as free as they think they are or would like to be. It is enough that they believe they are. Of course, such concepts of individualism and free choice do not enter people's heads by magic. They reflect common-sense judgments; they seem plausible to people; they rest on aspects of reality of the modern world. Modern technology, very notably, has shaped the environment in which people live, and therefore the way they look at the world. Technology is power—over the material world. It opens up a range of choices; it liberates the individual. An ordinary modern person—a barber, a factory worker, a secretary—has a kind of access to the wider world, at the wheel of a car, talking on the telephone, watching television, or on board trains and planes, that the ordinary person never dreamt of in the past. The world of choices, then, seems real and in some sense *is* real; the persistent drumbeat of advertising makes it appear more real, perhaps, than reality itself. Even people who complain that machines have tyrannized humanity use machines to spread their demands for liberation; the machines have helped create the mental world, the world of unlimited possibilities, that those who feel unfree use to define the freedom they lack.

But if technology is power and opportunity, it is also a source of problems, in ways the Luddites never imagined. A technological world is a complex world; this is a truism, but an important one. The world is complex in the most literal sense: crowded and interactive. It takes technology, including social technology, to sort things out in a human environment crammed with active, working, moving, functioning people and machines; to manage an environment of radical mobility in which individuals have been set loose from ancient bondages and moorings, to take off in all directions. Thus the paradox we began with—that rules, regulations, and laws become dense and pervasive in an age otherwise profoundly individual—seems less of a paradox. Many people believe that society *needs* a thick network of rules and rule-structures for the very purpose of protecting freedom of choice. The average person does not question the need for drivers' licenses, traffic police, stop signs, or speed limits. She values the right to drive whenever and wherever she wants, but that right would be almost useless, she feels, if the streets and highways were left unregulated in a state of anarchy. She also approves of rules to filter out blind, drunk, immature, and incompetent drivers. The right to drive would be much less real and worthwhile if the roads were clogged beyond measure, or were too dangerous. We need rules to prevent these situations. Ordinary men and women may be individualists; they are most definitely not libertarians.

In other words, one reason why there are so many rules and so much law is that some rules are necessary to defend or realize individual choice in the modern world. Rules create the framework of the state and hammer into place the planks and boards of the legal system itself. Secondly, some rules are "traffic" rules, rules of the road, which prevent choice from collapsing into anarchy—a state that would destroy the reality of choice. This is the function of traffic rules, taken in the most literal sense, that is, the rules of streets and highways. We could not get along without these rules, especially in big cities, and on highways and arteries in the countryside. But there is traffic and traffic. Any rules that make for orderly access to scarce resources are traffic rules in a sense. There are innumerable examples of allocation rules and rule-systems in modern law, which have this very purpose; for example, regulation of access to television channels and radio frequencies; air traffic control laws; regulation of wilderness areas; laws about hunting and fishing; laws to protect lobsters, abalone, fur-bearing animals; laws about energy conservation and energy sources.

This is one root of the multiplicity of laws. Civil rights laws exemplify another type, which also serves to realize individual choice. A vast proliferation of rules has grown up on this subject in many countries. Its fundamental notion is the uniqueness of the individual, the right of everyone to be judged and valued solely on his or her own merits as a person, rather than as a member of some ascriptive group. In the United States, the most pressing issue, historically, was race; and the civil rights movement carried the banner of a race-blind or race-neutral society with stunning success in the years after 1950, and in particular after the case of *Brown v. Board of Education* (1954), which desegregated the public schools.[1] The movement aimed primarily at closing the appalling gap between black and white in rights and opportunities, eliminating American *apartheid* and opening closed worlds of justice and privilege to blacks. In the *Brown* case, Chief Justice Earl Warren delivered a ringing message of praise for education in tones characteristic of his times. Education, he wrote, "is a principal instrument in awakening the child to cultural values, in preparing him for later professional training, and in helping him to adjust normally to his environment." Segregation, on the other hand, "generates a feeling of inferiority," which in turn affects "motivation to learn." The sin of segregation, then, was its failure to allow full development of the souls of black children. The distinct melodies and nuances of expressive individualism echo clearly through the screen of legal language.

The civil rights movement was only the beginning of a trend. Next came a new and revitalized women's movement, followed by the uprising of the "sexual minorities" (notably, gays and lesbians), and by strong claims to benefits and power by a whole cluster of groups: the handicapped, the elderly, prisoners, students, immigrants, and others. In other Western countries there were similar movements, taking of course different forms, moving at a different pace, and enjoying different degrees of success or failure. Each country had its own demographic and ethnic mix, its own special brew of resident minorities.[2]

The civil rights movement, broadly conceived, has deep historical roots. Its intellectual basis goes back to the Enlightenment, if not earlier. Like most liberation movements, it has framed much of its rhetoric in historical terms—the recapture of long-lost rights. The texts and slogans used to buttress or vindicate fundamental rights need not be modern texts at all; some are as old as the American Constitution, or for that matter as old as the Bible. Nonetheless, there are important differences between the "rights of man" as Thomas Jefferson conceived them, and the "civil rights" of the mid-twentieth century.[3] The altered form of individualism, the altered meaning of choice, and the peculiarly modern emphasis on freedom to shape and constitute a unique and fulfilling self account for these differences.

Civil rights law and the civil rights movement are crucial illustrations of the theme of this book. Individual autonomy, as an ideal, is incompatible with group stereotypes. Individualism of the contemporary type stresses what is unique about each human being. Groups such as women's groups, or black groups, apply group pressure on behalf of individual autonomy. The official line in Western countries insists that differences of language, race, and culture do not reach the essential core of human beings and are no excuse for discrimination or oppression. In the real world, of course, group stereotypes are stubborn and persistent. Hatred and war among races, nations, tribes, and language groups are positively epidemic, and in some places threaten to tear the world apart. Everywhere prejudice is strong and ancient; powerful laws are needed to combat it, backed by powerful social movements. The results at best are partial and mixed.

Moreover, groups that claim protection and toleration are often in conflict with each other. Minorities may put forward claims that contradict each other; those who assert rights collide with those who resist rights. For instance, Jews, liberal Protestants, and nonbelievers want the schools to be neutral as to religion; they want an end to preaching, prayers, and indoctrination. Fundamentalists then argue that the secularists have driven God out of the schools, abusing the rights of religious people. A humble Nativity scene on city land touches off an ugly squabble. Society has to cope somehow with this tangle of rights in conflict; and it does so through a hierarchy of traffic rules—rules to monitor and choose among competing claims; to rank them in some logical or popular order; to place them somewhere in a social queue.

A certain contradiction may have arisen between the *individualist* strand and the *separatist* strand in civil rights law. On the one hand, there is the claim that blacks (or women, gays, the handicapped, and so on) are "just like everybody else," and should be treated accordingly. On the other hand, group solidarity develops and takes the form of black nationalism, radical separatist feminism, gay pride, and the like. These are assertions of *group* claims; but of a special nature. They always contain an element of individual choice or affiliation; they reject stereotyping and discrimination from the larger society and assert the right of the black, woman, gay, or ethnic to embrace a total, all-encompassing culture of exclusion. Separatism also usually involves the idea that members of oppressed and wounded groups best develop their selves under conditions of isolation and cocooning. The argument is that the dominant culture is so inveterately repressive, so consciously or unconsciously stained with prejudice, that blacks (women, gays) can reach fulfillment only within a social or spatial enclave. In either case, a framework of civil rights strongly supported by hard-edged legal institutions is a vital necessity; though of course there is endless controversy over what these rights ought to be, and how the institutions should behave.

Regulation and Individual Choice

Less obvious to the general argument is the relevance of that tremendous body of rules and institutions that regulate or deal with the economy—the apparatus of the modern regulatory state. Still, as one patiently excavates bits and pieces of social history, themes and facts about business regulation come to light that are indeed germane to the republic of choice and very much of a piece with the legal culture as a whole. Regulatory laws have a political history that is often quite complex. Particular kinds of regulation sometimes keep their popularity precisely because they invoke themes and slogans of choice or individualism. The welfare state is a regulatory state, and thousands of rules put shackles and restraints on businesses, employers, and landlords. The public does not in general object; on the contrary, the public agrees that enterprise must be controlled, power curbed, and the public interest asserted. Banks, railroads, and large corporations should be reined in for the sake of small business, or to preserve the independence of farmers, small merchants, shopkeepers, and the consumer.

This theme, very notably, appears in the history of many of the great regulatory laws, for example, the Sherman Anti-Trust Act (1890).[4] This famous statute was passed against the background of intense agitation, even panic, over "trusts"—giant industrial combines that formed during the late nineteenth century. There was fear that the great monopolies could squeeze the life out of their competitors, driving small businesses into ruin or industrial servitude and threatening to attain intolerable power over the lives and affairs of ordinary citizens. The same impulses and energies motivated many of the laws directed at the economy. The Robinson-Patman Act tried to tilt the scales toward small business by forbidding price discrimination—discounts and rebates that might "lessen competition"[5] In the 1920s the rise of chain stores provoked another wave of agitation and legislation. Almost half the states passed special tax laws aimed against these stores. The point was to keep the giant food chains from turning the United States "into a nation of clerks by depriving individuals of the opportunity of establishing their own businesses and, in that way, impairing individual initiative, since standardized merchandising operations tend to make of employees mere routine workers."[6]

Whether or not these laws made economic sense or were even effective is not the issue here. It does not capture the cultural meaning of these laws to describe them purely in *economic* terms. Self-interest, as always, goes a long way to explain the motives of the most passionate exponents of these laws—in fact quite long enough. But proponents always added a broader argument. The laws were necessary to preserve freedom—theirs and other peoples—to keep small businesses alive and to preserve the right to choose one's occupation. Echoes of this theme sounded in the battle to achieve strong regulation of railroads. Small merchants and farmers cried out against what they saw as the crushing power of railroads. The "little man" was totally powerless against the mighty "octopus"; law was the only countervailing force.[7] Arguments that stressed choice, independence, and autonomy went beyond self-interest in the crudest sense. Slogans and leitmotifs were so phrased as to appeal to neutrals and enlist them on the side of those who had the most at stake financially. These slogans and leitmotifs were not and could not be random; they had to express basic themes of the legal culture.

Similar themes pop up in the rhetoric surrounding the economic programs most richly represented in modern welfare states. Many countries, for example, subsidize farmers and support the price of key crops. These programs are bothersome economically and politically. The laws are strongly protectionist, yet the ideology behind them draws strength from the myth of the sturdy yeoman—the family farmer, the autonomous peasant proprietor. The propaganda images and the ethical slogans about a romanticized rural way of life are necessary to recruit political support from city people who, after all, pay the bills for the sturdy yeomen in the form of higher costs for milk, bread, cotton, rice, and tomatoes. The farmers insist that subsidies are guarantees of independence and constitutional frameworks of a way of life, rather than simply devices to cushion them from economic shocks—least of all welfare or charity, which farmers despise and reject.

It would take us too far afield to examine the ideology (or rationalizations) of the welfare state. The welfare state is, in essence, tremendously popular and has spread all over the Western world, yet welfare itself is not popular. Indeed, "welfare" is a dirty word, and more so among working people than among elites, intellectuals, or perhaps even businessmen. To some extent, the concept of "social insurance" acts as a figleaf for welfare in the welfare state. The most popular programs—old age pensions, for example—are presented and accepted as insurance benefits, that is, something paid for, not a handout from the government or anything so degrading as charity. Some programs label benefits as *earned*, that is, as a kind of compensation—for service in the army or navy, for example, or as payment on account of work injuries. Legally, the benefits take the form of entitlements, which cannot be divested and are not subject to bureaucratic whim. They are solid, untouchable *rights.* At the very least, they are transfer payments that support, justifiably, an independent way of life.

In any event, the culture explains and legitimates its subsidies in terms of freedom and autonomy, not welfare or dependence. A minimum standard of living, and social insurance in general, are not charity; they are rights that inhere in human beings because food, shelter, and health are necessary conditions for the uses of freedom. Freedom itself means having many options. Of course hunger, cold, disease, and poverty are evils in themselves. But beyond this, they are enemies of freedom. The average person probably disagrees sharply with those on the left who claim that "bourgeois freedom" means nothing to the poor and the downtrodden. But the same average person would agree that those precious freedoms cannot be realized or enjoyed to their fullest without some sort of guaranteed minimum standard. In this way, an important part of the modern *corpus juris* absorbs legitimacy from the enthronement of choice; the norms that compose it are defined as protecting and fostering choice. Just as the state provides police, streets, and traffic lights to make free travel a reality, so does it provide programs that guarantee enough money, health care, and shelter to maintain a world in which people have options and can choose their destiny. To argue that these social insurance provisions are reductions of freedom because they regulate and tax would strike most people as profoundly misleading.

The maximization of freedom is, in fact, the very core of the welfare state. This is not a point about historical development—at least not literally. I am not arguing that maximization of choice was the sole or perhaps even the dominant impulse behind the original package of programs, doctrines, and institutions out of which the modern welfare state developed. Each of them, in each country, has had its own special history. From the political standpoint, pride of place may well go to a more primitive impulse: the desire for a decent standard of living, for food on the table, for bread and pensions in old age, for dignity and support for the sick, the unable, and indeed for the average worker. But at some invisible point these impulses melded with the new legal culture, the culture of choices and options, the culture of expressive individualism. The welfare state reconstituted itself in terms compatible with that culture. It became a prerequisite of freedom and of choice.

Some conservatives and libertarians, to be sure, honestly believe in a simple, linear relationship between freedom and law: the more rules and regulations, the less freedom. These people assert that freedom and (regulatory) law are sworn enemies; freedom means holding law at bay, shrinking it to the barest minimum. This minimum is a skeleton framework of law and order, enough to protect property from marauders and to enforce people's contracts. It takes some sort of judicial system, a few jails, and a certain amount of policing, but that is all. Beyond that, the state should do nothing.

In one sense, the basic libertarian proposition is true by definition. Any rule or regulation which tells me what I cannot do, or can only do in a certain way, diminishes my freedom. One classic definition of freedom is the absence of restraint. But freedom may also refer to concrete possibilities, to a range of options, and this, we believe, is part of its meaning in modern legal culture. Of course, a range of options implies an absence of restraint within that range; there has to be freedom to choose. But absence of restraints is only the starting point. Full realization of freedom requires *having* the options—a basket of goods, situations, or activities from which to select freely.

Freedom in the new sense, like many facets of the modern world, arises out of a consciousness shaped by technology, including social technology. Modern men and women live in a world of high technology, and its influence on their lives and minds is simply incalculable. But the technology itself and the institutions that flow from it either demand vast infusions of law, or are at least historically associated with such infusions. An advance in technology which (to put it schematically) increases "freedom" in the sense of creating new options and opportunities will almost certainly evoke or induce a body of rules and regulations as well. In the abstract, then, freedom is lessened, because there are bushelsful of fresh rules, but the increase in options and choices may be far greater than the decrease in freedom which the rules bring about. If so, then it is realistic to think of an increase in freedom at the level of society.

The automobile is a case in point. The automobile was invented around the turn of the century. It was at first a toy of the rich. Gradually, its use trickled down the social scale. By now, in wealthier Western countries, most households own or have access to a car of some sort. This opens up an enormous range of possibilities, which would have been far beyond the realm of hope a century ago. A French worker or farmer can drive to the mountains; live in the suburbs of Paris; vacation in another European country; visit historic sites; drop in on relatives who live in Provence or in Lille; move from city to city without cutting off old roots and ties completely; come and go as she pleases. The automobile also opens up chances for jobs and locales, chances at neighborhood and living conditions, that would have been difficult or impossible before. In a real sense, then, the automobile dramatically extends the range of options. On the other hand, it also generates a huge quantity of rules. There were rules of the road and traffic laws before the automobile, but they were nothing compared to the scope and scale of traffic law today. And the motorized society generates innumerable other rules: about the sale and marketing of cars, about drivers' licenses, about car repairs, gasoline stations, seat belts. The incredible number of cars and drivers forces the state to build and maintain a vast network of roads; this generates still more legal activity, on condemnation of property, highway construction, road repair. And so it goes.

The modern world is a place of freedom and a place of law; this is inevitable in so intricate a society. The complexity of modern society is a cliche, a truism. But what makes society so complex? It is the range of possibilities, the rainbow of choices, due at least in part to modern technology. This range of possibilities in a real sense *is* freedom, in the sense of mobility, socially, psychologically, and otherwise. Life has an open texture, at least in comparison to prior societies.

But an open texture has two aspects—subjective and objective. Objectively, stone walls *do* make a prison, and iron bars a cage. A prisoner is not free; the citizen is. Equally important, however, is the subjective sense: the way a situation feels. For most people, beyond a doubt, there are aspects of modern life which are objectively open-textured, compared to life in the great autocracies or in tribal societies, squeezed by the rigid constraints of custom. In *this* sense, people in the West take their brand of freedom for granted; it is all they know; a life of tyranny or tribalism is unthinkable. They are not necessarily complacent, however. They may worry about aspects of freedom that cross-culturalists or scholars who write about the whole sweep of human history would consider rather marginal. Hence the great outcry over threats to extended freedom, the concerns over the fragility of privacy and the more arcane civil liberties. From the perspective of life under Attila the Hun, in ancient Egypt, or in Hitler's Germany, one is surely unimpressed with the flaws of Western civil liberties. But to many of us freedom may seem precarious, a plant in need of constant watering and protection. We are aware of the dark shadows: threats from computerized data-banks, the convulsive effect of market forces on personal security, and the like. Our base of comparison is not tyranny or tribalism, but life in the republic of choice. Hence the need for strong buttresses built up out of rights and law.

A Society of Strangers

One consequence of modern life is the increased number of interactions among strangers; this may be part of the very essence of mobility. Such interaction generates a felt need for law. I say "felt need" somewhat cautiously; perhaps one should be courageous enough to say that the need is real. There is certainly a strong case for traffic rules. If millions of people in the cities or on country roads drove as they pleased, and when they pleased, racing off in all directions, at great speed, the roads might be jammed with wrecked cars, there would be insupportable carnage on the highways and gridlock in the cities. There was a weaker case, or no case at all, for stringent and elaborate rules of the road when people went about on foot, creeping along at what strikes us as a snail's pace; or when a few horses and carriages trotted along at a leisurely, upper-class gait; or when people were generally tied to some small, narrow environment, out of which they rarely moved.

A good deal of law, of course, cannot be explained literally or figuratively as rules of the road or rules of welfare or civil rights. In the modern state there are literally thousands of rules and regulations on every subject. There are rules about taxes, about securities regulation, about land use and planning. There are rules about which chemicals, drugs, pesticides can or cannot be marketed, about how much cotton dust is allowed in the air in textile mills, what flowers we are forbidden to pick, what animals cannot be hunted.

Many of these rules are extraordinarily technical. They are designed by experts, and perhaps only experts understand them. But rules in the modern state, no matter how technical, ultimately rest on much broader norms, which may or may not be explicitly stated somewhere in the code-books, or even in the decisions of judges. These broad norms support the whole structure of rules and regulations, even the most technical. Take, for example, a rule that certain chemicals may not be added to food, for highly technical reasons. Such a rule rests on a more general norm, usually expressed in a statute outlawing dangerous ingredients in food products. This norm in turn depends on more general norms—people should not cause bodily harm to other people, and a quick profit in the market is not sufficient reason. And so it goes. Ultimately, all norms are moral norms.

For some purposes, it is useful to distinguish between technical norms and overtly moral norms, the stability of which rests on different footings. A technical norm is vulnerable on technical or factual grounds. If an agency bans a food chemical, a manufacturer can attack the rule by proving that the chemical is actually harmless. Moral norms are less vulnerable on factual grounds; there are no "facts" than can impugn the laws against murder or rape. Yet in all cases legal norms depend on social norms and moral ideas.

It is important to recognize this dependence and to be aware that in this sense, then, there are no purely technical rules. Technical they may be, but never purely. Nonetheless, we are entitled to ask why there are so many technical rules; why legal regulation is so dense and pervasive. The rule-system must reflect some central features of social life as we live it, that is, in a modern and (comparatively) democratic society. (The density of regulation in a totalitarian society may reflect quite different features of life; at any rate, we leave this issue to one side.) Our argument has stressed the fantastic advance of technology; this is linked to the extraordinary interdependence of life in modern society. To be sure, members of every society, no matter how simple its social organization, are profoundly dependent on each other. *Homo sapiens* after all is a social animal. People are agglomerative beings; they live in groups, packs, families; they are not solitary hunters or hermits. But modern society has a feature almost completely lacking in simpler societies: dependence on strangers.

In the contemporary world, our health, our lives, and our fortunes are at the mercy of people we have never met and will never meet. We open packages and cans and swallow food made and processed by strangers, in far off places; we do not know the names of these processors or anything about them. We move into houses that strangers have built—skillfully, we hope. We spend a good deal of our lives locked inside dangerous, swift machines—cars, buses, trains, elevators, airplanes. One false move in the manufacturing process, one simple act of "human error" by pilots or drivers, and our lives are at risk. In a real sense, we as individuals have no power over aspects of life—and they are legion—in which we use machines and machine-made goods. We are in thrall to the machines; hence our lives are also in the hands of those strangers who make or run the machines. There is no direct way to ensure that canned soup will not poison us, that the elevator will not plummet to the ground and crush us, that boilers will not explode in our houses, and that the buildings we work in will not collapse and bury us under tons of rock and steel. There is no guarantee that the strangers who made these things are competent, and they are not bound to us by human ties and normative connections. To prevent all sorts of horrors and calamities, we need powerful methods of control over strangers and their instrumentalities. This cannot be face-to-face control. Nor are people satisfied to leave control to the pressures of impersonal markets. They look for more direct control in advance, through a strong third force—the state. In other words, they want control through law.

To the man and woman on the street, the rules and regulations that embody this control are entirely necessary; they are not inconsistent with freedom, or even with individual choice. In the republic of choice, modern life presents a situation of weird duality. The republic promises the individual complete control of his life-chances; yet, at the same time it puts him at the mercy of strangers, beyond the ambit of his personal power. Modern society seated us at the wheel of the car, and it gave us the wonderful gift of locomotion. But is the car soundly made? Is the highway safe? Other drivers are racing all around us on the highway; do they really know how to drive? If not, then the freedom and the choices are illusory, or come at too high a price. The way out of the dilemma is through control—control through regulation, through powerful, effective rules of law over all these instrumentalities.

Libertarians, as expected, argue that the rules diminish freedom. A powerful strain of economic thought advances the view that regulation, on the whole, is inefficient and self-defeating. To the average person these arguments seem abstruse, unrealistic. The average person knows very little about efficiency in the economic sense, and, subjectively, does not feel that she or the polity suffer when manufacturers or suppliers are regulated closely. Regulation enhances, in fact, the actual range of options when it requires producers to list their ingredients on the package and prove the ingredients harmless; or insists that drugs sold on the market should be free from poison unless the label clearly says otherwise; or when government controls the training and licensing of airline pilots and bans from the cockpit drunks, drug addicts, and people who have fits of madness. Few of us want or need the freedom to manufacture canned and frozen foods, or to market antibiotics without government regulation; few of us miss the freedom to fly a commercial jet without a license. But almost all of us are consumers, and passengers, and go in and out of tall buildings; and we want to do so without worrying that we are taking our lives in our hands.

In no way, of course, is this an argument that regulation is good, desirable, or efficient in any particular case. It is merely an attempt to understand those aspects of legal culture which support regulation *in general.* The specifics are another story. There is certainly no demand for red tape, let alone an argument that red tape enhances freedom of choice; the very opposite seems obviously true. The case for any particular regulatory regime—control of the airwaves; antipollution measures; restrictions on the marketing of drugs—can be completely misguided, and no doubt often is. In any event, the argument has to be selective. Deregulation of airline ticket prices seemed to promise greater freedom of choice, but there is no demand to deregulate the stringent rules about airline safety.

Trends and Countertrends

Our thesis is not that everything in modern law, and in modern authority systems, can be reduced to a single proposition about the primacy of choice. That would be, of course, incorrect. The thesis is, rather, that the concept of choice, the desire for choice, and the experience of choice pervade modern life and reconstitute modern law to fit the culture of choice. In some areas the dominance is so great that even exceptions, or countertrends, only confirm the fact of dominance. Nobody reacts against a dead or figurehead king.

Freedom of choice is in fact restricted in modern law in more ways than anyone can count and measure, even if one ignores the libertarian point discussed in the prior section. In some ways the areas of restriction seem to have grown in size, and during the very period in which the republic of choice seems to have won its greatest victories. This is, as we noted, the period of the welfare state. Arguably, the welfare state does not represent the enthronement of choice, but quite the opposite: the quest for security, for a safe harbor, a cocoon, the insurance society, risklessness, and social guarantees; comfort instead of chance. It can be argued that the republic of security is the primary state, and the republic of choice a secondary, lesser phenomenon.[8]

No doubt this point has some validity; the modern state has both aspects, intermeshed so tightly that they cannot be disentangled. My own view is that choice is primary, security secondary; that security can be seen as a framework or prerequisite to choice. The argument cannot be resolved one way or another. Some critics point the finger of scorn at the security arrangements of the welfare state; they sneer at their contemporaries as conformist sheep, they discuss the "escape from freedom," deplore the passing of the true individual, and look back on the golden age of liberty; or, from a similar angle, celebrate the end of the unregenerate market, the passing of laissez-faire's dark ages, and the demise of brutal, untamed capitalism. My aim is to make the other case, to decipher the messages of legal culture so as to demonstrate the underlying culture of choice, which gives meaning to countless aspects of law and life—even aspects that at first glance seem connected to the contrary impulse, the republic of safety and security.

To take a simple example: occupational licensing laws. Restrictions on occupational choice have an ancient history—the medieval guilds are a well-known example. By 1800 or so, these older restrictions had all but vanished. A person was free to choose to be a doctor, nurse, pharmacist, or architect without special leave, and without a license from the state. Occupational freedom was one of the glories of the liberal state, which buried the guilds and estates. Yet today every modern country restricts occupational freedom sharply. In the typical state in the United States dozens of occupations and professions are closed to the general public. A state board or agency grants licenses to practice these trades, but only to those who have undergone training and passed a test. Tennessee, for example, has state boards for accountants, architects, engineers, barbers, cosmetologists, dieticians, funeral directors and embalmers, general contractors, land surveyors, auctioneers, collection agencies, pest control operators, private investigators, and lie-detector operators, along with doctors, nurses, lawyers, veterinarians, psychologists, speech pathologists, dentists, chiropractors, druggists, and those who practice "the art of body massage, by hand, or with a mechanical or vibratory device."[9] This phenomenon is by no means purely American. Occupational licensing is pervasive throughout the Western world.[10] For certain types of occupation, the licensing movement may have peaked, or even entered a period of mild decline. But licensing remains an important aspect of labor law; no one expects it to be eliminated entirely. The major professions, and a raft of occupations, are closed expect to the few who are licensed.

Yet to most people, the "freedom" to be a doctor, architect, or a lawyer, or to pilot a jumbo-jet, is not a realistic option. A person cannot choose to be a doctor in the same way she chooses a brand of soap or even in the way that she chooses a hobby, a religion, or an ordinary job. Most people are not doctors; they are consumers of doctoring services; and the services of pharmacists, architects, and so on. People depend on these services, just as they depend on the unseen makers of food products, cars, or elevators. Dependence on strangers, as we have seen, is a cardinal fact of modern society, and it is one of the factors that legitimizes the increased volume of regulation and law. A similar point can be made with regard to dependence on professionals and experts. Thus the ordinary person accepts the idea that only those with training and skill ought to be doctors; and the unskilled must, at all costs, be kept out. People like the idea of *certification*—the license tells them that every doctor meets certain standards; otherwise they would be choosing in the dark. Licensing laws, like traffic laws, are also accepted as ways to keep markets orderly, to regulate flow and supply, to sustain quality; and this can be perceived (rightly or wrongly) as the enhancement of sensible choice. What the citizen demands for herself is the freedom to compete for a place in medical school regardless of background, race, age, sex, or sexuality, rather than the naked right to practice medicine. The menu of legal options tends to reflect this point of view.

Occupational choice is a crucial part of the sphere of the work life, but twentieth-century individualism, on the whole, emphasizes most strongly those aspects of life outside of or supplementary to the realm where one earns one's bread: the whole personality, the whole life, not merely the work life. Work of course is important. Ideally, work strengthens the self; ideally it is part of a general scheme that leads to personal fulfillment.[11] But that fulfillment, through the exercise of choice, is at all times the primary goal. Moreover, other trends in modern society—for example, the fluid life cycle and the receptiveness to second chances—act as countertrends to the countertrend of regulation; they have opened up new occupational choices for millions of people. These trends more than cancel out the narrowing of choice, which occupational licensing causes.

Occupational licensing began in earnest in the United States in the late nineteenth century.[12] The licensing of doctors and lawyers goes back somewhat earlier. The roots of occupational licensing are no mystery: the laws came out of orthodox logrolling and interest-group politics. Not all attempts to secure the blessings of licensing succeeded. The laws that were actually passed were compromises between contending interest groups; they do not require us to assume some sort of consensus or some fundamental postulate of legal culture. Moreover, the literature of those who fought for licensing is full of themes of general resonance, themes of independence and choice. Lawyers, plumbers, doctors, farmers, and other groups banded together, formed organizations, lobbied for friendly regulation and the like, not because they believed in a corporatist state, but in defense (they claimed) of the public good; they spoke as little as possible of self-interest, and when they did, they defined it in individualistic terms. Excessive or unfair competition were evils because (among other things) they threatened the independence of the practitioner, reducing a profession to a mere business and a free worker to a serf.

Beyond a doubt, many choices in modern life are subject to what we might call mandatory brokering. There are situations where the law requires you to use a lawyer, a doctor, or some other professional; or leave off doing. For example, one cannot buy many drugs and medicines without a doctor's prescription.[13] Some brokered choices are controversial, yet on the whole society accepts them with surprising ease. People are aware of their awesome ignorance. A right to choose drugs without understanding what they are, what they do, how to use them properly, what side effects they might have, would strike most people as a hollow choice. When the law requires a prescription, it does so, roughly, on the assumption that no amount of disclosure or explanation would ensure a rational choice, except through the brokerage of a doctor.[14]

Thus one could at least construct an argument that prescription laws do not interfere with the power of consumers to make choices. The argument is not necessarily specious. And in general, the doctor-patient relationship has moved in the opposite direction, that is, toward more choice and autonomy for patients. The doctrine of informed consent (Chapter 9) is one sign of this trend. Some women now choose to give birth at home or to use a midwife; in general, one sees a mild trend toward increased independence, increased resistance to professional hegemony.

Brokered choices are bound up with the larger problem or problems of information—the bewilderment of choice, which runs parallel with the virtues and advantages of choice. A Westerner who visits Poland or Bulgaria is usually struck by the wretched state of shops and markets; the helpless consumers have only a few, pitiful choices. People from the Eastern bloc, on the other hand, express dismay at the obscene multiplicity of choices in Western supermarkets; seventeen brands of toothpaste leer and call to them from the shelves. How *does* does one choose? Taste dictates whether we buy mint-flavored toothpaste, or plain; white toothpaste or green. But what brand is best for the gums? Toothpaste is hardly a burning issue; buying a car or a piano or a house is much more serious. The wide array of choices in modern life assumes that the chooser is competent to choose and that no one can do the job of choosing for him. This is obviously true for mere matters of taste, but the domain of choice is much broader and more serious; it includes many decisions (about sexual behavior or religion, for example) that were once brokered or dictated, socially speaking. People recognize, as they must, that in some areas of life they face decisions they are simply not competent to make, or nowhere near *as* competent as experts. This is because of the complex, interwoven structure of society, the sheer amount of scientific and technical knowledge, and the secrecy in which some social actors cloak their actions.

Thus an unavoidable tension builds up, at various points of the legal order, between the dictates of choice and the facts of consumer ignorance. Sometimes the norms tilt toward brokered choices; sometimes toward a sink-or-swim freedom to choose. Often, too, we find some sort of middle way. When we buy a car or a piano on the installment plan, modern law tends to dictate various forms of disclosure; sellers must tell consumers what they ought to know but have trouble finding out on their own. Under the truth-in-lending laws,[15] sellers are required to set out precisely how much interest they charge, and what happens when a buyer misses payments. Securities law insists on full, fair disclosure to the investing public. The consumer does not view such laws, of course, as in any way restricting choice, but rather as the enhancement of choice, since they provide him with information that would otherwise be hard and costly to get. (Truth-in-lending laws probably have little impact on consumer behavior; securities regulation, on the other hand, may have a strong effect on the market in stocks and bonds.) Rules that dictate what must be told, and how—that concern the flow of information—are felt to be necessities in a world of unrestricted choices. A chaos of choices, like chaos on the highways, generates a situation that breeds, legitimates, and supports rules of the road.

A person who goes on trial for murder or is about to be cut open for a coronary by-pass is in a much more serious situation than someone shopping for a car. Legally, these situations of deadly earnest are likely to be the situs of brokered or monitored choices. Only the trained professional is allowed to do heart surgery or handle the defense for an accused murderer; and the patient/defendant understands the need for this kind of brokered choice. The patient/defendant may retain control of the ultimate decisions, but day-by-day *technical* decisions are taken out of his hands.

In the broadest sense, information and access to information are essential to free choice; hence problems of the free flow of information are pandemic in the republic of choice. The public understands this; it is one of the arguments that justifies an unimpeded flow of speech on any and every subject. Originally, the justification for freedom of speech was largely political; current law of course goes much further than political speech, and the culture tends to support this expansion. The state cannot suppress argument and expression on *any* subject. It is even hard to ban pornography (this subject of course remains highly controversial). What Jefferson or Locke would have thought about pornography as a problem of "free speech" can be readily imagined. But today an enormous range of sexual options has been legitimated; hence information about these options, and even pictures of them, claim legitimacy.[16] The law has also blurred the line between information (in the sense of facts) and expressions of emotions, fears, and desires. Jefferson and Locke were thinking primarily of rational argument, of works of serious art, of the "market place of ideas," but freedom of expression in the modern world has raced past these conceptions. The right of expression now concerns the market place of *selves* and their various components.

Choice, Contract, and the Welfare State

No social trend in the Western democracies, over the last century or so, has been so important as the rise of the welfare-regulatory state. Country after country has retreated from the "liberal" policies of the nineteenth century—away from the minimal state, the state that does not interfere in markets, especially labor markets. In each country there is now a vast corpus of protective labor legislation on hours of work, conditions of work, vacations, benefits, pensions, unemployment, and minimum wages. Country after country has enacted huge, expensive programs of welfare; in some countries, the state administers benefits from cradle to grave.[17] At birth, the child gets (indirectly) a tax break or subsidy as a reward for entering this world; old age is cushioned with pensions; death triggers a final burst of cash for burial. The United States is supposed to be a welfare laggard compared to England or France, but it has in fact moved quite far in this general direction. The New Deal of the 1930s was a great watershed; in retrospect, it was only the beginning of a massive infusion of welfare and social insurance. In all societies of the West, all strata of the population, with the exception of a few diehards, accept the idea of minimum standards, guaranteed by the state and paid for out of taxes. A decent society does not let anybody starve; it provides free schooling for all its children;. it guarantees, in some countries, basic housing, and in most, some sort of medical care.

The regulatory apparatus of the modern state is also impressively large and growing larger. Typically, a massive labor code controls the terms and conditions of the labor contract; there are also laws on consumer safety, environmental protection, anticompetitive behavior, occupational licensing, and a host of other subjects. In the famous passage already quoted, Sir Henry Maine (1861) spoke of the evolution, in "progressive" societies from "status" to "contract." Maine wrote with the classic liberalism of England in mind. Some scholars detect or decry a strong trend backward toward status, or, in any event, away from the regime of free contract.[18] Every regulation of business, to a degree, diminishes the realm of free contract for that business or industry.[19]

True and yet not true. As we argued, regulation can be and often is felt to be an enhancement of freedom, in a society of interdependent individuals. What about the regime of contract itself? It is commonplace to assert that this too is in decline; that the welfare-regulatory state is its mortal enemy. Grant Gilmore has written about the "death" of contract.[20] Patrick Atiyah, in his masterly book on the rise and fall of freedom of contract, more or less agrees. Over the past century, he writes, there has been "a continuous weakening of belief in the values involved in individual freedom of choice." He notes one "paradoxical" exception:. "all matters concerned directly or indirectly with sexual morality." Here there has been "a significant increase in the respect accorded to individual freedom of choice."[21]

But perhaps Atiyah has missed the mark here. One could argue the very opposite case: that is, the "values involved in individual freedom of choice" have gotten more robust over the years. Either thesis probably overstates the point or runs the risk of slighting counterexamples. But "contract," in the sense that Maine and Atiyah use the term, has three distinct meanings. One is the sense of the formal, lawyer's law of contract—contract as it is studied in law school and described in treatises of law. There is also the actual *regime* of contract—agreements in the real world, especially business agreements. Atiyah may have blurred the line between these two; "decay" or "decline" in apparent freedom of choice in the highly atypical cases that populate law school texts or are decided by high courts is not at all the same as "decline" or "decay" in the regime of contract, in the real world of affairs.[22] Moreover, there is another sense or at least a cluster of overtones, in which the essence of contract *is* choice; contract means free and voluntary movements and arrangements, so that a social order based on contract is a social order which exalts the individual and his options above all else, a regime in which individual choice is the measure and legitimator of all things.

Atiyah's statement implies a definition of contract and of choice that runs counter to definitions implied in modern legal culture. The problem arises if we equate business regulation or the apparatus of the welfare state with restrictions on choice. Regulations in one sense do restrict choice, but some of the innovations and restrictions have, as we have seen, quite the opposite feel; and in many regards the range of options permitted by law and supported by custom and culture is much greater in the 1980s than in the period when "freedom of contract" ruled the roost. Choice holds a position of much greater *value* than it did before. The case of "sexual morality," then, is not some weird anomaly; it comes closer to the norm in the republic of choice than Atiyah realizes.

In the struggle for, and about, the welfare-regulatory state, contract has, to be sure, been a major (ideological) actor. Liberal economists made a fetish of freedom of contract, which they saw as the cornerstone of liberty and the touchstone of the market. Since the nineteenth century, the critics of classical economics have subjected the ideology of freedom of contract to a constant barrage of criticism. But most of those who criticized the norms and institutions of contract law as it developed in the nineteenth century, and who criticize it today, have never in principle opposed a regime of contract in the sense of free, voluntary choice among alternatives. In mainstream thought in Western countries, choice and consent are rarely attacked directly, and there is no particular quarrel with free bargaining when it occurs. The critics argue, rather, that in certain crucial contexts choice is illusory; or the bargaining is unreal or coerced; that people are placed in morally objectionable situations, or their options are exercised under circumstances such that one cannot truly speak of voluntary choice. A worker with a choice between starvation and a dangerous, dirty job, has no real choice at all, at least as modern culture defines it.

The case law, statutes, and treatises on contracts today reflect these ideas. They are full of discussions of "inequality of bargaining power"; special rules govern contracts with tricky fine print; and the law has become sensitive to the danger of sharp operators and fast-talking salesmen who take advantage of customers, especially poor customers.[23] One useful concept has been the *contract of adhesion*, a European term which successfully crossed the Atlantic.[24] A contract of adhesion is a take-it-or-leave-it contract; in modern case law, the adhesion contract is legally weaker than the freely bargained contract, and it is subject to more regulation. Lawyers and jurists have depicted it not as the expression of choice but as the negation of choice, as a set of terms imposed on buyers of goods or services. Friedrich Kessler, in a classic article which introduced the concept into American jurisprudence, spoke of contracts imposed by the strong on the weak; these standard contracts allowed "enterprisers" to "legislate by contract . . . in a substantially authoritarian manner" and threatened to become "effective instruments in the hands of powerful industrial and commercial overlords enabling them to impose a new feudal order of their own making upon a vast host of vassals."[25]

Within this somewhat overblown language is the heart of the critique of contract law. This critique has itself been criticized as economically and conceptually vacuous, but of course we are not concerned here with the rights and wrongs of the critique. What is interesting is the nature of the argument itself. The form (so goes the critique) is the form of free choice, but the substance is imposition of will and negation of choice. The helpless, ignorant buyer does sign the contract, lease, or bill of sale, and a signature usually indicates consent; but in these cases consent is doubly unreal—the buyer has no real choice in the first place, and in the second place, neither knows nor understands what he is signing.[26] Yet few people in the West, though they may level devastating criticism against the "myth" of freedom of contract, seriously question freedom or contract as such; they do not argue for a system in which tenants are bound to their landlords, unable to leave the apartment when their lease runs out; or a system in which workers are not totally free to quit their jobs. Few if any people in the West like the idea of internal passports or other trappings of societies which in fact *do* reject mobility and free choice as ruling principles.

Those who favor government regulation or welfare state programs speak much the same language of individualism and choice as do those who speak out on the other side. But "interventionists" tend to claim that under this or that condition no real choice is possible; that certain forces and powers have squashed or stifled the freedom which should be the people's birthright; unless these forces and powers are brought under control, true freedom cannot be realized. Farmers and small merchants in the American Middle West made such arguments when they demanded regulation of railroads, grain elevators, banks, and insurance companies. They never portrayed themselves as enemies of free choice and individualism; they expressed themselves on the whole in conventional, nineteenth-century terms. The hated monopolies blocked choice and threatened economic independence. Perhaps there was an element of self-deception, or even hypocrisy. But one senses a core of sincerity: true independence, true individualism, required the framework of policy they demanded. The same culture underlies, generally speaking, the rhetoric (perhaps also the reality) of most nineteenth-century struggles over law and the economy. The Sherman Anti-Trust Act and occupational licensing laws can be cited again as typical examples.

Individuals or Entities: The Paradox of Choice

Nineteenth-century legal (and social) theory conceptualized choice in a characteristic way. In labor relations, for example, the worker had the right to come and go as he pleased; he could hire on to the job or leave off, as he saw fit. No free man, it was felt, ought to be bound to the job; slavery was an anomaly and an abomination; other forms of bound labor—indentured servitude, apprenticeship—rapidly decayed after 1800. But the employer had a correlative and symmetrical right: the absolute right to hire and fire. Both worker and boss were individuals who had full freedom of choice. To many people this seemed a perfectly realistic way to look at employers and workers. Businesses at the time were mostly small. Moreover, free contract stood in sharp contrast to older systems where apprentice, servant, or slave were bound to the job; custom circumscribed the employer's or master's rights, but these rights were much greater than the servant's or worker's rights; the two statuses were definitely not symmetrical.[27]

Larger-scale business changed the social meaning of the neat, symmetrical rules of the nineteenth century. Increasingly, employers were wealthy and powerful corporations; formal symmetry no longer seemed fair, the scales seemed tilted toward the employer's side. During the nineteenth century workers organized into unions, and a labor movement developed. The unions voiced demands for job security, higher wages, better work conditions, and social justice in general. In England and the United States unions waged battle in the courts as well as on the streets.[28] But nineteenth-century judges, drawn as they were from the upper levels of society, were often hostile to the interests of labor.

In a number of important cases in the United States, courts showed their hostility by striking down protective labor laws as unconstitutional. The law formally recognized the rights of corporations. Corporations were "persons" and their liberty and property, like those of other persons, were under the sheltering wing of the Fourteenth Amendment. No legislature could infringe or impair those rights without "due process of law," an elastic phrase which the Supreme Court and many state courts expanded magically. They discovered inside the phrase hidden powers to block pro-labor legislation.[29] In a few egregious cases "due process" was construed, for example, to mean that the constitution protected "liberty of contract." Hence any law that regulated work conditions had a shadow cast over it; any such laws cut down the "right" of workers and employers to enter into contracts. In the infamous *Lochner* case (1905), the Supreme Court struck down a New York statute which, among other things, set maximum work hours for bakers: not more than sixty hours a week, or ten hours a day. "There is," said the majority, "no reasonable ground for interfering with the liberty of the person or the right of free contract, by determining the hours of labor, in the occupation of a baker." The Court declared the statute void,[30] over a famous dissent by Oliver Wendell Holmes, Jr.

Interestingly, some of the most notorious cases used language which stressed the *worker's* rights in the very process of striking down laws which organized labor had fought for. In *Godcharles v. Wigeman* (1886), the highest court of Pennsylvania declared void a law that required mines and factories to pay their workers in cash. The law, said the court, was an "infringement alike of the right of the employer and the employee . . . it is an insulting attempt to put the laborer under legislative tutelage, which is not only degrading to his manhood, but subversive of his rights as a citizen . . . He may sell his labor for what he thinks best, whether money or goods."[31]

In time the welfare state, without curtailing in any way the worker's right to quit his job at will, cut back on the "individual" rights of employers to deal with workers as they pleased. "Freedom of contract" died as a constitutional principle in the United States.[32] The result was an apparent asymmetry. The worker had "freedoms" which the employer lacked. But the average person sees nothing inconsistent or unfair about this imbalance. On the contrary, it seems perfectly natural and just.

The reasons lie in the legal culture. The beliefs and attitudes of most people do not necessarily cohere or hang together; are not necessarily correct, if by correct we mean some sort of rigorous correspondence to the facts; and do not by any means live up to standards of logical analysis. People think of freedom, choice, and individual worth primarily in terms of individuals, or people like themselves; they do not think of them in terms of organizations or business enterprises except for small and personal ones—a mom-and-pop grocery, for example. This is an important point about legal culture, since, after all, laws that enhance the freedom of "individuals" often do so by restricting the freedom of businesses or government agencies.

This is strikingly true with regard to civil rights laws. These laws were passed to protect rights and extend opportunities for racial minorities, women, offbeat religions, gays, the handicapped, and so on. They laid down rules about "equal opportunity" in housing, jobs, and public accommodations. They created new bureaucracies and agencies to enforce and implement the laws. This legal activity certainly extends the range of choice for blacks, women, gays, and others who suffered and still suffer from discrimination. It forces open doors that had been tightly shut before. But from the standpoint of large landlords, business corporations, and government agencies, civil rights are not rights but duties—not privileges, but burdens. Civil rights laws are full of commands to do this and not do that, restrictions on hiring, firing, leasing, evicting, serving customers, and controlling business decisions in general. Companies can no longer simply indulge the whims of their managers; implementing the rules imposes, at the very least, a mound of red tape on industry. The zone of freedom and discretion for managers of companies is definitely circumscribed.

But General Motors or Fiat are not "individuals" whatever their legal status may be, and people do not think of them that way. Putting a straitjacket of rules on giant corporations is simply not the same as telling individuals what they can or cannot do, regardless of what economists or economic theologians may think. Curtailing a landlord's right to throw out tenants is not the same as taking away the tenant's right to shut the door in the landlord's face. This is especially so when the "landlord" is not a person, but a mega-corporation, which may own or run apartment buildings thirty stories high and with thousands of tenants. Landlord and tenant simply stand on different planes.[33]

When economic conservatives and libertarians argue against civil rights laws or rules restricting landlords or the like, they tend to phrase their arguments in terms appropriate to ordinary individuals. The rhetoric is significant. They might argue (for example) that a landlord should be able to rent space in "his home" to anyone he wants. Similarly as to employers: the state should not tell me whom I can or cannot hire to work in "my store." In one notorious case (1908) the United States Supreme Court struck down a law which, among other things, made it a crime for a railroad to fire a worker for joining a union. Government, said the Court, should not "compel any person, in the course of his business and against his will, to accept or retain the personal services of another," or "compel any person, against his will, to perform personal services for another."[34]

Of course, such arguments strike us as somewhat specious, when the "home" is a forty-story apartment building, the store is Macy's or Harrod's, the "business" is not a fruit stand but a giant interstate railroad, and the expression "personal services" does not exactly fit a factory worker; but conservatives insist the principle is exactly the same.[35] They appeal to symbols and talismans of individual choice, personal privacy, and integrity.[36] Thus Milton Friedman reduces race discrimination to a question of individual "taste," which trivializes it as a social problem and makes it a matter of personal preference, like choosing a partner at a dance. "Is there any difference in principle," he asks, "between the taste that leads a householder to prefer an attractive servant to an ugly one and the taste that leads another to prefer a Negro to a white or a white to a Negro, except that we sympathize and agree with the one taste and may not with the other?" Of course, Friedman is aware that businesses and institutions discriminate, as well as individuals with "tastes," but organizations that discriminate do so merely as conduits or vessels for their constituents; they are "transmitting the preference of their customers or their other employees."[37]

Whatever the validity of such arguments, they are out of step with the legal culture, not to mention the actual course of legal and social development. The contemporary person does not define choice and taste as Friedman does, but thinks of free choice as a noble right that inheres primarily in individuals as individuals, and relates to whatever touches their lives and personalities. The converse is also important: an entity which is not an individual, which is not literally a human being, a personality, does not have, and need not have, the *same* free range of choice.[38] And, as we shall see, the moral basis of antidiscrimination law is very much in tune with the general legal culture. A taste for prejudice is not the same as other tastes because it restricts and injures *individuals*—it prevents them from exercising their own options. It stunts and ghettoizes them for being black, a woman, gay, or in a wheelchair—aspects of the person which have no basis in individual choice. Hence we must consider the issue of ascriptive or unchosen status, and its place in the republic of choice.

Organizational Man (and Woman)

The central argument here concerns the rise, flowering, and dominance of a certain form of individualism. But the golden age of that individualism—our times—is also, quite obviously, the age of the organization, especially the large organization. How are these two social facts to be reconciled?

The role of organizations in modern society is a large and difficult topic. Certainly, most individuals today work for big entities—government, or giant corporations—rather than for a family business, a farm, or for themselves. Many people live in large apartment houses; others tend their own garden, own their own nest, but even so, the chances are that nest and garden are mortgaged, and that the mortgage is held, not by Uncle Harry, but by a large or largish bank. Everywhere in society public life moves and works through organizations; labor unions may be past their prime, but they are mighty still, and so are the various trade associations and farmers' groups. Some scholars even see a kind of neo-corporatism afoot, especially in Europe.[39]

This does not, I believe, impair the central thesis; indeed, it strengthens it. These organizations and groups claim only parts of peoples' lives; they are not "total institutions"[40] like prisons or nunneries; they demand a pound of flesh or a lease on the soul, but never all the flesh and soul, even in Japan. In traditional society, the individual was locked inside the prison of the primary group. Nineteenth-century "society," with its rigid norms and its emphasis on discipline and control, was a kind of total organization in its own right.

Many of the groups and organizations of modern life are voluntary; moreover, they are *horizontal* interest or status groups. They act as vessels for expression or mobilization of the self, whether they are clubs of stamp collectors, radical feminist study-groups, or a league for the advancement of rice farmers. (There is more on the subject of these horizontal groupings in Chapter 7.) There is also a great variety, a veritable riot of organizations of these horizontal types; much of the job of expressing the self takes the form of choosing from this market place of organizations. This is to a certain extent true even of work choices—IBM, Phillips, or Shell are not identical in culture, structure, or habit. In general, group identities of all sorts, as Richard Merelman puts it, becomes "matters of individual choice, which can be changed without stigma."[41]

There is, to be sure, such a thing as the "organization man" and, more and more, the "organization woman": pressures to conform, rigidity, and petty tyranny on the job, not to mention bureaucracy, red tape, and the constant nibbling of minor regulation. Millions of workers suffer the subjection to red tape and bureaucracy. Alienation at or from work is common enough, though we leave to others to sort out exactly *how* common. But such alienation, whether mild or severe, makes the contrast between work life and nonwork life all the more vivid; the domain of expressive individualism swells by virtue of the very fetters that work settings impose. The radical separation of domains, to be sure, presupposes enough space—enough money and leisure—to indulge the self outside the work setting. The nineteenth-century factory worker, whatever his inner inclination, simply spent too much energy and time, from dawn to night, day in and day out, to afford those inclinations, nor did he have the safety net to encourage them. The twentieth century is incomparably richer and fuller in this regard.

Birth, Status, and the Immutable

The culture stresses choice, but some aspects of the individual are or seem to be beyond the realm of choice: race, sex, age, birth, height, general appearance, body structure (to a degree), color of eyes, and everything else that comes as part of the genetic package. I have no control over whether I am white, or black, or Asian; male or female;

young or old, and so on. These are so-called "immutable" characteristics.

Immutability as a concept has played a part in American constitutional law. In a sex discrimination case, for example, the Supreme
Court duly noted that "sex, like race and national origin, is an immutable characteristic determined solely by the accident of birth."[42] The
fundamental laws of Western nations, generally, outlaw discrimination based on race and other ascriptive bases. It is possible to analyze
modern rights laws in terms of immutability. No person should suffer
disadvantage because of race, sex, and other inborn traits. And why?
Because they are immutable, or, in other words, because the culture
does not see them as matters of personal choice. It is one thing to turn
down a job applicant who has no skill, no training, and a fistful of bad
references; these are his own "fault"; they are matters of choice (or
are thought of that way). Race is beyond the worker's control. Here
too the solemn discussions at the top of the legal system distill ideas
that have a more popular origin. As individualism, with its emphasis
on contract, choice, and consent, pervades legal culture, it becomes
the body and blood of living law. The rules reflect this master principle: disadvantage should not flow from situations or from aspects of
the self that are not within a person's choice or grasp.

In fact "immutability" is not so obvious a concept as it seems at first
glance. Popular beliefs and legal culture cannot be equated with facts,
the real world, or even with the way sociologists construe the world.
Analytically, we can distinguish three senses in which an aspect of
the self may be immutable. To begin with, brute fact is immutable:
something which simply is, or which has happened once and for all
and cannot be undone. That I was born on such and such a day, in
Chicago, Illinois, is this kind of brute fact. Once the event has
occurred, I can in no way undo it; consequently, it would be "unfair"
to penalize me because I was born there, because my mother was
twenty-five or thirty-five when she gave birth; or because my family
lived in an apartment instead of a house.

Race is immutable in a different, more complicated way. It involves
two other meanings of "immutable," one biological and one social.
The two are intertwined. Most people think of race as biology, pure
and simple; racial identity is immutable because it is inborn, genetic.
But race is basically a matter of social definition. In the United States,
the child of a white mother and a black father is black; even a single
black grandparent is enough to make the child black. This clearly has

nothing to do with genetics. It would be just as logical to call the person white; more accurate to call her mixed. In American society people of mixed blood are automatically black. With regard to ethnicity, the situation is different. The child of an Italian mother and an Irish father might simply say "I'm half Irish" or "half Italian." But there is no such thing as "half white." In England, whites lump Pakistanis and Indians together with blacks, which defies conventional (scientific) classifications of race.

The decision to attach consequences to certain genetic traits and not to others is almost entirely social. Nothing turns in society on whether you are brown-eyed or blue-eyed—traits which are in fact genetic—but the cluster of traits defined as "racial" is exceedingly significant. Race is a basic social category; race has played a crucial, tragic role in the history of nations and in the destiny of individuals. Other aspects of the self may be biologically determined and carry social consequences, precisely because people do not see them as utterly beyond choice. For example, there is a great deal of discrimination, conscious or unconscious, against fat people, but for millions of suffering dieters, body fat either is genetic or might as well be. It is the social definition that counts, not the genetic situation.

Sex differences are biologically rooted in a way that is deeper and more significant than race, but the same cannot be said for sex *roles*. These are largely, if not entirely, sociocultural. In fact, most immutable characteristics are not biological at all; they are simply defined that way. But the idea that these characteristics are defined *socially*, not biologically, is a bit too sophisticated for many people; they prefer to think of race, sex, and so on, exclusively in biological terms. Social definitions, at least in the short run, are as pervasive and difficult to change as biological facts; they are thus equally "immutable" from the standpoint of the person in question. The massive power of some *social* definitions—race or gender, for example—is more than any woman or black can overcome in the course of a lifetime. In the past such definitions consigned women and blacks to fixed and inferior roles; in many ways they still do so—egregiously so—in many countries. The law, however, defines traits as "immutable" precisely to draw one notable consequence: they lie beyond the power of individuals to choose. In modern legal culture choicelessness, like choice, is a fateful fact. A norm of growing power, working its way in the direction of consensus, posits something to this effect: it is not right to inflict any disadvantage on people by reason of aspects of life that are completely immutable, that is, beyond the reach of choice.

To many of us living in the 1980s this seems self evident; the very cornerstone of morality; it is hard to think of another, competing ethic. But in fact the social and legal consequences of immutability are fresh developments—products of contemporary legal culture. What was immutable in, say, the eighteenth century did not thereby become the subject of civil rights law. Quite the contrary: it simply fixed a person's place on the social ladder, usually beyond any hope of alteration. Immutability of traits and factors did not signal an ethic of nondiscrimination; rather, it was the key to one's station in life, not to be questioned or altered. In a society with primogeniture birth order was one such trait; sex roles were generally fixed in most societies; caste, race, or ethnicity was determinative in other societies; religious affiliation in the Ottoman Empire and elsewhere. The United States and most Western countries have today largely reversed this situation. Large bodies of law and great systems of rules purport to outlaw discrimination on the basis of race. These rules play their most prominent role in the United States and other countries with large racial minorities. Sex discrimination, too, is an almost universal subject of concern. Western countries generally lay down rules that mandate equal pay for both men and women[43] and outlaw other forms of sex discrimination.

A growing body of rules extends the principle to other groups. Religious discrimination, for example, has been widely put to the ban. The same principle can be extended to ethnicity, sexual preference, and physical handicaps.[44] Each of these is a vast subject in its own right, and has its own plateful of political and social complications. Each occupies a special niche in the cultural fabric of the republic of choice. Religion, for example, has a peculiarly double aspect. It is, in the first place, a matter of birth. Almost all of us are born into specific religious heritages. For many people religion borders on ethnicity, so that it is hard to disentangle the two. Judaism is a prime example; neither Jews themselves nor antisemites bother to distinguish between practicing Jews and born Jews. The Third Reich defined Jewishness as a racial category and sent everyone who had Jewish ancestry, whether atheists, Christian converts, or orthodox rabbis, to a common end in the gas chambers.

In the United States and other Western countries religion still often has this ethnic, ascriptive flavor. This is true for many minority and non-Western religions—Buddhism or Islam. But, as we note again in Chapter 9, religion has also become a matter of personal, individual choice. People choose freely from a broad menu of spiritual and cultural patterns. Religious discrimination is thus condemned on two distinct, somewhat contradictory counts: first, because for many people it is *not* a matter of choice, but rather of immutable destiny; second, because for others it *is* a matter of free choice—an aspect of their style of life, an elected pattern of belief and behavior, which the modern republic is bound to protect.

Sexual preference, too, is a mixed aspect of personal status. The basic sex drive is believed to be instinctual. It is not clear what determines sexual orientation, but in any event it develops early in life. People in the West have grown somewhat more tolerant of minority patterns of sexual behavior. They are less likely to condemn homosexuality as mortal sin. "Sodomy" was once punishable by death; it has now in many places been totally decriminalized. The subject still arouses passions on both sides, to be sure. The Roman Catholic church and conservative Protestant churches are bitterly opposed to any further laxity; they want the laws and customs to condemn homosexuals and homosexual behavior. Many people who may or may not approve of same-sex relationships believe that the behavior is the product of personality defects, illnesses, neuroses, some sort of malfunction in the human machine, perhaps arrested development, but in any event beyond a person's control.

Yet sexual preference, like religion, has also taken on something of the flavor of voluntary choice in modern society; it has become, for certain people, an elected "life-style." Thus though the basic idea is "can't help it," an element of choice comes to be associated even with fundamental patterns of sexuality. The phrase "sexual preference" hints at this element. And indeed it is true that the precise menu of sexual acts—and the cast of characters eligible for partnership—is often literally a matter of preference or choice; by no means is this only true for "sexual minorities." After all, even the "sexual majorities" though they take their "partners" from a socially approved list, were once much more limited, legally speaking, as to *which* partners they could choose and when, and what to do with them. Free choice of sexual practices was hardly the nineteenth-century ideal. In modern legal culture, it becomes harder and harder to argue with free choice.

Discrimination on the basis of *wealth* has been one of the trickiest legal issues in American constitutional law. The Supreme Court moved boldly, after the 1950s, to ban race discrimination and, after 1971, sex discrimination. It based its decision on the Fourteenth Amendment, which guaranteed to everyone the "equal protection of the laws." The question arose: did the Constitution also forbid legal distinctions based on income or wealth.? Were these too denials of "equal protection," or of due process of law?

Wealth discrimination is pervasive in Western society—one might even say fundamental. Thus it is no surprise that the Court has treated the subject quite gingerly. In a number of cases, starting in the 1950s, the Supreme Court seemed to be groping toward some sort of principle which limited the right of the state to discriminate against people without money, or to favor those who had it. In the famous cases of *Gideon v. Wainwright*,[45] Gideon, accused of a crime in Florida, was too poor to hire a lawyer. He demanded that the state pay a lawyer to defend him. Florida law said no, but the Supreme Court said yes. In another case, the Court declared the poll tax unconstitutional.[46] The Court struck down a number of laws as offensive to the Constitution because they discriminated on the basis of wealth. These decisions rested on this or that clause of the Constitution, read in a somewhat creative way. But the Court was never willing to go the limit and find in the Constitution a *general* ban on wealth discrimination.[47] The case-law moved hesitantly a few steps toward this goal; the Court stalled, back-tracked, and the theory vanished from the stage of doctrine.

The reasons are obvious. The Court cannot strike down wealth discrimination in the same way it can strike down laws that discriminate against women or blacks. Taken literally, a ban on wealth discrimination would turn the whole social structure topsy-turvy. Wealth discrimination is unavoidable; it is a permanent form of inequality in Western societies. Law and social policy may set a floor under misery and poverty, or a ceiling on woe; they can guarantee, or try to guarantee, basic decencies of life. But legal action cannot, as things stand, eradicate the advantages of a fat bank account, a sound portfolio, and (perhaps most important) a privileged upbringing.

What legitimates these inequalities in society? This is a complex issue, and there are many answers—including, of course, the observation that for some people *nothing* legitimates inequalities. Yet many people, even poor people, do seem to endorse the system of inequality and label it as more or less fair.[48] They do so for a number of reasons. One justification is worth noting here. In myth and story, and in the opinion of at least some people, wealth is the product of merit—it is earned, in other words. Of course most family wealth in society (perhaps 80 percent) comes from inheritance;[49] in the past the percentage may have been even higher. There is also accidental wealth (winning the lottery). Finally, there is earned wealth, created wealth, self-made wealth, one-generation wealth. A popular theme in literature is the rise from rags to riches. Inherited wealth fascinates the general public, and the very rich have celebrity status (see Chapter 7). But popular culture prefers to focus on forms of wealth specific to mobile societies. In fairy tales and older myths, the poor shepherd boy and the servant girl turned out as a rule to be found-lings, lost heirs, princes and princesses of the blood. Success, wealth, and honor were matters of breeding; "princess" was an ascriptive, inborn status, whether in a hovel or a palace. Blood will out. Today's rags-to-riches story leaves out this ending; the shepherd or frog never turns into a (literal) prince. Princedom is more or less something plain money can buy, and so is celebrity status. If one is rich enough, after all, one can always *buy* a palace.

A good start in life—a middle-class or upper-class background—is still tremendously advantageous; similarly, to be born into a poor family, especially in the slums or ghettos of big cities, is a tremendous handicap, which only a heroic handful ever surmount. But popular literature and popular opinion tend to gloss over or ignore this point; it is buried beneath the rubble of an ideology stressing merit, choice, and desert. In one American survey more than twice as many people felt that people who fail "are lazy and lack self-discipline," than felt that such people "weren't given a good enough chance to begin with." The rich, on the other hand, were "models to be admired and imitated," rather than selfish, ruthless, ambitious men.[50] Thus the rich are defined on the whole as people who have deservedly "made it," who have earned what they have; and the culture reinforces this basic ideology in hundreds of large and small ways.

SIX

The Chosen Republic

THE LEGAL culture rests on certain basic social norms that are not easy to map out or measure. These norms are vague and variable, and the evidence for them is distressingly "soft," especially with regard to time periods before the blessings of survey research. But it is impossible to give a good account of social structure and behavior without taking into account the power and reality of these norms. "Legal culture" is a phrase conveniently used for norms and ideas about law, but it is an abstraction, and a slippery one. Each person's attitudes and values are distinctive; no two people share exactly the same set of ideas, just as no two fingerprints are the same. "Society" is an even looser abstraction. The term is useful and unavoidable, but we must constantly remind ourselves about its limitations. No country or community is an undivided whole, with a coherent, uniform spirit that pervades everyone and everything. The danger is always that terms like society and culture will mask or gloss over splits, dissensions, and struggles within a community and smooth out ethnic, racial, gender, and class divisions.

A few pages back we discussed the civil rights law and its relation to legal culture in terms of the underlying norms favoring the primacy of choice. The goal was to distill general legal and social norms underlying developments in civil rights. Such norms do *not* imply social consensus. No such thing is or ever was. Every step of the way has been bitterly contested. Every litigated case has at least two parties and at least two sides. Public policy, crystallized into formal laws, now firmly condemns race and sex prejudice, declares "discrimination" an outlaw concept, and punishes violations of civil rights norms. Enforcement is another matter. And prejudice, of course, does not vanish at the stroke of a pen. It has retreated, but it is still a powerful, sinister force. Civil rights remains a major issue in American politics, though the forms of the issue change. It is also a major issue in other countries; from the standpoint of racial equality, many of them lag behind the United States. What has been described, therefore, is *relative* and *comparative*—trends, directions, flowing currents. The baseline is the not-distant past.

General tendencies in the flow of attitudes and behavior are nonetheless important; they must be dealt with and mapped out. The job is to peel off the outer husks and get to the kernel of norms; to describe and catalog those basic principles that saturate modern legal culture. These are, of course, abstractions—distilled and inferred from behavior patterns of legal actors, from expressions of attitudes, and from the language and content of rules of law. I put the following forward as among the ruling legal ideas within the republic of choice. They are not, of course, *everybody's* ideas; this must be emphasized. A complex society has a complex legal culture. But these are powerful ideas within the law, with powerful forces likely to lie behind them.

1. People should not suffer harm because of events, traits, and conditions over which they have no real control.[1] When there is no real choice, no real losses, disadvantages, or punishment should attach. A person should accept the legitimate consequences of free choices. But any calamity or misfortune is unfair if it is *not* the result of free choice and is "undeserved"; and any suffering that ensues is a form of injustice. Injustice cannot be tolerated in a just society. Hence occurrences of this kind should give rise to some sort of claim of right, some mode of compensation—some arrangement to restore the prior or proper situation.

2. Law should allow, provide, and guarantee a wide range of choices for those situations where people can or do have control. Only in this way are people able to live rich, free lives they fashion for themselves; only in this way can they develop their own personalities and individualities to the fullest.

3. Within the zone of choice, all options should be treated as equally good or equally available. Nobody should suffer because he or she exercised a choice, so long as it was within the permitted range. People should be able to decide whether to wear blue shirts or green shirts; to be religious or not and what religion, to live in the city, the suburbs, or the countryside, to marry or not, divorce or not, and so on.

The formal law of Western nations—and the legal practice even more so—reveal the workings of these and other norms. Of course, these norms are highly abstract; they are principles, or perhaps super-principles, that serve more or less as patterns and templates, out of which more specific rules are carved. The basic terms of these super-principles and the master ideas that underpin them—choice, consent, merit, fault, and so on—are constantly redefined, subtly and unconsciously; the actual working code is modified accordingly. The words and ideas that make up the content of these norms are commonplace, even trite. But these bits of ordinary thought and language differ in critical ways from the words and ideas used and understood in older and other systems of law.

Modern law is a system of *rights* and entitlements. This is yet another reason for the proliferation of law: more rights and more entitlement *mean* more law. A regime of discretion can do with relatively few (formal) rules. In theory, it is possible to reduce a total dictatorship to one single formal rule: the word of the leader is law. The *Fuehrerprinzip* in Nazi Germany, the ultimate principle of legitimation insofar as that system had one, is a rather chilling illustration of the possibilities. The will of the leader in the state as a whole, and the will of the leaders of each sub-part, constituted law. This was an invitation, eagerly accepted, to act ruthlessly and arbitrarily in the name of a regime as evil and unprincipled as any in the history of man.

Legal systems have always been concerned with *rights*, particularly rights of one person or group against another. But the modern citizen is said to be peculiarly rights-conscious, meaning that she is more apt to make use of, enforce, and invoke rights than did citizens in past societies; in particular against the *government* and other bulky institutions. In any event, where there are many rights there are also many rules, setting forth those rights; and rules defining the rights, and procedures for claiming and enforcing them. There are also rules to regulate *conflicts* among rights. A domain of many rights, frequently and rapidly used, makes social space into a kind of crowded street; rules of the road become necessities. A good deal of modern law is explainable in these terms. The law arranges rights and duties in hierarchies and deals with open or covert conflicts among duties and rights.

And why is society so *rights*-conscious? It is because a system of choices is meaningless unless a citizen can convert the choices into entitlements. "Mobility" in the spatial sense is a social fact; it depends on trains, planes, automobiles—all the modern modes of transport, but it also means the *right* to go from place to place. The machinery is useless without the right. And the other, more subtle and metaphorical forms of mobility—social and economic mobility; the mobility implicit in the right to change jobs, hair styles, sexual behavior, religious orientation, sense of self—also depend on or imply entitlements and would be meaningless or futile without them. Conversely, the entitlements are meaningless without the choices; the *right* to travel becomes rich and full only where there are open choices about how to go and where.

Of course, the term "entitlement" is usually used in reference to concrete claims, especially claims within the welfare state. These are, indeed, of enormous importance as a kind of "safety net": a term that became popular in the United States in the 1980s to describe basic welfare programs. It is an apt and significant phrase. Most of us would not get up the nerve to walk on a tightrope, unless there was a net underneath. The net, in other words, permits and encourages behavior too risky to try *without* the net. One by-product, then, of the social safety net is that it stimulates rights-consciousness in our society. What we will describe as *loser's justice* has the same tendency. Clearly, expressive individualism depends on the safety net; without it too many options would be forced, and the punishment for failure or deviance would be far too great.

Rights-consciousness is also the product of a specific historical development and a specific legal culture. Although this culture is extremely complex, it can be parsed, analyzed, and synthesized. It rests on certain pervasive basic principles, including the general expectation of justice. The social, scientific, and technological transformations of the Western world in the last century and a half have given birth to modern legal culture. The scientific revolution has, among other things, radically reduced certain types of life-uncertainty. Science and technology brought with them new problems and undercut old assumptions, but they give humanity a gift of enormous value—greater power over nature, more control over the brute, inanimate world. For example, antibiotics now cure a list of diseases that had ravaged humanity for centuries. As a result, the way people look at the world has changed radically. The *sense* of control and the possiblity of control are as important as the actual control. Many things once impossible now seem quite possible through use of the proper mechanisms, including legal mechanisms.

Control, of course, is an essential aspect of choice. One cannot choose something which is beyond one's power. Life under water is not a realistic option. Options have to be within reasonable reach. This explains the close connection between the scientific revolution, the centrality of choice in modern law, and modern authority structures. Choice means *individual* choice, but people need collective arrangements to make choice possible and meaningful. The freedom to drive into the country generates a demand for road building. But individuals do not construct highways, viaducts, bridges, and overpasses by themselves. The power of science requires collective measures so it can be translated into forms that people can use. If better sewage disposal, pure tap-water, and mass inoculations can rid a community of cholera, smallpox, and other plagues, a demand will arise for these measures. But the demand will be addressed to public authorities; it will call for government action; in other words, for an expansion of law.

Thus a cycle begins, and rights and expectations change in the process. As legal rights and protections expand, as government takes on more and more jobs, fresh expectations are created—an upward spiral of demand and response. The first stage, for example, produces public health authorities and rules and instruments to make sure water is drinkable and pure, to quarantine infected people, and to curb epidemics. People then come to *expect* these arrangements; they form part of the environment. Insofar as government measures are treated as normal and necessary, people hold the collectivity responsible for any shortfalls and failures. The many rules and regulations do not feel like burdens, at least not to the ordinary citizen. If they are socially inefficient, the inefficiency is invisible—an odorless, tasteless gas. What *is* palpable is the base-camp feeling, the safety-net feeling. At the end of the process—at what seems to be a climax in our time— a new, full-blown legal culture emerges, and its keystone is the general expectation of justice. This, in turn, is an essential element of the republic of choice.

Just Desserts

Choice is a central concept in modern law and legal culture. The converse is also true, that is, important consequences flow from the *absence* of choice. A person can and may choose his life and life-style; and one takes the results, for better or for worse (more on this in a moment). But, when we face situations that are *not* of our choosing, it is not right that we should suffer adverse consequences. This is the first of the "principles" mentioned earlier in this chapter. This idea underlies the astonishing efflorescense of civil rights laws and their analogues in society after society. Birth or other "immutable" characteristics should not bring disadvantage. The same general idea undergirds the equally astonishing explosion in tort law, especially products liability and medical malpractice, in the United States and (to some extent) in other countries.[2] The twentieth-century mind does not accept "accidents" fatalistically. It looks on calamities as examples of injustice—evils that a victim did not choose and does not deserve. When injustice occurs, of whatever kind, the law must provide a remedy—some sort of entitlement, perhaps some scheme of compensation. At a deeper level of legal consciousness, all forms of disadvantage coalesce; historical disadvantages of birth merge with the disadvantages that fate hands out in the course of a lifetime. Since these all lie beyond choice, they should also lie beyond disadvantage. Medical malpractice suits and civil rights laws are sisters under the skin.[3]

The general expectation of justice ties together aspects of modern law which seem very different on the surface. A new and rapidly growing field of law concerns the rights of the handicapped. Beyond a doubt, there is discrimination against the handicapped; people avoid them and stigmatize them, perhaps out of embarrasment. This prejudice to be sure, is mixed with sympathy for the blind, the deaf, and people in wheelchairs. But sympathy is one thing, entitlements another. The civil rights movement changed the situation dramatically. One form of entitlement seemed to lead to another, lending support to claims for new modes of right. In the 1950s, black people boycotted segrated buses in the South and demanded equal access. A generation later, people in wheelchairs demanded the right to get *on* the bus in the first place; since the design of the buses made this impossible, they demanded rebuilt or new-built buses to meet their needs and desires.

This progression from one bus right to another was political and social, not logical or conceptual. To talk blandly about the "influence" of the civil rights movement misses the point. What joined the two was a shared sense of calamity, choicelessness, and injustice; the ever-spreading consciousness that injustice cannot be legally permitted in the republic of choice. The duty of law and authority is to remove injustice of all types, or if that cannot be done, to provide money or a substitute for money; the substitute may take the form, when need be, of ramps and lifts and retrofitted buses.[4]

Second Chances

Twentieth-century people are inclined to go easy on themselves in another regard: legal arrangements betray a pronounced bias against *irreversibility*—against choices and arrangements that cannot be undone. At first blush, such a tendency seems either to fly in the teeth of norms that stress free choice, or seems to allow people to have their cake and eat it too. If we permit people to change their minds, they escape from the consequences of choices, which in a sense undercuts their choices freely made. But the presumption against the irreversible means that people should not, at all costs, blunder into choices which foreclose *future* choices; and certainly they should not be forced into such choices. Nobody, for example, is allowed to sell herself into slavery.

One can ask why not, if the decision to choose a slave's life is truly voluntary. Of course, there are strong reasons to be suspicious of any such arrangement; arguably, nobody could possibly choose slavery at any price; if someone seems to make such a choice, we assume some unacceptable pressure or coercion must be lurking in the background. But in fact there is no reason to assume this is universally true, and the rule *does* limit freedom of choice, at least to a degree.

Choices and options which are irreversible, which preclude further choice, nonetheless bear the stamp of illegitimacy. Some such choices are banned outright; they are "against public policy." Irreversibility is one reason for the horror with which most people regard drug addiction, especially as a trap for their children; even people who favor free choice in (almost) all aspects of personal life do not apply the principle to use of a "habit-forming psychoactive drug that alters the user's perspective as to postponement of gratification and his desire for the drug itself."[5] The drug, in other words, creates a kind of enslavement; it robs the addict of his precious stock of free will. There is also no right to destroy oneself, nor a right to sell one's body or one's life. A living donor cannot authorize transplanting his own heart, under any circumstances, and for any reason. One kidney is as far as one can go.

Of course, there is no absolute general norm against the irreversible. Every contract and every choice a person makes is in some sense, and at some point, irreversible. Life is a series of tickets that cannot be refunded. Irreversibility is not thought of as an evil in most ordinary decisions of our daily lives. It becomes questionable only as to major choices, and only those that preclude others, in an endless chain of choice.

The norms that oppose the irreversible choice are vague and shapeless; they do not take the hard, gem-like form of rules. They are all subject to exceptions and countertendencies. The presumption does, however, appear in many disguises in the law. It is a weapon, for example, in the battle against capital punishment; the death penalty is arguably an invalid form of punishment precisely because it cannot be reversed. Of course, when an innocent person rots away in prison, no one can ever restore the lost years, but at least compensation can be paid. More pervasive, perhaps, is an attitude of legal leniency toward people's mistakes and neglect that is particularly characteristic of contemporary law. In the nineteenth century, for example, the victims of accidents could not recover if they had been "careless" themselves, even slightly careless. This was the doctrine of contributory negligence; in practice, it punished victims severely— the word "punish" seems entirely appropriate—for small misdeeds and mistakes. The law was even harsher toward victims defined as "trespassers." The behavior of courts toward (say) men who wandered onto railroad tracks, accidentally or on purpose, and were hit by trains, was nothing short of savage. These rules, in part draconian, in part merely nasty and niggardly, have now almost totally evaporated.[6]

A straw in the wind was the doctrine of last clear chance. It is usually traced to an English case, *Davies v. Mann* (1842).[7] Plaintiff "fettered the forefeet of an ass belonging to him," and "turned it into a public highway." A wagon drawn by a team of three horses came along rapidly, and struck the animal. Plaintiff had clearly been careless, and this should have ended his case, but the court held the wagon-owner liable. He had the "last clear chance" to avoid the accident. Later on, other judges extended the doctrine. It became useful to litigants who got into dangerous situations and were unable to get themselves out. In modern American law, the doctrine of contributory negligence has been largely replaced by comparative negligence, which seeks to balance the carelessness on both sides and makes the plaintiff's slips less consequential.[8]

Less literally about irreversibility, but more important in practice, is the law of *bankruptcy*; this is the commercial version of the impulse to allow second chances. Without bankruptcy, or some analogous arrangement, an entrepreneur whose business failed badly, or who sank for any reason into a quagmire of debt, might be ruined irreversibly. Bankruptcy is a complex legal arrangement. One of its goals is to make sure that whatever the bankrupt has left is fairly divided among the creditors. But it also guarantees a clean, frest start for the bankrupt. Bankruptcy is essentially a modern idea. It grew out of mercantile custom, to be sure; at one time, it was a privilege reserved for merchants, rather than for the public at large.[9] Under the present system, quite ordinary people can cleanse themselves of debt and emerge like newborn babies. Insolvency arrangements go back at least to the eighteenth century; the present American bankruptcy law, which sets up a national standard, was passed in 1898.[10]

Many other examples of "second chances" appear in modern law, particularly in criminal justice. The system treats first offenders with special leniency; they are much more likely to be put on probation than to be sent to prison. In many American states the arrest records of young offenders can be "sealed" and kept secret in this way; youthful mistakes will thus not work permanent harm.[11] Probation, which gives second chances to first offenders, dates from the late nineteenth century; California enacted an adult probation law in 1903.[12] Juvenile courts were established around the turn of the century in Cook County, Illinois, and in Denver, Colorado,[13] spreading rapidly to other parts of the country.

There are various reasons why modern law segregates young people who commit crimes or fall into trouble, and why it treats them in a special way. To begin with, childhood is socially defined as a period of trying things out; a time of trial and error. The self, in process of formation, may take quite wrong turns, and society tends to tolerate and forgive these, at least among children of the middle class (much less, on the whole, is accepted from the children of the underdogs). The facts of birth no longer play a conclusive role in fixing status; neither do the facts of childhood. Of course, society must draw a line, ending the try-out period, and fixing the time when a mature self has emerged from its chrysalis. This is the age of majority. Adulthood is of course not the end of a period of free choice—quite the contrary, more is permitted to adults than to children, but the toleration of *certain* mistakes comes to a halt. Juvenile court, then, is a symptom of an attitude toward children—more accurately adolescents—which reflects norms against irreversible moves.

The general idea of "second chances" continues to spread in society. The norms are shaped by the social taste against irreversibility. People wish to keeps their options open and to a certain extent society keeps the options open for them. Educational theory in the United States rejects the idea that students should be permanently sorted, tested, graded, and labeled, like slabs of meat in the supermarket. They must not be irreversibly assigned to "tracks." Of course, tracking persists, formally or informally, and it is devilishly hard to get rid of. But the system also allows and fosters second-chance institutions. High-school equivalency tests and community colleges provide paths of mobility for "late bloomers," for people who "wake up" relatively late in life. Educational systems in England and Europe are much more prone to life-labeling; this no doubt reflects a deeper sense of class and caste. But in many countries the irreversibility of educational processes is under attack, and even the English and French systems are becoming looser, less class-bound.[14]

The norm that implicitly works against irreversible steps also affects the life-cycle itself, and renders it, as the phrase goes, more "fluid". The passage of time is, alas, irreversible. There is no way to hold back old age; but some consequences of the ticking clock need not be quite so fateful. In North America, there are laws against age discrimination as we shall see. The norm against irreversibility has left a strong imprint, too, on the law of marriage and divorce—or rather, the law of easy divorce. The master theme of free choice has transformed legal culture and the texture of rules and practices; it has turned authority systems on their head, and reworked institutions, all in order to give greater play to the dominant motif of open options. We return to these examples in Chapter 9.

Loser's Justice

In the game of life and the game of law—in every lawsuit, every claim, every election—there are inevitably winners and losers. The norm against irreversibility puts a social limit on the punishment that can be imposed on a loser, literally and figuratively. Some "losers" will not suffer punishment at all, even though they had the gall to challenge the system. This too is a common feature of modern legal systems.

Most societies, past or present, have not respected loser's justice. A person foolish enough to speak out or act out against perceived injustice, if he failed in the attempt, ran the risk of a second catastrophe. Political losers sometimes forfeited their heads in the bargain. In Western democracies today losing an election is hardly fatal. The loser keeps his profession, his social status, and his family; often, losers try for office time after time and some losers turn into winners at the next election. A university student who demands changes in the curriculum, disengagement from South Africa, or better allowances for students may or may not succeed, but win or lose, the student stays a student and is not usually punished or expelled. A tenant demands more heat from the landlord or wants the stairway and boiler repaired; the landlord refuses, and the tenant complains to the housing authorities. The tenant may or may not get results, but win or lose, she expects to stay in the apartment. A striking worker does not expect to be fired, and is not, normally. In most times and places and under most systems none of this could be taken for granted. The price of asserting or claiming rights was high—sometimes prohibitive. In the nineteenth century, for example, an American or British worker who was injured on the job and dared to sue his employer could expect to be summarily fired.[15]

Loser's justice, then, is the widening of the social definition of permitted forms of dissent and opposition and the narrowing of the definition of permitted forms of retribution and response. Loser's justice is in some ways the core conception of democracy. It is closely related to the "safety net" idea, which underlies the modern welfare state. The safety net is an economic cushion; loser's justice is a social and personal cushion, a protection against reverses in pursuit of rights and claims. It is comparable in concept and consequences to such diverse legal arrangements as bankruptcy and unemployment compensation. Like the safety net, loser's justice may have far-reaching effects on behavior and attitudes. It encourages a kind of claims-consciousness, a kind of feistiness; it is a great stimulant to modern forms of individualism. After all, most people are not heroes by nature. They do not battle for their rights. They prefer peace and security. The modern protester—and here I mean not only people who riot in the streets, but also people who sue their bosses, criticize the government, or struggle in various ways to make radical changes in society—may or may not be heroic. Many protesters are courageous, but they also respond unconsciously to institutions of loser's justice, which form part of modern legal culture, and which protesters take for granted. Fewer people are likely to join the opposition in a society where the wages of opposition is death. Loser's justice reflects the general expectation of justice, and, not incidentally, the norm of irreversibility. In modern society asserting rights, demanding justice, and expressing opposition are legitimate options, and in the legal and popular view it would be wrong for them to drag in their train overwhelming or irreversible consequences.

Loser's justice is therefore not merely an expression of the ordinary rules of the democratic game. It is an important social phenomenon in its own right. It engenders and encourages individualism, but it is also an effect of the individualism of personal options and choices. Most likely, it is neither cause nor effect; it interacts and interlocks with the new individualism. Of course, the point should not be carried too far. The modern West is no paradise for the offbeat. Troublemakers are unpopular in any society. People who complain and criticize on the job are still likely to be shown the door. A regime of loser's justice does not mean that democratic ideals of tolerance coincide with reality. The discussion omits gross exceptions and yawning shortfalls. Peers and the state still visit real punishments on loners, troublemakers, whistle-blowers, gadflies, and others defined as nuisances or worse. Those who are out of step are likely to suffer stunted careers and misery in personal affairs. The point is thus a relative one. Loser's justice reflects a subtle but important shift in the *definition* of a troublemaker; it modifies social judgments about the rights which are or are not forfeited through asserting oneself or making trouble. Loser's justice is related to the changing nature of life-cycle, as we shall see in Chapter 9. It is also affected by the nature of social relationships.

Tenure, Citizenship, and Exit

A striking feature of contemporary law is the tendency to strengthen job and tenant security. This trend is more pronounced in Europe than in the United States. Two principles of legal culture are at work here: *tenure* and *quasi-citizenship*. The tenure principle gives special weight to long-term relationships.[16] That is, additional claim values accrue with the passage of time. In many countries tenure is literally the rule for teachers and other civil servants. After a probationary period, civil servants have job security; professors can hold their positions for life or until retirement. But tenure-like notions crop up in other parts of the social order, too. When a married couple splits, the duration of the marriage makes a difference; a wife married a long time may have stronger property claims than the wife in a shorter marriage.[17] Under some modern labor codes workers have strong rights—almost property rights—in their jobs. The employer cannot fire without notice; severance pay is guaranteed, and some workers cannot be terminated at all, except for cause.[18]

In the United States private employers have a great deal of freedom to hire and to fire, but even here the passage of time brings fuller rights, with regard to pensions, for example; the law also favors seniority rights, though indirectly. Significantly, too, recent American case law has begun to recognize new causes of action for employees "unfairly" or "unjustly" dismissed. A British statute forbids "unfair dismissal"; American courts have improvised a similar doctrine on their own. In most cases the complaining parties are white-collar workers or junior executives, and so far the cases are not much more than straws in the wind. Still, the trend seems to be strengthening. In some states it is a recognized wrong to get rid of an employee "in bad faith"; courts have dreamt up a number of theories for granting damages to employees who have been dismissed for bad reasons, or for no reason at all.[19]

Long-term employees probably win the most sympathy in these cases. But the attitudes expressed by the judges go beyond tenure. Courts seem eager to find liability in situations where the termination strikes the judge—and the average person—as unfair: women fired for resisting a lecherous boss; workers fired for complaining about noxious work conditions; "whistleblowers" fired for exposing graft or corruption; salesmen fired to save the boss the expense of commissions or pensions. The idea that a boss or a landlord should have dictatorial power is inconsistent with a culture that emphasizes justice, leeways, and choices, and disapproves of penalties imposed on these leeways and choices.

Some legal relationships are easier to break off than others. Today, a wife can divorce her husband quickly and cheaply, and a worker can quit her job in a flash; a citizen cannot break off from his country so lightly, however. Anyone born in the United States is by law an American citizen. Not all countries have such a principle, but in any event, in most countries, the bulk of the citizens are citizens from birth and stay that way. A citizen who opposes her government, criticizes it, even sues it or harasses it, is nonetheless a citizen. Citizenship is not a relationship of intimacy; it is not so brittle that it breaks at the touch, or because one party or the other wants it to break. Initially at least, citizenship is ascriptive; it is not a relationship of choice. The option of "exit" (to use Albert Hirschman's term) is simply not readily available. This may increase the chance that dissident citizens will use the other option, which Hirschman calls "voice"—the option of protest from inside.[20]

Other relationships in law have acquired traits that resemble citizenship in some ways; we might call these *quasi-citizenship* relations. I will use the landlord-tenant relationship as an example again. Suppose a tenant in a gigantic complex, a whole city of apartments, quarrels with the landlord over rent, conditions on stairways and elevators, or over the landlord's duty to provide heat or air-conditioning. The quarrel is serious and unresolved; the tenant complains to the authorities and finally sues the owner. Certainly, she hopes to win; but even if she loses, she does not expect to be thrown out of her apartment. In fact, the law protects her right to stay; she cannot be evicted merely because she tried to assert her rights.[21] And tenant security, like job security, is even stronger in European law; some parts of France are still subject to rent control, and in both England and Germany tenants have broad rights of security of tenure.[22]

In other words, the relationship of landlord and tenant tends toward quasi-citizenship. It is not the atomized, symmetrical relationship of nineteenth-century theory; still less a kind of feudal symmetry, which binds rather than loosens both sides. The new relationship can be analyzed as a form of loser's justice, especially the ban on retaliatory eviction. Landlords in big cities are usually not "persons" at all but corporations and institutions; the relationship between landlord and tenant is a business relationship; it lacks intimacy or emotional connection. Twentieth-century law protects, more and more, choices and relationships that are "personal," "individual." For this reason, too, people do not mind the asymmetry between landlord and tenant, at least in large housing developments. The tenure principle protects the individual side of the bargain. It also redresses what is considered an imbalance in power and resources. As the law deepens its protection of quasi-citizenship rights, as it buttresses loser's justice, it lays the foundation for further individualism, boldness, and consciousness of right in at least *some* rights-holders. The legal protections act as a kind of "base camp," or sanctuary, a kind of physical and psychological insurance against harm. The citizen can bivouac in the base camp, in perfect safety, before and after mounting the assault on a higher, more dangerous peak.

At first glance, these protective principles and assurances seem oddly discordant with individualism. Partly for this reason, we hear so much about the decline of individualism and so many people talk about a passion for "collectivism" or "security" which has (they say) replaced individualism in the twentieth century. But this opinion depends on a specific reading of "individualism." Contemporary individualism implies as large a menu of choices as possible for each human being; only in this way can people freely develop their selves, their personalities, their central core of being. This is different, to be sure, from the rough-hewn economic and political individualism of the nineteenth century, a sink-or-swim individualism. Modern individualism is far from inconsistent with security; indeed, it thrives on security, it depends on security. The individualism of the nineteenth century began with an uprooting; it tore people out of traditional settings and shipwrecked them on an island world, a locus of isolation; it exposed them to deep economic and social insecurity; they were forced to make their way or die untended and alone. The world of modern individualism is still cursed with loneliness and isolation, but it *presupposes*, in the West, a certain base of wealth and leisure, and, what is more, a basic floor of guarantees, entitlements, social services, and rights.

To be sure, many institutions of the welfare state appear *logically* as the very opposite of choice and institutions of choice. But the social sense of these institutions is not a matter of logic. Free education for children is free in the money sense; it is also compulsory. This constrains parents who (for example) might prefer to exploit their children for money wages, or perhaps teach them themselves, or not teach them at all. A logical argument can be made that forced savings and old-age pensions (provided by the state) reduce the rights of individuals to make their own arrangements or, perhaps, to live the life of the grasshopper, instead of the life of an ant.

But these institutions simply do not *feel* that way. Education feels like a necessity: a start in life everybody must have, without which no fruition of self can be possible. Pensions and other social programs do feel like the lifting of burdens; like a social safety net; they enlarge the sphere of leeways, options, leisure, choice, and remove the crushing weight of obligation and uncertainty.[23] Modern individualism, in other words, rests on, comes from, and desperately needs its supporting pillars: the guarantees of the welfare state, provisions for second chances, the tenure principle, and loser's justice. These make it possible to choose and lose, and choose again. A person has realistic choices and options only if "wrong" choices are not fatal and irreversible, if they do not lead to desperate, calamitous outcomes. Otherwise, most people could not work up the courage to choose among available options.

In short, tenure and the other super-principles of modern law form part of what we have called the "base camp." The system permits experimentation and free choice, because it frees the individual from the paralyzing fear of total calamity. There is also a kind of base camp of social tolerance; a broader, more extensive zone of legitimacy; the "mainstream" is wider, and more encompassing; certain old and new minorities have more mobility and exercise more of their options than they could in an environment which once constrained and squeezed them into a narrow and oppressive slot.

Of course, the norms against irreversibility, and the doctrines of tenure and loser's justice are general trends, not absolutes or "laws" without exception. Bankruptcy, for example, was mentioned as an example of the tilt toward second chances, a sign of how irreversibility is disfavored. But of course one does not go through bankruptcy completely unscathed. And bankruptcy itself is in one sense the very opposite of a second chance: it is the final act in a drama of debt; it signifies that the doors of credit do not stay open forever. At some point, yes, losses and debts become an irreversible burden, and the choice is between bankruptcy and ruin.

Moreover, the concept of "the public" is a great abstraction; while political and social support for specific norms, policies, and principles is quite concrete. There is no magical consensus. The norm against irreversibility, for example, is a rhetorical and normative pillar of the movement against the death penalty. But not everyone has joined this parade. In fact the death penalty itself is, alas, quite popular; large segments of the population here *prefer* the irreversible; they want the door slammed shut; they want a quick and ruthless end to the lives of the most rotten of criminals. This anger and rage are social facts. "Loser's justice" too is a matter of more or less. The tenure principle applies in a spotty way. Workers cannot be so easily fired as in the nineteenth century, but even in Europe a sour economy costs workers their jobs (the high unemployment rate is proof of that);

lawsuits against "bad faith" termination have little or no effect on job security, and the enfeeblement of the labor movement in the United States—and perhaps in Europe as well—more than offsets whatever gains this litigation accounts for. In short, the norms and phenomena described in this chapter are real and significant but they range from straws in the wind on one end to pervasive phenomena on the other. It all depends.

I do not wish to suggest, even for a moment, that the principles of the republic of choice necessarily serve the public interest, whatever that might mean; least of all that such principles are economically efficient. This may or may not be. Lopsided landlord-tenant laws—in England for example—may destroy the market for rental housing. Rent control and tenant security may do more harm than good; may help along the rush to convert flats to condominiums; or depress the housing stock. Determining whether each trend is good or bad is a separate issue.

Neither am I arguing that the norms of legal culture are "principles of justice" in some timeless and absolute sense. Quite the contrary. They are absolutely culture-bound. Nor do they, even in their own terms, necessarily succeed in their aims. Oppression, hopelessness, despair, and grave failures of justice still occur. The point is that these losses are measured against a different baseline. Satisfaction and frustration, complacency and unrest, take place within one and the same cultural framework; it is that framework—the republic of choice—which these pages attempt to describe.

SEVEN

Gods, Kings, and Movie Stars

I N THIS chapter, I consider the transformation of authority in contemporary times and the effect of this transformation on modern law and on the social order generally. This exploration leads us, inevitably, to a consideration of what has been called the celebrity culture. If we are right to assume that traditional authority is crumbling, what, if anything, has come to replace it? Social systems do not tolerate a vacuum, and new forms of authority replace the ones that weaken or disappear; new *legal* structures are prominent among them. American office-holders swear an oath to the Constitution, a legal document. Before the American Revolution, they swore allegiance to the British king.

Law is, on the whole, rather cold and bloodless; it cannot replace traditional authority in the expressive, emotional sense. The word *authority*, after all, refers to a kind of bonding, a link of legitimacy between someone or something that commands and the subjects who follow or obey. It is possible to worship the idea of law; but law does not hold authority in the modern world because of its grip on the emotions. Rather, law is a form, a framework; a mode of organizing and translating authority which has become diffuse and multiplex. But what is that diffuse form of authority?

Observers have pointed out that authority in the modern world, compared to other periods, tends to be organized horizontally rather than vertically. To a great extent, in other words, it is the peer group that exerts authority, rather than parents, teachers, and rulers. David Riesman described the members of the group as "other-directed."[1] It is, of course, no easy matter to pinpoint the locus of authority; certainly no one would assert that parents exert no authority over children in the modern world; but Riesman's proposition seems to have a certain resonance. The peer group *has* gained, one feels, relative to parents and other rulers. But the peer group is not an independent authority; it is a flock of sheep, with what seems to be an invisible shepherd. If we ask who are the new heroes, the new models, the shepherds, the most obvious answer is not peers, but famous people, or, in a word, celebrities. *Celebrities* need not be authorities in the literal sense of the term. But they are, more and more, the models of expressive behavior.

It is not easy to define the term "celebrity." Fame is the core notion. The emphasis is on fame itself, rather than on whatever activities produce it. A celebrity is anybody who, for whatever reason, is known to people who read newspapers, listen to the radio, go to movies or concerts, or watch TV. A person can be famous simply for being famous. Most celebrities, of course, are famous because of some concrete achievement, or because of their position in society; they are movie stars, musicians, sports figures, politicians. Or they are rich and powerful, or simply rich.

In the 1980s information and gossip about the personalities and lives of the rich and famous constantly bombard the public. The most admired people in America seem to be sports champions, rock stars, movie stars, TV actors, a scattering of political and business leaders, a few wives of Presidents and the like, and a religious leader or two— the Pope or Mother Teresa. Millions of people read *People* magazine and similar gossip and scandal magazines. *People* is a spiritual descendant of the movie magazines (which still exist), but it is broader in scope; it is devoted to celebrities in general. *People* itself helps promote its subjects to celebrity status. If one thinks these magazines are an exclusively American disease, one need only look at the tabloids and magazines that crowd the kiosks in France, England, Italy, or Germany. Intellectuals, of course, scorn all of these, but they are a genuine social phenomenon. News about celebrities is to be found everywhere—in books, on TV shows, and in the *New York Times*. The public appetite for celebrity news seems totally insatiable. This appetite affects the arts, intellectual life, popular culture, and books. In the *New York Times*, in November 1985, Russell Baker pointed out that the "top five books on the *New York Times*'s list of nonfiction best sellers" were all by or about celebrities. The number one best seller at that time was *Elvis and Me*, a book by the ex-wife of Elvis Presley.[2] Elvis Presley, needless to say, was a celebrity of celebrities.

Why are people so interested in celebrities and what impact does this curiosity have on social behavior? The attitude towards celebrities does, to be sure, contain elements of sheer curiosity and envy. But neither curiosity nor envy seems to capture the prevailing mood of a celebrity culture. Admiration comes somewhat closer. And admiration leads to *emulation*, an important aspect of celebrity culture. The celebrity is a model. People imitate celebrities in matters of style, dress, and habits of life.

Emulation is a powerful force, a behavioral magnet—a mode of social bonding. In the Victorian period the middle classes emulated the clothes and manners of the upper classes, and the upwardly mobile crust of the lower orders emulated what they could of the middle class. This was almost certainly a new factor in social history. Emulation signifies the blurring or melting of social boundaries. A traditional or status society is not, and cannot be, a society of (upward) emulation. People see their betters, they obey them, willingly or not; they observe and absorb differences in classes, ranks, strata; but they cannot imagine their own selves other than as they are.

An emulating society presupposes a certain fluidity between strata, including moral and cultural strata; it presupposes the possibility of rising and falling in the social scale. Emulation also has its sinister side. A characteristic crime of the modern world is the confidence game—frauds that depend on simulated identity: people passing themselves off as bankers, noblemen, salespeople, and prospective suitors to take the money of dupes and gulls. Frauds that depend on false identity are unlikely or even unthinkable except in a society where there is movement between classes and strata, in which emulation is a *possibility*. Today, some people even make a living out of emulation: imitators of stars, "Elvis Presley look-alikes," and so on. It is hard to imagine such goings-on other than in a celebrity culture.

Emulation is, therefore, an important social fact; it has an influence on the way people act, the clothes they buy, the food they eat. Many people, especially young people, try to remake themselves into copies of their heroes; they want to walk like them, talk like them, cut their hair like them. But a celebrity culture goes deeper than emulation.

To begin with, there is a certain ambiguity about the cult of the celebrity. Celebrity culture seems, in a way, quite inconsistent with modern individualism; similarly, Riesman's "other-directed" personality seems inconsistent with individualism; and so too of the passion for conformity which so many social observers think they see in modern society. But if we sort these notions out a bit more carefully, the inconsistency disappears. One basis for the cult of celebrity is that the celebrities live in another and magical realm; as F. Scott Fitzgerald put it, the "very rich are different from you and me."[3] As we see them on television or in the pages of popular magazines, celebrities *are* different: they lead luxurious, exciting, pampered lives; their love affairs and divorces are the stuff of romance and of soap opera, far from the humdrum daily lives of most of us who form their audience.

Yet in another sense the celebrity is (spatially and emotionally) quite close to the ordinary person. Celebrities are mostly people who excel at what ordinary people do, only not so well. The paradigm celebrities are the "greats" in sports, in (popular) music; hosts of TV shows; actors in movies. They are only heightened forms of ourselves, of the common woman and man; admiration is linked with a kind of kinship. For millions of people the admiration is quite probably colored by a subconscious feeling of wistful regret—they themselves might have been celebrities if fate had dealt them a slightly better hand of cards; if they had been able to throw a ball a bit further, twang a guitar slightly better, act a little better, sing more in tune.

The key to the celebrity culture is thus a certain paradox: being different means being just like us. After all, every one of us is different from everybody else. Uniqueness is what makes us human. Each of us is part of the crowd, and at the same time essentially individual. The celebrity "gods" are also humans; they are more like Wotan or the gods of Greek mythology—gods who eat and drink and make love—than the terrifying, abstract, unseen divinity of medieval times and the churches. Celebrity culture reduces the distant, awesome, and powerful to *personal*, familiar terms. The strange and the remote are redefined, reconceptionalized, so that they come within the orbit of ordinary experience. This is not a statement about religion or belief in the supernatural. The supernatural is still very much with us, but it is molded strictly in twentieth-century terms. Medieval man believed in devils, witches, and miracles but these were part of *standard*, institutional religious beliefs. Today we have the right to pick our own *personal* supernatural. This may involve following a guru, becoming a guru, or preparing for some form of reincarnation. It is we who decide and choose according to our taste.

The attitude of our times toward celebrities is part and parcel of more general attitudes toward otherness. A case in point is the way popular literature and the movies treat one form of the remote and the mysterious: "aliens" or creatures from outer space. At one time in the literature of science fiction, invaders from other worlds were almost always dangerous, sinister, and totally inhuman. Science fiction was a form of horror story. The aliens threatened the very existence of our planet. They came to conquer and destroy. The literary projection was xenophobic, paranoid, deeply fearful.

This strain continues, but in recent years popular culture has presented a counterimage—it has painted a sympathetic picture of the alien. The movie *ET* is a classic example. ET, the extra-terrestrial, is utterly foreign, utterly strange in his appearance; but underneath he is just another living creature, and a lovable one at that, a kind of child from outer space. Movies like *ET* treat invaders from the great beyond with a gentle tolerance. It is the tolerance we are expected to show for people of other races and cultures, for people who are handicapped or have different life-styles and sexual preferences; it is, in fact, the tolerance others are expected to show to us. We would want to enjoy the same understanding and acceptance on ET's planet that the good people, the liberal people, show him on ours. Indeed, we would like to have this acceptance right here on our very own planet. That is the message of ET—a message of pluralism, of "civil rights."

To be a celebrity is just another way of being "different." Someone who can run a four minute mile, sing pop tunes better than others, bat .350, or serve as President is not *qualitatively* different from a person in a wheelchair, a foreigner, or someone who goes to a different church. Modern societies are pluralistic; the term refers, literally, to a mix of peoples, cultures, races, and religions. This pluralism also implies the existence of many "ways of life"; a society in which even stratification and the distinction between rich and poor is redefined as just another form of different-ness.

Of course, in another sense, celebrities *are* different; in the republic of choice, they are, or seem to be, the people who have the most choices, options, potentialities; they are able to make their dreams come true; they have already done so. The public sees them through the magic eyes and ears of television, wonders about them, adores them; they have a marvelous glitter and glamor; they enjoy the scope and freedom everybody wants, but few people actually get. Yet at the same time, celebrities are bound to their public. They are celebrities—

they have fame—precisely *because* they have a public. It is the public that defines their status and provides them with the richest of their gifts.

In the modern world *authority* has been reshaped in the image of the celebrity. To be sure, celebrities are not necessarily authorities; no one would call Elvis Presley an authority, dead or alive. The argument here is rather as follows: face-to-face authority (including family authority) has eroded, partly because of the influence of the mass media, which breaks the monopoly of face-to-face influences and models; authority which is *not* face-to-face has been recast in celebrity terms. Even the surviving institutions of traditional authority have been fundamentally rearranged to take on the aura and the habits of a celebrity culture. Pope John Paul II is a good example of this process. The Pope wields considerable power; he is head of a vast and influential organization. But his authority depends more and more on his celebrity status. It is perhaps for this reason that the current Pope has become a world traveler, concerned with TV and public opinion, unlike his predecessors.

The Queen of England, who wields no power, has become almost entirely a celebrity. The Queen, of course, unlike a rock star, actress, singer, or sports hero, has hardly any visible talents. She is also not a monarch in the old-fashioned sense: over the centuries, the English monarchy has lost almost all of its political authority. All the talk about what the Queen symbolizes and what functions she performs for the nation and Commonwealth does not account for the fact that millions of people in the United States, France, and West Germany have as keen an interest in the Queen and her relatives as the British do. In fact, the Queen is best described as a kind of hereditary international celebrity.

The essence of celebrity status is exposure to the public; celebrities cannot remain celebrities without publicity and the mass media. *Most* celebrities are "people just like us"; many start out as ordinary people from ordinary families and then become celebrities because of achievement or merit, good fortune or bad. Others, like the Queen of England, are celebrities from birth. Nonetheless, the Queen's publicity stresses how "human" she is, how "ordinary," how much she is like us, despite the glamor and the mystique. Half the time she is seen in a tiara; the other half in a kerchief, acting like a housewife.[4] There are other, more transient, born celebrities—the Dionne quintuplets, for example; or Baby M.[5] Thus a celebrity is an ordinary person, transformed through some magic into something more, but nonetheless akin to the rest of us. It can be the magic of birth that works the transformation; or the magic of talent; or the magic of tragic or fortunate events.

It is characteristic of modern Western society that even ordinary people have chances in life to climb the celebrity ladder. This was not true of traditional societies, where status was fixed once and for all at birth. Traditional stories and folk-tales, as we noted, reflect this idea; if a hero or heroine was poor and humble at the beginning of the tale, he or she was sure to be revealed as a secret prince or princess at the end—a foundling, abandoned as a child, or subject to some strange enchantment. Charismatic leaders owed their power and authority to the supernatural; and it is supernatural force that transfers the spirit of the dead Dalai Lama to a newborn baby, born perhaps in a peasant's hut.

Today celebrity status can strike the common man like lightning, either through positive events like winning the lottery, or negative events—falling victim to some terrible disaster. A little girl who falls into a well is a celebrity, at least for a time. The victim of a notorious rape can be a celebrity too. The archetype celebrity has a deep kinship with the viewing and reading public; the celebrity is a fantasy (or nightmare) image of our very own selves. Circus freaks are fascinating because of this duality; they are ordinary people underneath the amazing beard, the bulging muscles, the tower of fat. The American showman and charlatan, P. T. Barnum, was a pioneer in exploiting freaks and promoting stars. As Leo Braudy points out, Barnum exhibited the "private lives" of his stars "primarily to celebrate the unthreatening normality under the surface strangeness."[6]

The celebrity has thus been touched by black or white magic, but only in some particular regard—in other respects she is one of us; we see ourselves reflected in celebrities as they live the glittering and romantic life, or the fearful, fateful, tortured life, portrayed in shows, movies, and television. Most political leaders—Ronald Reagan was an excellent example—are pure celebrities. They are hardly charismatic in Max Weber's sense at all. Their political powers of enchantment are exactly the opposite of Weberian charisma. They are not superhuman beings, but lucky or exhalted versions of the average man. Their leadership strength, such as it is, comes from their kinship with the commoners.

It is amazing how much we know (or think we know) about celebrities; not only what they look like, but what they wear, what they think, who their friends are, their habits, their thoughts, their sex lives. Of course much of this "knowledge" is public relations nonsense or outright lies. But the public does know a good deal more about prominent people than was true in the past, or under other systems of government. A striking difference between politics East and politics West has been the degree to which their leaders have celebrity status. Russian and Chinese rulers do not parade their families before the public. Stalin's wife, or Brezhnev's, were not written up in gossip magazines. Raisa Gorbachev has carved out a different role, but the idea of a "first lady" in the People's Republic of China still seems totally ridiculous. Western experts often are ignorant of the most basic family facts about high Russian or Chinese officials—whether they are married, whether they have children, where they live.

The celebrity status of leaders in the West did not happen overnight. It is the gradual product of a political transformation. In the United States George Washington came to be virtually deified, but this deification was not the same as the celebrity treatment of modern Western leaders. One cannot imagine a statue of Ronald Reagan, or Winston Churchill or even of de Gaulle, posed in a classical toga. The social meaning of fame has altered over the years. For the founding fathers, the tradition of fame was "neither ethically blind nor morally neutral"; fame was directed at lasting achievement, at the judgment of posterity.[7] This is, of course, strikingly different from the modern celebrity culture. Today fame is intense, current, fleeting, and connected with "virtue" tangentially or not at all.

To be sure, the public in the past had also been interested in the backgrounds of its leaders. This was perhaps inevitable in the case of officials in the United States. Abraham Lincoln's campaign capitalized on his humble birth, the log cabin, the rail-splitting. But presidents in the age of Lincoln and later had a degree of privacy, a distance from the public that now seems part of a dim, innocent past. In the late nineteenth century President Grover Cleveland underwent a serious, dangerous operation in total secrecy. Woodrow Wilson suffered a serious stroke; the public was kept largely in the dark. Franklin Roosevelt, a master of media manipulation, suppressed any photographs that showed him sitting in a wheelchair. The public knew he was crippled, of course; but his handicap was not paraded blatantly before them; it was kept in the background.[8] Other heads of government enjoyed the same sort of privacy.

Today the President's bowels, spleen, blood pressure, and prostate glands are the subject of daily bulletins when he is ill; television chronicles even the slightest ailment; hordes of reporters circle about the hospitals of state. Of course, the public has a right to know whether the head of government is healthy or not. But the level of detail on this and other aspects of the leader's life goes far beyond any possible considerations of government; it reflects instead the celebrity status of leaders. A man may be President, command armies, and lead the whole Western world, but he has a colon, a kidney, a digestive tract; he has blood pressure and indigestion, just like the rest of us. If you tickle him, does he not laugh? If you scratch him, does he not bleed?

Politicians (and even the Queen of England) are treated in the media like other contemporary celebrities—the stars of movies, sports, or music. They are special, but also really "just like us," or like us "down deep." In a famous incident, Senator Roman Hruska of Nebraska defended a man nominated for Justice of the Supreme Court by President Nixon against the charge that the man was mediocre. There are "a lot of mediocre judges and people and lawyers," the senator said, and they "are entitled to a little representation, aren't they?"[9] It was a foolish remark and widely scorned, but nonetheless diagnostic. Americans, as James Bryce pointed out long ago, do not want intellectuals to govern them. The "ordinary American voter does not object to mediocrity" in a President.[10] The voters want people like themselves. Intellectuals or not, leaders *are* like ourselves. Thus we are interested in their aunts, wives, nephews, cousins, their hobbies, what food they eat, what cars they drive; what they like and dislike, and why. We want to see them, hear them, know them, smell them. We even want to know about their sex lives and whether they are faithful to their husbands or wives. All this is supposed to be in the public domain; it is part of the public's right to know.

Celebrity culture is a complex phenomenon, not to be accounted for in one-dimensional terms. Obviously, a celebrity culture is of a piece with a mass society, in the sense of mass production and communications. It depends totally on modern technology, which can deliver messages to millions of people rapidly and simultaneously. This technology also fosters one of the nastier features of modern society: propaganda and manipulation of truth through control or corruption of media. Propaganda, as Terence Qualter defines it, is "the deliberate attempt by the few to influence the attitudes and behavior of the many by the manipulation of symbolic communication."[11] Propaganda is by no means confined to totalitarian countries. Every Western government is obsessed with image; propaganda is an instrument of image, and advertising is a form of propaganda. There were probably no instruments of propaganda before modern times, but there was also no *need* for them. In most societies the allegiance and enthusiasm of the millions was not an issue for the ruling class, except in extreme times and circumstances.

All governments lie, but they lie in characteristic ways. In the Soviet Union and in most totalitarian countries, lies are often pure suppression of fact; the government simply says nothing, hides what is happening, and keeps whatever it can as secret as it can. The lies of Western governments are often lies of replacement. The public is supposed to know *everything*; thus when Western governments lie, they pretend to tell the whole story, and instead tell half of it or the wrong story altogether. These are celebrity governments, which means that the public thinks of itself as their participant, or at the very least as a spectator with regard to every facet of national life.[12] The concern with image is not only a hunt for votes and support; it is part of the duty to be public, to act in the celebrity mode.

Celebrity culture would be unthinkable without the mass media. The celebrity culture evolved along with the instruments that make it possible. In the United States any history of this culture would put great weight on the rise of "yellow journalism," in the late nineteenth century—the sensational, scandal-mongering, popular press, notably the newspaper empire of William Randolph Hearst.[13] Then came radio, but a picture *is* truly worth thousands of words, and the influence of the movies, and especially of television, is incomparably stronger than the influence of the print forms, or even radio.[14]

Technology here acts as a tremendous motor force of social change. Radio and television did not create the celebrity culture as such. There is no celebrity culture in Bulgaria or mainland China, though there are mass media; yet the connection between the media and celebrity culture is so close that it is almost as if the casual chain were reversed: that is, that the celebrity culture called the mass media into existence. In earlier times rulers and members of the upper classes were not "celebrities;" rather, they were creatures apart—profoundly different from ordinary people by birth or breeding; and their position (they believed) had been established by God, or fixed by immemorial tradition. Their subjects looked at them through a misty lens of reverence. Political democracy changed the situation dramatically. As the suffrage was extended in country after country downward into the middle classes and lower, the hereditary and "inherent" ruling classes were consigned to oblivion. A new ruling class replaced them, whose tickets to power were luck, mobility, and money. The importance of "breeding" was destroyed, that is, the essential, ascriptive differences between "us" and our rulers; the process brought them down to our own level—which is, of course, also a way of bringing us up to theirs.

Fear and suspicion of authority do not vanish, of course, but the bad thoughts become displaced onto abstractions: the mechanism, the red tape, the bureaucracy. The celebrities at the top are not part of this demonology. Indeed, in the United States at least, clever politicians run for office by bashing the bureaucracy; they defame the very machinery they are so eager to operate and denounce the perquisites they so desperately want for themselves.

The process of turning rulers into celebrities began earlier perhaps in the United States than elsewhere in the Western world. It led to a certain insolence in "domestic manners," a kind of obsessive egalitarianism, which shocked Fanny Trollope and other gentle visitors to American shores in the nineteenth century. Mrs. Trollope's son Anthony, who came to the United States one generation after his mother (1862), observed the same situation. He was "pelted with the braggadocio of equality." American manners offended Trollope deeply, but he admitted that the United States must be a good place for the ordinary person to live. Though such people acted with "disgusting" familiarity, no doubt they had a better life than their servile counterparts in England; they certainly had more dignity.[15]

There is still a substantial chasm between England (and continental Europe generally) and the United States in regard to deference and civility, but manners everywhere seem to be changing. And political leadership shows a definite tendency toward Americanization. British and German voters do not elect heads of government directly, but celebrity culture has gained ground in politics nonetheless. People vote less for parties and ideologies than for personalities, for leaders—for or against Prime Minister Thatcher, for or against Chancellor Kohl. "Name recognition" is essential. Campaigns are briefer and less hysterical than American campaigns, but they too are turning into celebrity and media exercises.

The mass media have become powerful forces of intrusion and

dissemination. How many people in 1856 knew what President Buchanan *looked* like? How many Englishmen could have recognized Gladstone or Disraeli if they saw these leaders on the street? The face of Queen Victoria was, of course, familiar, but as a kind of icon on stamps and coins; this was perhaps true of American presidents, or candidates, through buttons and posters. In general, people knew little enough about political leaders and certainly nothing about their families. For the mass of the population, political leaders were dim and distant figures at the center. In the United States presidential candidates campaigned, and vigorously; they shook hands; they traveled about; but they could not cover all the ground and meet everybody in a country so vast. They reached only a fraction of the population in the flesh. In Britain voters chose members of Parliament who were local notables, and Parliament chose its leaders itself. Seats in Commons were often owned, practically speaking, by nobles and great landowners.

The structure of politics has changed dramatically in the contemporary world. Mass media and the celebrity culture reinforce each other. More to the point, this culture makes possible a continued, drastic shift in the structure of authority—a shift that comes about silently, almost secretly, without any consciousness or plan. In the old days the most powerful authorities and role models were people close at hand: the father, the teacher, the clergyman, the local lord or squire. Authority lived in the home or close by in the village; authority exerted constant, daily pressure; it was part of a little world whose boundaries were formed by what a person heard or saw and by the range of travel. Nor did the outside world or the central authorities interfere very much with the tyranny of local rule. The father's power within the family, the power of the local priest and of the school teacher were untrammeled; there was little to curb the authority of the squire, who lived in the great house on the hill, just beyond the village bounds. There were greater figures far away— kings, bishops, popes. But they had no personal presence in the cottage of the average family; they were sensed and felt from a distance, rather than experienced firsthand. These mighty authorities, outside the primary group and beyond the local community, were shadowy, mysterious, godlike—figures like the Emperor of Japan, the Czar, the Supreme Pontiff. They were totally beyond the ken and understanding of peasants and ordinary citizens.

Distance in this sense means nothing in the modern world.[16] A thousand miles is a millisecond away by satellite. Models and heroes march into the household across vast spaces. Queen Elizabeth, unlike Queen Victoria, is more than an icon; she is a familiar figure who moves, talks, and communicates. She is a celebrity. The current Pope, John Paul II, has become a world traveler and media star; it is hard to remember that popes, until recently, were virtual prisoners of the Vatican and almost never left its grounds. The late Emperor of Japan was a special case; he remained a mysterious figure, rarely seen and remote from ordinary contact. But the new Emperor is likely to be more accessible.

In any event, the Emperor of Japan and the Queen of England have no say in running their countries. Those who do—presidents and prime ministers—are part of the celebrity culture and are treated accordingly.[17] Indeed, it is the leaders of socialist states who have inherited the mantle of the czars. They live in walled cities or fortresses; their private lives are shrouded in secrecy; nobody chronicles their comings and goings; they disappear for weeks at a time. The Eastern bloc's "cult of the personality," like the deification of Hitler, is a throwback to premodern forms of authority-worship. And the phrase is misleading: what the object of the cult lacks is precisely personality, that is, the breath of humanity, the leveling touch of the ordinary and the familiar, which is vital to any celebrity.

Celebrity culture embraces primarily heroes of popular culture; secondarily, political leaders. It has expanded, however, to take in *all* the elites, including the modern businessman. Popular culture, certainly in the United States, but elsewhere as well, strongly emphasizes mobility—"rags to riches"; and this, of course, is a common pattern for celebrities. The history of attitudes toward businessmen in Western society is varied, passing through a number of phases. In the nineteenth century some of the very rich, like John D. Rockefeller, were bogeymen, demon-figures, famous for evil. Yet on the whole American culture treated businessmen with enormous respect. They were *the* American elite—practical, worldly, hard-working, successful. The business of America—so went the slogan—was business;[18] and the businessman belonged at the apex of society.

There was always a radical and populist strain which demonized the rich, but it seems to have lost much of its virulence. One no longer hears much about "malefactors of great wealth."[19] Hatred of big business as such seems confined to a tiny segment on the far left. There are still business villains—wheelers and dealers, inside traders, currency speculators—but they are treated as deviants, not as class-monsters. In part, the welfare state has defanged big business; managers and owners have had to learn to treat the public with respect, or have at least improved their public relations. Behavior itself has probably changed as well—big business leaders are less inclined to give off messages of contempt, less likely to say openly, "the public be damned." It would never do today to strike a posture of despising the consumer.

Moreover, business behavior is under considerable state control. It is watched and guarded and hemmed in by rules and regulations. The most blatant swindles have been outlawed. No one would claim that business invariably follows the rules. Scandals and news of corruption abound; far more, no doubt, lies beneath the surface. But businessmen nowadays break the rules in secret, like ordinary thieves, not defiantly, like autocrats. And leading businessmen, like the very rich in general, have become celebrities themselves: Lee Iacocca is an excellent example. There are plenty of stories about businessmen in *People* magazine.

There are also, of course, business magazines, and they often run feature stories about businessmen who are particularly interesting, successful, or colorful. Recently, business magazines have begun to run lists of the richest men and women in the country or the world. Customers snap up these issues; they are eager to learn these wondrous names and to read about the fabulous wealth of these people. The tone of the stories does not differ much from the tone of stories in entertainment magazines, in *Sports Illustrated*, or in *Quick*. Recently, too, magazines for the legal profession have sprung up in the United States, strikingly different from the older professional journals. The new legal journalism is full of gossip about law firms and feature stories about colorful, interesting lawyers.

Wall street lawyers once shied away from publicity; they hid behind a protective curtain of gray. Only criminal, divorce, and tort lawyers—practitioners with "one-shot" clients—had any need to parade before the public; any taste for newspaper copy and flamboyance. They needed the publicity to ensure a steady stream of business. But modern practice, even at the Wall Street level, has become highly volatile. In any event, leading business lawyers today do not seem to relish the quiet life in the woodwork quite so much. They do not reject celebrity status out of hand—at least not within the profession itself.[20]

Celebrity Culture and Authority

Celebrity culture has thrived on the accumulation of knowledge (real or imagined) about authority figures and role models. This tends to change the *nature* of authority as well. At the most general level, the celebrity culture makes possible, or at least reinforces, the peculiarly modern form of individualism centered on creating one's own life, personality, and style; the crafting of a unique, fulfilling self through the free exercise of options in a glittering field of choice.

The same technology that spreads celebrity culture also transmits, with stunning rapidity, styles, fashions, and fads; it presents a bewildering succession of models, goals, wishes, habits, behaviors, ideals. Authority is presented horizontally and synchronically, instead of appearing in its older and more vertical posture. Authority once worked slowly and methodically, through glacially powerful processes—socialization within the family, neighborhood, and village. Authority once hinged on local centers of power, and it was the product of years of training and learning, much of it unconscious.

In traditional society, and well into the nineteenth century, the self was handed over to the almost despotic control of face-to-face authorities. The individual was molded and shaped within a protected environment, and when he or she was let loose into the world, so to speak, it was as a fully formed personality, a butterfly released from its cocoon. The modern personality, on the contrary, is exposed from the outset to the outside world in all its power, its incredible wealth of images and colors, its infinitude of models and suggestions. This begins virtually at birth, especially in the television era. The child has barely learned to distinguish shapes and voices when it confronts the great box of pictures, the images of today's floating world.

Law—like authority—was vertical in traditional society. Its operations were powerful, custom-bound, immemorial, and reinforced through local authorities; its origins seemed remote, mysterious, meta-human, emanating from unseen realms of higher authority. Nothing strikes the reader so strongly in descriptions of medieval or tribal culture as the sense of the narrowness of life, the sessile nature of existence. The individual and his clan seem to inhabit a tiny circle of light. the known and familiar, surrounded by a world that was immense and unknown, full of shadowy spirits of evil and good. But in the most miserable hovel today, a beam of great power and magic intrudes from the outside world. And modern law, unlike its predecessors, is horizontal and kaleidoscopic; it is constantly in flux; it is a mosaic of aggregate choices in a society theoretically made up of peers, none better than any of the others, all of them freely making and unmaking their lives in accordance with models and images displayed before them.

Within that modern legal system, no influence seems more potent than the role of organized interest groups; it is their pressure that creates the norms at the legislative level, and, through class-based litigation, in the courts or through the courts. Law seems more and more to be the product of social movements.[21] Yet this is the age of the individual. Is there a contradiction here? Not really. Television, as Ulrich Beck has put it, both "isolates and standardizes." It loosens traditional patterns of living, and it exposes great masses of people to identical experiences "from Honolulu to Moscow and Singapore"; it creates a world of "isolated, hermit-like masses."[22] Yet the patterns of living these masses observe on television—though they do not of course display the full range of geographical or cultural diversity— are ineffably more varied and cosmopolitan than the patterns and models available in the closed, narrow world most of the audience would otherwise inhabit.

Television both fosters and permits the formation of horizontal "interest" groups. Such groups do not easily arise in societies without means of horizontal influence and communication. In modern society individuals make a difference in public affairs largely through groups to which they belong, or which represent them. The groups themselves may be purely voluntary associations: a national league of stamp collectors; the trade group of turkey farmers; friends of prison reform. Other groups are made up of aggregates of "immutables"—feminist or racial groups, for example. But even in these cases the decision to join the group and to be active in a particular cause is a matter of individual choice. There is enormous scholarly debate on the role that interest groups actually play in making law and in shaping public affairs. Is Western society really pluralist, in the sense of a genuine market place of group formation, or is it run by visible and invisible elites, who hide behind the illusion of multiplicity? None of the parties to the debate would deny at least *some* role to pluralism and the array of interest groups; for some observers, these groups overshadow everything else in the modern polity.

The very existence of pressure groups is a tribute to modern communications. The group members may be spatially remote from each other. What they share is a kinship of choice. They talk to each other, if at all, by means of newsletters, brochures, and telephone messages. They exert their force electronically, not by rioting in the streets and not in compact geographical clusters.

The keystone of modern individualism is the concept of choice. Even "conformity," so-called, is at bottom a matter of choice; people choose the group they wish to conform to. What conformity means is a more or less voluntary association with some particular peer group. The very concept of "conformity" is distinctly modern. It implies that it is possible *not* to conform. In a truly traditional culture, there is no such concept as "conformity," since actual conformity to community norms is taken for granted. In traditional society, status is pervasive. The individual of course conforms—to his clan, tribe, religion, to the customs of the group; to the precise, detailed requirements imposed by sex and age roles. These roles and customs appear to be fixed and immutable and in the short run they are. The members of the group have accepted them, without question. The short run is all that most of us ever experience.

In traditional society there was no such thing as a "life-style." There were indeed styles of life, but they were not a matter of choice. In modern psychobabble, a life-style always carries with it the notion of choice, however dimly. The modern conformists, in short, though they may act like sheep, have at least chosen their flock of affiliation.

Thus the very concept of conformity is a sign of the primacy of choice in two distinct ways: first, in its sneering and pejorative tone, which implies that "conformity" is the mark of the inferior self; and second, in the recognition of choice as inherent in decisions to conform and in the selection of a group to which the conformist will adhere. The signals that bombard us—the radio voices, the images on television, the advertisements everywhere—present us with an amazing stock of information. There are so many models and cues that a person no longer feels she must stick with the old, inherited models and codes of the primary group. Even in the privacy of the home, or within the confines of village life, the outside world is with her. Celebrities are powerful vehicles for conveying information about new models and patterns. They are the living embodiment of choice in style of life.

Choice and consent are crucial to ways of life; the individual makes and remakes the self, at least in theory. Indeed this is supposed to be her main function and task in the course of a lifetime. The reality of it is another question. As we have said, choice can be a complete or partial illusion, and the making of the self—a cosmic undertaking—may come down to nothing more than the small, narcissistic decisions of everyday life, about clothes, vacations and record albums.

Still, the belief that modern life is a life of free choice has enough truth in it—or appearance of truth—to feed the attitude and keep it green. There *is* a measure of geographic and social mobility for great numbers of people; there *is* freedom to move from religion to religion, from place to place, from job to job, from hair style to hair style, from guru to guru, at least for the middle class. And even people who are rooted to a single spot socially and psychologically absorb messages of mobility from the media; they watch on TV and in the movies scenes from the world's boundless multiplicity; they observe a dance of motion all about them, conveyed through the enchanted screen. Thus the sheer abundance of patterns in the world, whether the viewers share in its riches or not, comes to be accepted as normal, natural, instinctual. At the very least, the ceaseless flow puts ideas into people's heads. These ideas are the basic stuff of legal culture, and the legal culture is the architect and mechanic of law. The celebrity culture expresses authority organized horizontally, rather than vertically; transmitted electronically, rather than through family or village models; expressed in constitutions of choice, rather than those of hierarchy and self-control. All this, of course, is a matter of more or less. The family is not dead; parental power is still awesome; old-fashioned religion and old-fashioned patriotism exert enormous pull on millions of people. There are, however, crucial differences at the margins; and this makes a difference in society itself.

There is no single pattern of reaction to the menu of vast possibilities. People see this menu as open to them, at least in part. Or if they see it as closed, it is because of their own choice or shortcomings. If one cannot sing like Elvis, at least one can dress like him or buy his records. But there may also be darker reactions, reactions of rage and frustration. They may be extreme enough to lead to violence and crime; the next chapter deals with this subject. There may also be reactions of apathy or despair. The world looks rich and many-colored, but the viewer's own surroundings may be drab, mean-spirited, unsatisfying. Yet this very despair comes in through windows open to a world of options and choice.

Manipulation and Dependence

Societies in the West are relatively open, and public opinion plays a powerful role in them. The argument here does not, as we have said, require that the choices must be real, and the public input dominant. These may be quite illusory; a conjurer's trick. Similarly, as to the give and take between media and audience. Which is in actual control? Do the media respond to the public, or are they expressing instead the wishes of hidden or overt power-structures? Are they shamelessly manipulating the public? If the consumers think they are choosing freely, is this a myth, or is it ideology?

These are serious issues, but they are basically beyond the scope of this work. A few comments, however, are in order. In the celebrity culture lines of force and influence seem to travel in two directions at once. Generally speaking, authority depends on its public. Market research, the vote, box office receipts, TV ratings, the market itself—all these are devices either for aggregating choice, or for determining what choices have been made or will be made by consumers. Authority *needs* this information. Its appetite is insatiable for knowing what the public wants or thinks. Governments hardly make a move today without consulting their oracles, the public opinion polls. A relationship of mutuality and reciprocal dependence ties leaders to their publics. The President of the United States, for example, is essentially a "popular leader," and the "rhetorical" task of the presidency is the very core or "heart" of the office. Presidents "have a *duty* constantly to defend themselves publicly, to promote policy initiatives nationwide, and to inspirit the population."[23]

Thus the public seems to be all-powerful. At the same time, only the naive think of leaders as humble servants of the people. In the very process of coaxing and consulting, the leadership manipulates its public. The whole point of all this rhetoric and public relations, all this uplifting and "inspiriting" is to mold the public like putty. It is to find out what image to project, what propaganda to use, what messages best persuade and deceive. Government becomes an exercise in public relations. Power, then, is interactive at best; it is hardly a pure emanation from the popular will. The press and TV are exceedingly powerful in modern society precisely because this interaction is so central to leadership. In some ways the media are as mighty as government itself, since government is so dependent on them.[24] Elites in Western society all enjoy and use celebrity status; this makes them dependent on the media, and through these on the public.

In advertising and "consumerism" in general the same kind of complex interaction takes place. Between the model and the person who conforms to the model, between leader and follower, there is no simple command relationship in either direction. Consumer sovereignty is, of course, a fairy tale. Nobody believes in it, not even the advertising moguls who use it to defend their social role. Yet the public is not simply a tool in the hands of media people. The audience can be monumentally fickle; customers change allegiance in a flash. The history of advertising and marketing is strewn with corpses of products that failed miserably, despite market research and millions of dollars in advertising and promotion.

Businessmen and apologists for the American system are thus not wholly hypocritical when they claim, in tones of injured innocence, that they do not trick the public or induce artificial, useless wants. Marketing, they say, is at the mercy of the public. They give the public what it wants. If the public wants green toothpaste, this is what they get. Clearly, no amount of advertising could persuade more than a handful of people to give up sex on the grounds that sex is dangerous to health or is a deadly sin. Advertising, however, *might* induce people to change brands of soap, or make them feel unclean unless they brushed their teeth after every meal; and, since the advent of AIDS, advertising has helped promote "safe sex." Advertising also spreads a message which many people welcome: that buying the right products can bring great gratification; that soaps, breakfast cereals, and underwear help make a satisfying self.[25]

Men and women in society are always subject to strong but invisible constraints which influence their choice, sometimes decisively. This is a central message of modern sociology and anthropology. The subliminal messages of advertisers may be important factors in constraining and shaping wants, but the ambient norms are far more significant. Here the hand of the puppet-master is skilful and delicate; and the puppets are unconscious of the strings. People like to feel that they are masters of destiny. And they may be right; possibly people in the West *are* masters of destiny and *can* exercise choices to an extent past generations would have found unthinkable. It may be equally true that they are manipulated and preformed to an extent they never imagine.

Relativism and determinism on the one hand; the subjective sense of choice on the other: these stand in a state of tension. The ordinary person is not a party to the great debate. People never see the axioms and postulates of their own society; these are too close up to be visible. Free choice and its values are among these axioms. The limits of free choice are even more invisible. "Choice" after all is choice among models. It is like choosing a wardrobe at the store. The choice is real, but it is constrained by price, range of styles, and supply of stock. The customer can only buy what sits on the rack—what stores actually offer for sale. Similarly, what is not *presented* by the media—or by society in general—cannot be chosen; the consumer never even knows these possibilities exist.

EIGHT

Crime, Sexuality, and Social Disorganization

HARDLY any issue so agitates the American mind as the problem of crime. In the United States violent crime, and perhaps crime in general, seems to have increased dramatically in the last two generations. Crime is much less of a problem in other Western countries—people walk in the streets of London or Rome with less fear than in New York—yet concern about crime is apparently on the rise in Italy and England as well as in the United States. As far as one can tell, the amount of crime has also increased in European countries, though from a lower base than in the United States.

It is never easy to measure crime; it does not normally advertise itself. Moreover, crime is to a large degree a matter of social definition; thus, a country can increase or decrease crime by adding or deleting items in the penal code. But these variable crimes, the items that go in and out of the codes, are not usually the ones that make up the "crime problem," though they may be important in other ways. If we confine ourselves to the more durable and less transient crimes—crimes like murder or armed robbery—the measurement problems become somewhat more tractable. Older statistics are much less reliable than contemporary ones, which makes the history of crime and criminal justice a tough book to read. For recent times, however, the historical evidence does point in one general direction. In the West violent crime in general declined in the nineteenth century; there were fewer murders, assaults, and burglaries per 1,000 population. But this happy state of affairs came to an end sometime in the early twentieth century. The crime rate then began to rise, though rather slowly, until about the end of the Second World War. At that point rates shot up dramatically. There is a surprising similarity in cross-national trends. The *amount* of crime may be different—New York, as we said, is vastly more lawless than London—but the shape of the crime curve looks much the same wherever the matter has been seriously studied.[1]

The progress (if that is the word) of crime since the early nineteenth century is full of big and small mysteries. There are dozens of theories about the causes of crime. Some stress this or that social or economic factor—the business cycle, urbanization, ethnic diversity, demographic patterns, birth rates and sizes of cohorts, employment and unemployment. Every single one of these factors is hard to fit to the historical crime curve without great juggling and squeezing. Yet serious crime and violent crime are obviously social, economic, cultural phenomena. If murder is less common in Japan than in the United States, this cannot be accidental. No doubt wars, recession, the rise and fall of cities, the number of young males in the population (to mention a few obvious factors) do explain some dips and bulges. But the *baseline* remains unexplained. This must be responsive to matters deeply embedded in the social fabric. Changes in forms of culture, of the kind we have been discussing, changes in ways of looking at the world and in types of individualism should also, in theory, deeply affect the rates and forms of crime.

What seems clear is that "all explanations of crime that locate its source in the social web reduce to a description of conditions that weaken moral community."[2] There are, to be sure, biological theories; theories that crime begins in the genes and the chromosomes. Not many scholars today believe in "born criminals," though this idea was once very popular.[3] Rather, a criminal is a misraised, mistrained person, unsuccessfully socialized, who does not recoil from committing acts which society condemns. There are, to be sure, many motives for committing crime—sheer hunger, for example. Self-preservation is a higher law than obedience. Hunger was once a major stimulus to theft. In England in 1800 hundreds stole to get bread or to feed their children—people like Isabella Fell, who stole three handkerchiefs from a shop counter in England in 1830 because she "was in great distress and was without bread for two days"; or Mary Ann Ward, who stole a blanket, a candlestick, and two pillows, among other things, from a lodging house: "I had a blind mother and I would not sit and see her starving."[4] General prosperity and the welfare state, whatever their failings, have changed the picture.

Hunger and the desperate struggle for physical survival are no longer *major* factors in explaining why people steal in the modern West.

Current theories look elsewhere for explanations. "Moral community" and its weaknesses are at the core of arguments made by James Q. Wilson and Richard J. Herrnstein. Wilson and Herrnstein point the finger of blame on changes in socialization. In the literature on child-rearing there is no longer any emphasis on "the importance of inculcating moral and religious principles." At one time people thought of children as "endowed by nature with dangerous impulses that had to be curbed." No more; the new theme is about "harmless instincts that are yet to be developed." The point of socialization used to be to develop *character*; today, the point is to develop *personality*. The nineteenth century was able to dampen crime, they believe, because it put heavy emphasis on "impulse control." But in contemporary society, "the importance of teaching self-control has been to some extent supplanted by the value of stimulating self-expression."[5] Parents and teachers, in other words, once believed in repression as an essential element in building character. Today the repression of instincts is considered positively evil. The child is taught individuality instead of obedience; creativity, rather than conformity. At least this is the argument. A shift along these lines in theories of child-rearing and education has taken place in many cultures.[6]

In short, Wilson and Herrnstein argue that the enthronement of choice, individual volition, and life-style at the expense of order, discipline, and hierarchy must bear the blame for the explosion in crime. From this vantage point, crime can be called the price society pays for stressing individualism and choice. Their argument is certainly plausible; the shift from an emphasis on self-control to an emphasis on expressive individualism more or less fits the data underlying historical crime curves. The intense value placed on discipline, regimentation, and moderation in habits; the rise of disciplinary institutions—police forces, penitentiaries—and the increasing *universalism* of penal codes may well have helped reduce the incidence of serious crime in the nineteenth century. (We will return to these themes.) The rise of expressive individualism in the twentieth century may have had the opposite effect.

Thus the failure to impart an "internalized commitment to self-control"[7] may be one plausible root of the explosion of crime. Individualism and its contemporary variant, personalism, make people "self-centered" in a literal sense. The culture does not teach people to submerge or melt themselves in some larger group, entity, or cause. Rather, the primary duty is to the self, and the primary job in life is development of this self. This is not a job that everyone does well, measured by any standard. Not everybody crafts a way of living that brings personal satisfaction or the good things of life. Personal short-comings and various combinations of personality, family structure, and the social context produce a dismal crop of (self-assessed) failure, and along with failure, radical discontent.

In some instances these failed selves turn to crime, which seems a better or easier way to achieve gratification than any of the obvious alternatives. An anonymous criminal, interviewed by Jonathan Casper, justified a life of theft in these frank terms: "There was things I wanted . . . like a new car and nice clothes, and maybe some day . . . a nice house and stuff. I know just working take twenty years, ten years to get these things . . . I wanted a car . . . I felt, boy, how am I gonna work and save a thousand dollars and another five hundred dollars for insurance. Boy, by the time I do this, then I'll be an old man."[8]

But whatever the merits of this argument, the whole blame for crime cannot be pinned on socialization and its failings. After all, most people remain perfectly law-abiding in the 1980s despite the stress on self-expression. Permissive, indulgent parents do not neces-sarily produce criminals; if they did, society would have to build a million new jails. Indeed, crime comes out of violent, harsh families rather than soft, permissive ones.[9] It is important, then, not to mistake the argument made here, which is not the same as the old-fogey argument that strict parents raised better children than loose parents do today. Rather, the argument is that crime is a *social* phenomenon related to changes in the general culture—specifically, the emphasis on gratification and the self rather than on self-control and discipline. Perhaps in fact loving and indulgent parents do better than cold, harsh parents precisely because they do not go against the grain.

Moreover—and this is essential—what has to be accounted for are small, marginal differences. It does not take many people to cause a crime wave. The search for the causes of crime is, in a way, looking for a needle in a haystack. If the number of burglars doubles, there may still be only a handful, but twice as many houses and stores get pillaged; homeowners and shopkeepers begin to notice the differ-ence. The crime problem arises when a small number of people decide to embark on crime. Some people made decisions for crime in older and more traditional societies, but apparently there were fewer of them, and their reasons may have been different. The causes of crime do not necessarily remain constant or stable over time and across cultures, any more than the definition or nature of crime, the *modus operandi* of criminals, or the sheer number of lawbreakers.

There are other responses to failure besides crime—dropping out, lapsing into depression—and some failed selves simply try again and again, or end up with cheerful acceptance of their lot. What distinguishes these people from lawbreakers is hard to say. Obviously, the surroundings, the peer group, and the neighborhood play some sort of role. Exactly how much is endlessly disputed. The role of the economy, of unemployment rates, of political events, is similarly important, but hard to assess. Still another possible factor—the criminal justice system—requires a further word.

The Criminal Justice System

Some students of the criminal justice system—and vast numbers of ordinary people—put some of the blame for high crime rates on the legal system itself. In the popular view, the system is not stringent enough. It has gone too far in the direction of "coddling" criminals. It has turned away from pure punishment, discipline, regimentation, and rigor; it insists (too much) on individualizing the offender. In the process it has lost its fangs, and thereby its capacity to deter the commission of crime. In contrast to these critics, liberals worry about the rights of the accused; they want to protect and expand due process. Every defendant is a unique human being; each case must be handled on an individual basis. The typical conservative, on the other hand, wants more toughness in the system—stiffer ways to handle criminals and punish crime. Herbert Packer described a classic tension between two models of criminal justice—due process and crime control.[10]

The two opposing views are both common; both are typically held in a muddled way; both reveal the influence of expressive individualism, each after its own fashion. The conservative ascribes crime to a corrupt will. He stresses individual *choice*, but it is the criminal's choice; he has elected a life of crime and must take the consequences. The conservative is also fond of pointing out that victims too have rights. Crime diminishes the victim's freedom; it robs everyone of such simple pleasure as a safe walk in the moonlight in the park. The

liberal sees the defendant's failure as society's failure too. Circumstances beyond his control predestined him for a life of crime. The
defendant is probably poor, probably comes from a background that
has thwarted and stunted the self and removed the *reality* of choice.
Poor education, broken homes, inadequate modeling, and social disorganization must share the blame along with the individual himself.
The liberal theory is a social theory, but it treats the criminal as not
quite *sui juris*, perhaps because of the corrosive effects of squalor,
early privation, and a defective family. These robbed the man of
those choices which ought to be the birthright for all.

In fact, many experts on the criminal justice system feel that its
impact is marginal at best;[11] that the public overestimates how much
the system can reasonably accomplish. Perhaps if there were *no*
system at all—no police, no judges, no jails—the crime rate would
suddenly balloon. This is hardly a testable proposition, though there
have been a few "natural experiments" during police strikes, for
example; and John Philip Reid took a close look at the living law of
the overland trail in the American West, where travelers were for
months beyond the reach of law and order.[12] But even these instances
are not firmly in point. The real question is the impact of a "soft"
system compared to a "hard" system; more accurately, how much
more deterrence could be achieved by tightening the screws in
Western systems. The impact could very well be small; some measures might even be counterproductive. It is not really possible to
tighten the screws a lot. Neither law nor public opinion would allow
mass arrests, preventive detention on a grand scale, or the return of a
busy gallows. Socialization will count far more in making or braking
the crime rate, or to be more precise, in fluctuations in the crime rate,
than fluctuations in the criminal justice system.

The system, however, is under attack; it faces vigorous and
scathing criticism from all sides. Undoubtedly, in various places the
systems are rife with contradictions in policy and practice, are sometimes corrupt, and teeter between the poles of inefficiency and
oppression. Opposing and contradictory forces push and pull at
these systems. In Western societies individualized justice is defined as
a fundamental right; the public respects this norm in principle, but in
practice the norm is offset and neutralized by deep public cynicism
about criminals and the possibility of reforming them. Demand is
strong for cheap, efficient ways to handle masses of criminals. It out-
rages the citizens if guilty men are released on technicalities; if

murderers or rapists get out of prison, no matter how long they have served.

In modern (liberal) theory, a person accused of crime must be tried as an individual. Each act, actor, and victim should be regarded as unique and judged accordingly. We must be sure the defendant is guilty, not the victim of some awful mistake. Even if society is ultimately responsible for its black sheep, degrees of guilt should be carefully balanced in every case; judges, juries, and other actors should assess punishment and blame in the light of particular facts.

Against this is the crushing weight of numbers: the sheer volume of men and women to be processed. There is extreme pressure to speed up, to routinize. Hence liberal theory remains, alas, in the realm of theory. The practice is otherwise: rushed, standardized, slipshod, underfinanced, careless, except for a handful of "significant" cases. Especially is this true when defendants are poor. "The model of a zealous advocate," willing to "fight tooth and nail so that the prosecution is forced to prove guilt while adhering to due process," only rarely gets fulfilled in the United States. For structural and financial reasons, lawyers for the poor rarely act as "gung-ho advocates" for their clients.[13]

One mode of routinization is the notorious practice of plea bargaining. It substitutes a form of consent or choice—often a sham form—for the more expensive and protracted system of trials.[14] Plea bargaining is the subject of an enormous literature, mostly a literature of invective. It is essentially an American phenomenon, though it has been described in England as well;[15] and it has analogues in other systems. The plea bargain can take many forms. Typically, the defendant agrees to plead guilty; in exchange, the prosecutor drops some charges or asks the judge for a lighter sentence. The judge, of course, goes along. Largely as a result of the plea bargaining system, actual trials are relatively rare in the United States. In a recent study of nine counties, actual trials accounted for less than 8 percent of the cases sampled.[16]

Plea bargaining may be a charade, and most defendants think of it that way. But it is an interesting charade; it mimics consent, participation, and free choice—mimics, in other words, an actual arm's-length bargain. Plea bargaining is a common law device; it depends on the fact that the common law insists that the accused must enter a plea of guilty or not guilty. After a bargain, the defendant formally accepts some or all of the charges and pleads guilty to them. In other systems, the bargain—if there is one—takes a different form. In West Germany the "penal order," which is faintly analogous, is in widespread use. This is a "court order prepared by a prosecutor and signed by a judge," which describes the crime, sets out the evidence of guilt, and specifies the punishment. If the defendant "does not object in writing or in person within one week," the order goes into effect and has the same consequences as conviction at a trial.[17] The "penal order" shares with plea bargaining the *appearance* of consent.

The emphasis on consent is not, of course, exclusively modern. Many systems have placed great stock on confessions, and some systems have been so eager for confessions that they extracted them through torture.[18] There are, in other words, confessions and confessions. The modern confession is supposed to be completely *voluntary*. A coerced confession, let alone a confession induced through torture, is unlawful, invalid.[19] Systems that use torture seem utterly barbaric.

But those who used torture in the past were not necessarily barbarians (modern torturers probably are); they merely inhabited a different cultural world. The confessed criminal, even when confession came about on the rack, reaffirmed the norms he had broken, and his smashed body joined together the stratified community whose inner order he had dared to defy. In this lay the value of confessions. In the republic of choice confessions are still quite valuable; they still affirm and legitimate the proceedings. But consent is all. The law insists (sometimes hypocritically) that a confession must express the purest free will or else it is utterly worthless.

Problems and difficulties of all sorts plague criminal justice; perhaps the basic source of trouble is the antinomy between crime control and due process, to use Herbert Packer's categories once more. Modern systems vacillate uncomfortably between theories of stringency and theories of leniency. The tension is not new. English criminal justice in the eighteenth century, as described in Douglas Hay's marvelous essay, tempered its bloody code with generous doses of mercy: pardons and commutations within the grace and favor of the crown and high officials. It thereby achieved a degree of efficacy neither extreme was capable of.[20] Modern law rejects classic modes of leniency; they are too overtly patriarchal, paternalistic, and hierarchical for modern tastes. Precisely those aspects of eighteenth-century mercy which made them functional for crown and aristocracy make them unsuitable in the republic of choice. In our times leniency is even more widespread, but it takes institutional forms:

due process itself, second chances, bureaucratized parole boards, time off for good behavior.

Deviance and Control

The enthronement of individualism and personal choice, as one would expect, has dramatically affected definitions of crime and modes of punishment. Each society has its own way to deal with forbidden behavior. The story of crime and punishment is interesting and important in its own right; it is also a book of clues to social meanings. Penal laws make up a "code" in more ways than one: the texts carry hints and signs about the legal culture of those who call the tune in society and who write, enact, support, or interpret the laws. Whether a society labels this or that act as criminal is an important diagnostic trait. Popular ideas about the causes and sources of crime, and about ways to control and punish crime, are also social factors of great significance.

There is both continuity and change in legal culture. Murder, burglary, arson, and armed robbery have been proscribed and severely punished in all organized societies, and in every period relevant to the themes of this book. To be sure, definitions of these crimes do change slightly and enforcement practices most assuredly, but changes have on the whole been fairly subtle. To trace changes in more volatile parts of the penal code is probably an easier way to smoke out clues to legal culture. We will use for this purpose the so-called victimless crimes, particularly those that deal with sexual behavior. Deviance and vice have been variably defined over the last two centuries or so; and the enforcement efforts have swung from this side to that, and back again, in interesting patterns.

Such offenses as fornication, adultery, prostitution, and sexual deviance have been important concerns of public policy in Western societies. Almost all societies—and almost all legal systems—have drawn lines between allowed and forbidden sexual conduct. The boundaries have changed greatly over the years; currently, the tide is running strongly in favor of relaxing the traditional code, and against strict laws prohibiting many forms of sex between consenting adults. The law, in other words, tends to fix boundaries in such a way as to make *choice* a central criterion. Freely chosen conduct does not deserve the label of crime. The law should punish violent and coercive sexual relations or sexual relations with someone unable to make a mature choice—a child, most notably. For consenting adults, every-thing, or almost everything, should now be permitted.

This relaxation of rules against so-called victimless crimes stands in dramatic contrast to the laws of the past. Indeed, the very term "vic-timless crime" more or less prejudges the issue. The acts are volun-tary; no force or compulsion enters in; thus there is no victim and no harm. Fornication between willing adults is the classic example; as an offense, it has largely vanished from the statute books.

"Victimless crime" is a distinctly modern concept. No such idea was possible or even thinkable in Puritan Massachusetts, for example, or in eighteenth-century England. In the Bay Colony crime was equated with sin,[21] and since God sees all, knows all, and visits punishments on sinners and sinful communities, it would make no sense to call these acts "victimless." Society itself was the victim. Crime and sin offended an order which was divinely instituted; they also threatened to destroy the social fabric. A prime function of gov-ernment was to control and punish such behavior.

Fornication was very much a crime in the Bay Colony; in the seven-teenth and eighteenth centuries fornication was, in fact, the single most commonly punished offense in Massachusetts.[22] All in all, pun-ishment for fornication was not extraordinarily severe: whipping, fines, sitting in the stocks, and forced marriage (if that is a punish-ment). Nonetheless, the act of fornication was taken seriously. Crime control, as always, reflected the values of the colony's leaders and presupposed its forms of hierarchy. The elites of colonial society believed firmly in traditional authority—the authority of God, the Bible, and the magistrates, who ruled with divine sanction.

By the eighteenth century the aims and methods of criminal justice were already in process of change. Laws against fornication and adultery were less vigorously enforced. The moralism of the seven-teenth century ebbed. Fornication still figured in the pages of legal records, but these records suggest a different emphasis. Fornication laws were used to force fathers to support their bastard children,[23] that is, they were adjuncts of the poor laws. In the nineteenth century the laws against fornication and adultery were even more weakly enforced. Penal codes, to be sure, continued to denounce moral offenders. As far as we can tell, however, few people were arrested, convicted, and punished for morals crimes, either in England or the United States.[24] In part, social change made this inevitable. These "crimes" are not easy to ferret out, except in small, gossipy, inbred communities. In bigger cities, with a more or less transient population, sexual misbehavior is hard to expose; fewer people know or care about the morals of the people next door.

But enforcement problems do not tell the whole story. In many states, for example, courts granted divorces on the grounds of adultery, yet this did not mean that defendants were prosecuted for the *crime* of adultery. The texts of some penal statutes also changed in revealing ways. Under Illinois law, for example, adultery as such was not a punishable crime; it was an offense to live in an "open state of adultery or fornication."[25] Adultery, in other words, was a crime against public morality, rather than a sin against God. Criminal justice was not concerned with secret, hidden, occasional acts of adultery; it cared only about disgracefully overt behavior that thumbed its nose at conventional norms.

It is tempting to connect this change to nineteenth-century individualism. As we noted, individualism in that period meant freedom in work life and politics, together with a strong regime of self-control in personal life. The good man was hard-working, ambitious, forward-looking and followed the rules of conventional morality. The good woman was pure, obedient, domestic, and knew her place. Some deviant traits—notably the "vices"—were deeply rooted in human nature, hard to eradicate, and socially dangerous. They were dangerous in that they were failures or defects in self-control; they were *most* dangerous when they were offenses against self-control itself. Leaders of society feared, perhaps subconsciously, that the whole social order might unravel if people lost their grip on themselves, if they gave way to temptations and unbridled self-indulgence. Self-control was the main theme of laws that regulated morality. The policy was to craft a legal order and structures of authority that would keep self-control in the saddle and restrain people who lacked the will and the strength to restrain themselves, who threatened the regime of self-control by openly attacking the norms in word or deed, or who slipped from the ideal too far or too egregiously.

Respectable people in society, and society's leaders, were not so naive as to think it was possible to win the war against vice once and for all; sin, sexual excess, and general debauchery could not be stamped out completely. The aim was to keep these excesses within limits, to stigmatize them, to drive them underground, and in so doing to safeguard the structure of the normative order. Norms, rules, and practices had to make clear that deviant behavior was wrong and brand it as illegitimate. Rules of this kind, not incidentally, would also limit the sheer number of wrongful acts committed. It is easy to say that laws against vice were never enforced and cannot be enforced—it is conventional wisdom, for example, to dismiss laws against drinking or smoking marijuana as ludicrous failures. But if people cannot drink or take drugs, except illegally, then they cannot and will not drink and take drugs as freely and as often as if they could do so in broad daylight, so to speak. *Some* timid souls and some habitual law-abiders will think twice or desist from drinking or trying drugs because these acts are illegal.

At the very least, then, prohibition laws affect the time, mode, and manner of drinking and drug-taking. No matter how much effort society puts into enforcing repressive laws (typically not much), vice and gambling do not rush into extinction. But this does not mean the laws have *no* impact. They may have considerable effect, including effects on actual behavior. Drinking *did* decline during Prohibition, and deaths from alcoholism declined correspondingly. The ultimate point of many laws on morality is limitation and control, through delegitimizing.

People who called the tune in society groped, unconsciously, for an appropriate level of enforcement, for an equilibrium between invest-ment in controlling the behavior, and the quantum of control their investment could buy. It was the search for a balance between pred-ator and prey, between wolves and sheep. As we look backward, the laws and legal arrangements of the nineteenth century are apt to strike us as grossly hypocritical: legislators who drank passed laws against liquor; men who gambled and went to brothels passed laws against gambling and prostitution; men with extravagant, secret vices wrote books in praise of Victorian prudery. But the word "hypocrisy" does not capture the Victorian mood. These laws were not produced by cynics, and they were not *intended* to be futile. Legislators no doubt had faith in these laws, but as control devices, as acts of limita-tion, just as legislators today pass laws against speeding which they violate themselves. Yet these laws are neither hypocritical nor point-less.

The vice laws *were* meant to affect behavior, then. They were also meant to express social ideals, to label dangerous behavior as deviant, to limit such behavior, and most of all, to force it under-ground. This was the essence of what one might call the Victorian compromise. The older law had treated sexual violations as ordinary crimes. This now seemed harsh, theocratic, and in any event devoid of practical utility. Sin was not an overwhelming problem, so long as it kept its place; when it kept it place, it was not a *social* problem. The *open* practice of sin, on the other hand, was a genuine threat to the moral order, for such behavior demonstrated either a failure of self-control or, what was worse, contempt for self-control itself.

The Penitentiary

Other important changes in the system of crime and punishment after 1800 bear on our themes. One major change in the correctional regime was the rise of the penitentiary system. Imprisonment was not the normal mode of punishing serious crime before the nineteenth century. Jails were mainly used for debtors and for people waiting for trial. The system was slapdash and corrupt. The primitive jails were replaced or supplemented with great, grim fortresses built especially for penal purposes. These were the penitentiaries. By the middle of the nineteenth century they had become the norm in England, the northern United States, and France.[26] Some historians credit the United States with this marvelous invention. If so, the penitentiary spread rapidly to Europe or was reinvented there. Michael Ignatieff has given us a vivid picture of London's Pentonville in 1842[27] that is strikingly similar to descriptions of American prisons.

The heart of the penitentiary system was a ruthless regimentation. In the classic American penitentiary, prisoners were housed in solitary cells and lived out their terms in daily, deathly silence. Prisoners woke up in the morning, worked through the day, and went to bed in a pattern of total, monotonous uniformity. They walked in lock-step, ate the same food, and wore the same prison uniforms. Gustave Beaumont and Alexis de Tocqueville, who came from France to examine the new system, found it both admirable and effective. It was, however, surprisingly "severe." They observed a paradox: "While society in the United States gives the example of the most extended liberty, the prisons . . . offer the spectacle of the most complete despotism."[28] Nineteenth-century society, after all, was embarked on a radical experiment in self-government. Traditional authority had weakened greatly in the United States, and it was weakening elsewhere as well. People were supposed to govern themselves; freedom depended on their ability to control themselves in order to participate in organized society. Those who misbehaved were not fit to be citizens; they betrayed the principles which a free society assumed and needed; they had to be severely punished, both to avoid harm to the principles of a free society, and as a lesson to others. Beaumont and Tocqueville made the point: "The citizens subject to the law are protected by it; they only cease to be free when they become wicked." All societies take crime seriously, but a self-control society takes it *very* seriously indeed. Deviance threatens the pillars of the social order—the assumption that people are and ought to be free, and can be trusted to be free.

Thus the penitentiary was not merely a mode of punishment; it was a living embodiment of the nineteenth century's commitment to discipline, which was central to the key nineteenth-century form of individualism. It was also an extreme version of what that century saw as normal socialization processes. It was an exaggeration, a caricature, of childhood life: regimented, paternal, rigidly disciplined, designed to "break the will" of the criminal and coerce him back to normal behavior. Sound, strict training in childhood produced good morals; bad company, loose training, exposure to frivolous and sinful peers produced vice, intemperance, and crime. A general failure of self-control came about in this way. Theories of crime had become "environmental," to use Ignatieff's term. Regimentation and discipline were modes of reform; they were also, as David Rothman put it, "designed to carry a message to the community." The prison would "train the most notable victims of social disorder to discipline, teaching them to resist corruption. . . . The penitentiary would promote a new respect for order and authority." This was vital, because "social stability could not be achieved without a very personal and keen respect for authority."[29]

In general, criminal justice in the nineteenth century was, or aimed to be, rational, systematic, and orderly. This was an age of codification. In earlier times—in eighteenth-century England as Douglas Hay has described it—penal law and penal codes were anything but "rational" in a Weberian sense. They were chaotic, unsystematic, and unpredictable; personal ties and the unbridled discretion of magistrates and noblemen determined who lived and who died.[30] To be sure, the legal order had a kind of inner logic. The penal code was cruel, bloody, unyielding on paper, but in practice mercy and pardons, lavishly invoked, acted in mitigation. But only the high and the powerful had the privilege of extending mercy. Thus strong bonds of deference and obligation bound the lower orders to the ruling class. A savage formal law, combined with an informal system of mercy and discretion, produced social control more effectively than terror alone could have done.

Theories of punishment in the nineteenth century retained a strong element of paternalism. Kings and governors made liberal use of their pardoning powers. The criminal justice system still punished thieves with great rigor, in the name of respect for property rights and in order to reinforce a regime of individual self-control. Deference and hierarchy of course survived and flourished, but less in the United States than in England, both as to substance and style. There was no landed gentry in the United States. In England and on the Continent there was movement in the "American" direction. It is no accident, then, that the penal law evolved toward rationality, bureaucracy, and logic; and that the penitentiary began to supplant the old jails. A democratically organized society loosens the informal ties of a face-to-face and paternalistic order. It becomes heavily dependent on individual self-government; where the choices of free individuals must guarantee virtue and good order, one cannot rely on a traditional ruling class. Such a society turns away from open use of mercy and caprice toward a system of regimentation and uniformity. The stern but egalitarian life in the great silent prisons was both a symbol of nineteenth-century justice and a prime example of that system in full operation.

The Criminal: Born or Made

Just as there are popular or folk theories about modes of punishment—which ones work, and which ones do not; and why—so too there are theories about the nature of criminality: *who* becomes a criminal, and why. In the late nineteenth century theories that stressed a *genetic* element in crime became quite prominent. Both ordinary people and scientists tended to believe in "born criminals"—criminals by birth, defective human beings produced by generations of bad breeding. The eugenics movement took the view that humanity, like cattle and dogs, could be improved by "selective breeding." Conversely, "Degenerates beget degenerates, idiots beget idiots, criminals beget criminals."[31] A literature grew up around this point: chronicles of the horrible persistence of deviance, which made criminal families like the Jukes and the Kallikaks into household words. In these families generations of thieves, idiots, and prostitutes descended from a single bad seed. A "born criminal" of course was beyond reform or redemption, beyond the reach of social learning. The vice was in the blood.

Of course, it is a trait of popular thought in many periods to dichotomize criminals; one class consisting of offenders who could be reformed or educated, the other of those who were inherently hopeless. The born criminal was thus the functional equivalent of witches, vampires, or those who sold their souls to the devil. Ordinary punishment had no power over such people. The witch had to be burnt, a stake had to be driven through the vampire's heart; true incorrigibles had to be hung and quartered. The late nineteenth century no longer believed in possession by devils, but it continued to believe in incorrigible evil. Genetic theories of crime made it legitimate to treat certain criminals and deviants very harshly indeed. Genetic theories avoided environmentalism, which implied that something was wrong with *society*, and theories about rehabilitation, which did not seem to work. The worst criminals were born that way; the mark of Cain was on them from birth; they occupied a *status*, a brotherhood or sisterhood of those defective, of those not quite human. Genetic theories of crime bubbled up in the late nineteenth century, in a period of panic among old elites. The old order seemed to be tottering; the solid native stock, it was feared, was swamped by foreign riff-raff and worse. The theories of the born criminal led to such legal excesses as sterilization laws; ideologically, they lent a hand to racist theories and other forms of dark and sinister reaction.

Misuse of genetic theories is one reason, too, why the theories later fell into such deep disrepute. The approach seemed both racist and pseudoscientific. Yet the theories never quite died out. In the 1960s, for example, there was a flurry of interest in biology and crime; the extra-chromosome theory had a definite vogue.[32] Physiological theories are intensely controversial, but the general public probably believes in them, up to a point. There are also purely environmental explanations of crime—economic, social, psychological—based on slums, broken families, shattered dreams. These views are associated with the "bleeding hearts" of the left. They are unpopular with the majority. Environmental theories have a grave flaw: they are inconsistent with the culture of choice and responsibility. It is much more attractive to think of the criminal as a rotten apple in the barrel; as a human being without moral character, who has ignored the available and legitimate choices and elected to go down the crooked path.

Essentially, many people prefer to think that criminals are neither born that way, nor forced into crime by events and contexts beyond their control. Like the lives of decent citizens, the law-abiding majority, the lives of felons are crafted by themselves. All are citizens of the republic of choice.

Criminal justice, including the law of victimless crime, has gone through many gyrations over the last century or so. In recent years there has been a dramatic turn of the wheel with regard to victimless crime. Society has entered a period of decriminalization. This did not, however, follow immediately on the heels of the age of self-control. In the late nineteenth century and in the first part of this century, interest in control of immoral behavior heightened throughout the Western world. The movement achieved some remarkable legal results. In the United States, Puritanism appeared to rise from its grave—as if the stiff, dour magistrates of the seventeenth century were born again as late Victorians. Their counter-revolution lasted until at least the 1930s.

Signs of the counter-revolution appeared shortly after 1870.[33] In the United States, the so-called Comstock law made it a crime to send obscene material through the mails; the law also defined as obscene any information about contraception. At about the same time many states made abortion a criminal offense. Between 1870 and 1910 many jurisdictions tightened their laws against homosexual behavior, drug use, and teen-age sexuality. This last noble aim was accomplished by raising the age of consent. Legally, any intercourse with a girl below the age of consent was defined as rape, a crime that carried a heavy penalty indeed. The starting point, the common-law age of consent, had been ten. This strikes us today as absurdly low; but by 1918 California, had fixed the age of consent at eighteen, which is surely absurdly high. This was by no means an American exclusive. England and many continental countries also raised their ages of consent.[34]

In the United States the Mann Act, passed shortly before World War I, made it a federal crime to transport a woman across state lines for prostitution, "debauchery," or "other immoral purposes." At about this time, a strong social movement arose to stamp out the "red light" districts in American cities, and drive vice out of business.[35] The crowning victory of the morality movement was national Prohibition, the "noble experiment" which began after the first World War and lasted just over a decade. Prohibition was abandoned in the late

1930s, and the forces of righteousness began a long and weary retreat. The sinners, more militant and numerous, seem to have broken the back of the counter-revolution. But not completely; the hills are still full of stragglers and guerrillas who have vowed eternal battle against Satan.

Even the countertrends bore the mark of the transformations of legal culture that form the subject of this book. The new Puritanism was never quite the same as the old. The Mann Act, for example, was popularly and officially called the "White Slavery law".[36] The name reflected an important image, or fantasy: vicious men kidnapped and seduced young women; they drugged, coerced, or betrayed them into lives of prostitution and rampant sexuality. Lives of this sort laid waste the health and the souls of the women, who were thus condemned to guilt, earthly suffering, and early death.

No doubt there was some truth behind the overblown rhetoric. Sexual oppression and traffic in women were all too common in society. But the Mann Act was not concerned with male domination as such. The act, in language and theory, vacillated between two conceptual poles. It reflected the popular idea that sexuality was inherently dangerous; it echoed themes of traditional morality, and the "hydraulic" emphasis on self-control. Animal appetites had to be repressed. Moreover, a woman who lost her virtue was "ruined" for life; she was shut off from the only route to a respectable life, the normal marriage market. But the text and theory of the law also reflected emerging social definitions of choice and consent, in all their power and persuasion. To justify the law, women had to be portrayed as choiceless victims. A young woman who entered prostitution, even one that took a lover, *must* have been coerced; it was unthinkable that a decent woman might *choose* this way of life. This point of view was reinforced, of course, by the dogma of female passivity, the idea that women were typically "devoid of sexual feelings, desires, or needs."[37] For women, unlike men, initiation into sexual activity was a fatal and irreversible step. Honor and virtue, like virginity, once lost, were lost forever. The very term "slavery" attached a fateful label to those events and situations that the act was meant to cover. Sexual slavery, no doubt, existed, but the term suggested something broader, more metaphorical. For a woman, a life of sexuality amounted to a total loss of self, a selling of the self into slavery; it was an irreversible choice of the kind no human being should ever be allowed to make.

Democracy, Morality, and Penal Codes

The reactionary turn was a somewhat paradoxical result of the democratic revolution of the nineteenth century in another way. What we think of as traditional morality is often also labeled middle-class morality. The moral code and the legal code which gave it official status spread upwards and downwards from their origin within the middle class. Aristocracies had their own codes—codes of honor. The upper classes believed in their inherent superiority; they had the money and position to indulge themselves as they wished, and in any event they felt exempt from normal law enforcement. Who dared complain about a drunken duke, or the mistresses of an earl? The other end of the social scale was also largely exempt; the code never reached down below, or even tried to. People at the bottom were crude, dirty, unregenerate; they were "animals"; nobody expected respectable moral behavior out of such people. It would be ridiculous to think of imposing temperance or sexual moderation on the hordes that swarmed the London slums in 1700 or 1800.

Political democracy, as it grew in strength, empowered first the middle class, then the working class. Middle-class political strength laid the basis for enactment of the middle-class moral program. This meant rejection of the double or triple standard of morality; it blurred the class line in laws about morality, and, to a degree, complicated law enforcement. The legal code, as always, expressed the interests and ideology of the ruling class; but this now included the respectable middle class. Ideals of respectability and self-control became positive law. This explains, for example, why the age of consent was raised. The counter-revolution of the late nineteenth century was thus a kind of distant thunder, a delayed response to the political emergence of the republic of self-control; the middle-class moralists saw a chance to enact, enforce, and realize their code of conduct up and down the social scale. They, of course, considered the code timeless and universal, and to extend it to the whole population was to promote reform, rationality, and progress.

There is also a connection between the universalism of the penal code and the increased mobility of the century. The United States was a nation of immigrants; people traveled ceaselessly from east to west, from farm to village, from village to city, from south to north or the reverse. In Europe, too, old cities swelled in size; new cities sprang up like mushrooms. People abandoned their villages and farms for ports, mercantile capitals, industrial zones. Mobility has become even greater in the twentieth century. Every industrial nation (Japan excepted) harbors enormous numbers of immigrants, and everywhere (Japan included) natives shift their places of work and residence in a ceaseless process of motion.

Yet a mobile modern society is in a curious way unified within its complexity. A plural society does not necessarily have a plural legal code. Its divisions are not the fixed status differences of the past. Guilds, classes, estates, boroughs, and religious communities are no longer *legally* established; nationalism tries to level out cultural diversity and ethnic pluralism. The melting pot is one of the central images of American political theology.[38] In Europe, the nineteenth century was an age of nationalism. Ethnic pluralism meant disunity and thus conflict, which ended up either in national independence—the creation of a Czechoslovakia or a Finland—or assimilation. Mobility broke up old ethnic enclaves; it both created and reduced pluralism. Mobility led to a massive *legal* uniformity. This is no paradox. In democratic republics law centers on individuals rather than on groups. The individual is the *unit* of modern mobility. It is the individual, not the people or the tribe, who wanders through the republic of choice. Thus it is not surprising that law tends toward generality, toward universalism—that is, toward a single general code of conduct applicable to everyone within the jurisdiction. Hence the trend to suppress ethnicity and multiplicity in the nineteenth century—a trend that in some ways continues.

Today, in most European countries, the central government and the dominant speech and culture group still insist on ethnic assimilation. Internal migration, state-run education, and national television networks disempower the local dialects. They continue to shrink and impoverish the cultural domain of minorities trapped within national borders—the Welsh, low Germans, Frisians, Wends, Basques, Bretons, and Gaels. All are under enormous pressure to jump into the melting pot and become part of the national stew. Precisely this has occurred, though with major exceptions, and only up to a point. The exceptions are large, compact groups, like the French in Canada or the Flemish in Belgium. The point of resistance comes when the group becomes an active "minority" and demands its rights. But these are at one and the same time group rights and individual rights. The individualist strain has gained in recent years, and thus ethnicity has been making a comeback (see Chapter 10). In the nineteenth century romantic ethnic pluralism was not yet fully in vogue. The majority encouraged social mobility and condemned cultural pluralism. It especially disfavored the moral and penal codes of newcomers or minorities. The United States, for example, savagely repressed Mormon polygamy, which, as the Supreme Court put it, was suitable only for "Asiatic" or "African" peoples.[39] Polygamy for immigrants from Islamic countries was and is completely beyond the pale.

Some small minorities have already disappeared; others, like the speakers of Plattdeutsch or Breton, are probably on the road to extinction. But some of the old minorities have now reconstituted themselves in the form of *chosen* heritages—free affiliations, in other words. This is in fact the modern situation. No one, of course, is required to wallow in ethnicity, to glorify one's Irish or Swedish heritage in the midst of Cleveland, Ohio, to join groups in honor of the motherland, or to teach the old language to the kids. But many choose to do so. For that matter, no one is compelled to be a militant Basque in the Basque country, or a Welsh nationalist in Wales.[40] This too is now a matter of choice.

The Permissive Society

The recent reforms in the laws on victimless crime play against those last-ditch defenses of traditional morality which were so prominent in the late nineteenth and early twentieth centuries. Recent changes in the law have erased all the "gains" of that moral counterrevolution. Fornication, along with adultery, has vanished from the penal codes of many countries and in many American states as well. A California law of 1976, for example, legalized "sexual acts in private between consenting adults" and wiped off the books penalties for "victimless sex acts" such as "adulterous cohabitation, sodomy, and oral copulation."[41] Adultery—which arguably *does* have victims—is still a crime in a few American states, and some states continue to criminalize homosexual behavior.[42] But the trends in the last generation or so have moved strongly and clearly in the direction of permissiveness.

"Sexual deviants" have by no means won social equality. They still suffer from severe discrimination, and agendas of reform have met with firm and intransigent resistance. But on the whole sexual permissiveness in modern society has shot far past anything a nineteenth-century moralist could imagine in his most feverish nightmares. The relaxation of manners and morals is sometimes referred to as a "sexual revolution." The revolution gains strength from a broader movement of all underdog groups, including deviants and downtroddens of all shapes, stripes, and colors, and the consequent wave of "liberation" movements. This vast social development has probably not yet run its course. The Victorian compromise is out of step with twentieth-century thought and behavior. The sexual revolution and the general trend toward liberation reflect the influence of expressive individualism, and of the enthronement of choice. They are also manifestations of and depend on the easy development of horizontal groupings (examined in the last chapter) and are thus creatures of the modern mass media as well.

The continuing history of sexual regulation is a history of continuing complexity. Traditional moralists have lost many battles, but they have not hauled up the white flag, nor do they intend to surrender. Theirs is by no means a lost cause. Monarchists are extinct in the United States, and almost so in France or Italy; but the same cannot be said of religious fundamentalists. Moreover, nobody (well, hardly anybody) favors *total* decriminalization of gambling, vice, drug use, and indiscriminate sexual behavior. The emphasis on consent suggests one kind of limit on permissiveness: "consent" is not and never was a clean, simple concept. One person's consent is another's coercion. Consider, for example, the movement to strengthen the laws of rape and put more teeth in enforcement; to tilt the scales toward the victims of rape, rather than the men accused of this crime; to outlaw sexual harassment; and to remove legal barriers to prosecution of marital rape.[43] The effort draws some of its strength from the work of women writers, who have pointed out what sexual consent may really mean, in a world dominated by men. Considerable regulation and controversy still surround sexuality in the Western world. As the laws on sexual harassment show, the movement is not all in one direction. Control of sexuality and its limits stubbornly remains on the agenda of public debate; it is still a problem to the living culture.

The modern movement to decriminalize sexuality is much more than a reaction to the born-again prudery that flared up in the nineteenth century. It has a central place in the culture of personal choice. It is not merely a defensive tactic against the aggressive attacks of the moralists who want to stamp out sin or vice; the point is, above all, to achieve parity of *legitimacy.* Even at the peak of the reign of official morality, criminal justice never seriously threatened most victimless "criminals." Few people who gambled or used drugs were arrested. Prohibition did fill American jails, but it was all in all an expensive failure. Millions kept on drinking, and the authorities were powerless, unconcerned, and even complicitous. Laws against teen-age sexuality, not to mention the Mann Act itself, never made much of a dent in actual behavior. Laws against homosexual behavior led to distasteful episodes of blackmail or disgrace and occasionally to sweeps and crackdowns; there were always some prosecutions and a great deal of unnecessary suffering and disgrace. But no systematic enforcement was ever attempted, or ever could be, since so much of the behavior was private, intensely personal, and very often desperately hidden from view.

What sets contemporary "deviants" apart from Victorians is their refusal to accept the *label* of deviant with regard to activities which involve free personal choice. They do not accept the traditional morality of the Bible as binding—or any codes of conduct, including the legal codes, based on that morality. They do not reject all codes of behavior, but whatever codes one follows must be codes that one chooses freely, and which respect that freedom of choice. And *any* free-choice code, if it does not harm other people, deserves equality of legitimacy along with the others.

This is what differentiates our period from former times. The underlying *behavior,* after all, is not new; same-sex love, or fornication, did not spring up overnight in a permissive society. The psychological and social impulses which bend people toward nontraditional or "immoral" sexual conduct may, in fact, be no more common than before; there may be a more or less constant ratio of "sexual minorities" among the population at large. Historical research does not support the view that the twentieth century invented wholesale extramarital sex.[44] In fact, arguably it is the nineteenth century—the age of official repression, prudery, and exaggerated self-control—which is the real historical anomaly.

But the Victorian period was only yesterday; so vehement and swift a rejection of labeling seems startling. It is difficult to account for the rapid change without taking note of the rise to dominance of the notion of (expressive) choice. People have the *right* to choose their life-style—the right to express and act on their sexual preferences. This last phrase is not some mealy-mouthed euphemism. The choice of words is significant. Forms of sexuality, the phrase suggests, are matters of *choice*. One does not "prefer" something one cannot help doing.

Sexual orientation may not in fact be merely or even primarily a matter of choice. But choice most certainly plays a role in sexual conduct—as both sides to the argument over permissiveness agree. Preachers, including modern evangelists who thunder and roar against sexual deviance, have always assumed an element of choice. Otherwise it makes no sense to condemn sodomy, adultery, and fornication as deadly sins; God would not assign eternity in hell to those who cannot help themselves. No one fulminates against leprosy, against short people, or people with red hair. Psychologists and psychiatrists considered it progressive, therefore, when they defined homosexuality as a disease or a defect of maturation. Illness is of course not an item of choice, and neither is arrested development.

The gay *movement* decisively rejects the Biblical threats of hell-fire; but the illness label is also unacceptable. Psychiatrists and some of the clergy have now recanted.[45] This opens the way to treat patterns of sexual behavior as matters of choice. And, certainly, to live a gay life openly, to live in a gay community, to join gay groups, is within the realm of the chosen. What is chosen, then, and what is "preferred," is a style of life; what is rejected is repression. A person should not struggle against desires and inclinations, she should not squash patterns of behavior which represent the core of her being, her actual self that demands fulfillment.[46] Repression is wrong: first because it is futile and cruel, second because it stunts growth, retards personality, and restricts the range of legitimate choice.

These sentiments are certainly not confined to "sexual minorities." They are, if anything, stronger among members of the sexual majority. They reflect the same underlying cause—rejection of the ideal of radical self-control, so central to nineteenth-century individuation. People have or should have the right "to engage in forms of sexual expression" which are "central to the integrity of their intimate relations and personal lives." Laws criminalizing nonstandard sex prevent "responsible sexual fulfillment" and "callously" interfere with "personal aspirations."[47] Not that people of the 1980s have openly abandoned themselves to endless debauchery. Self-control is alive and well—is in fact epidemic, in the form of exercise, yoga, diets, and similar regimes of free-choice asceticism, including religious ones. But these are all seen as means to specific personal ends, rather than codes of behavior imposed from above and beyond or from outside. They aim to liberate the personality, not to submerge it in the will of some traditional shepherd.

A word should be said about the amazing increase in cohabitation. This bland Latinate word has replaced the word "fornication," an expression which already seems quaint and archaic. Cohabitation, whatever else it represents, is a decisive rejection of traditional morality. It is also a rejection of sexual repression—certainly of the idea that young men should wait until they are "settled" before getting married, and wait until they marry before they become sexually active, at least with regular partners; and that decent women must marry as virgins and should have no sexual life at all outside of marriage. Cohabitation, for many people, is a trial marriage; for others it is a rejection of marriage. In both cases it is an assertion that relationships are matters of choice, and a denial that marriage should be eternal and exclusive, a fateful and irreversible step. Cohabitation is amazingly widespread and popular in the United States and other Western countries; it has lost both its social and its legal stigma.[48]

In the twentieth century, what perhaps most clearly legitimates cohabitation is the fact that free choice and expressive individualism stand so high in our culture. Cohabitation is a style of life that gives people what they need sexually, emotionally, and financially, without closing too many doors or foreclosing too many options. The alternatives to cohabitation are simply not acceptable. It is sexual repression, not exuberant expression, that people now define as neurotic. The official line in the nineteenth century was the exact opposite: too much sex was considered dangerous to health. But today few people believe there can be such a thing as too much sex; sex, like sleep, is considered a natural and self-limiting process. The development of the full self, the use of all human potentialities, is not only desirable; it verges on the essential.

A society in which a powerful strand of opinion defines individualism in this way will tend to dismantle codes and laws which forbid and proscribe variant forms of "sexual preference;" traditionalists resist, as we have seen, with success in some arenas; but the battle over cohabitation itself is basically over. Cohabitation is perfectly legal; it may even give rise to property rights under certain conditions. This was the message of *Marvin v. Marvin,* decided in California in 1976.[49] Michele Marvin, who lived with a movie star, Lee Marvin, and even took his name, claimed rights to some of his wealth after the relationship ended. She relied on an (alleged) promise to share the property. Lee Marvin resisted, arguing that such an arrangement, if there was one, was immoral and could not be enforced. The trial court threw the case out, but the Supreme Court of California disagreed and sent the case back for trial, so that Michele Marvin would have a chance to prove the facts. The justices spoke frankly about the changing moral code and the sheer frequency of cohabitation. In England, under the inheritance law of 1975, a live-in lover, if actually dependent, can claim a right to maintenance out of the dead cohabitor's estate.[50]

From Deviance to Minority Status

Just as the term "sexual preference" is revealing, so is the phrase "sexual minority." The term assimilates gay men and lesbians, for example, to a status somewhat similar to that of racial and religious minorities. Minorities in modern society are not supposed to be inferior to majorities in rights or in dignities. In the United States the civil rights movement was particularly important in hammering home this idea. As we noted, the movement won some major legal victories against segregation and race discrimination. Other types of discrimination based on sex, ethnicity, religion, and age later came under increasing legal attack. The unrolling course of events proved a powerful, concentrated lesson in the strength and meaning of the new pluralism.

By the 1970s other groups—oppressed, deviant, or outside the mainstream—had moved onto the brightly lit stage of demand and controversy. Each group argued its case; each tried to draw analogies between its cause and aspirations and those of groups that had already won their battles or at least won recognition. Of course each "minority" was differently situated and put forward a somewhat different claim: gays and lesbians, the handicapped, offbeat religions, prisoners, ethnic groups. Each group was far from monolithic in ideology and in its political wish-list. Within some groups factions advanced different, even contradictory claims. Some feminists, for example, placed their main emphasis on women's traits which (they claimed) set women apart from men in fundamental ways—women's special voice. Other feminists insisted on parity with men in ways that explicitly or implicitly denied any radical differences; they ascribed disparities in role and position to social labeling and male domination. Sexual minorities vacillate between the emphasis on inborn drives which determine their basic orientation and the right to express their free choice among variable patterns of sexual behavior, that is, the right to follow out their desires, the demands of their nature, rather than suppress them in humility and guilt.

What unites all the groups is their resistance to stigma, to the label of deviance, the mark of Cain, the ascription of sin, the void of illegitimacy. This lies at the heart of all "liberation" movements. Deviance was the common denominator of their former status, though of course being black was "deviant" in a different sense than being gay or criminal. It was never against the law to be black, but it was a status of permanent inferiority and stigma, all the worse in that it was totally visible.

The war against deviant status has been vigorously waged since the 1950s, with very mixed results. Traditional norms and authority, as is obvious, do not lie down and play dead. Prejudice is persistent and endemic. Every thrust provokes a counterthrust. To the guardians of traditional morality, the women's movement and sexual permissiveness destroy family life and corrode moral values; they see ahead of us a dark night of Godlessness, putrefaction, and destruction. Gay rights ordinances fail to pass in discouraging numbers. But the "minorities" have achieved a great deal in a relatively short time. The idea of choice and the goals and thoughts of expressive individualism are more powerful than the opposing concepts. Even among fundamentalists, the most tradition-minded people in the West, the *language* of hierarchy and status has fallen into disfavor. They express old norms in a modern language—a language of equality, of free and equal choice. Legally as well as politically, society is no longer pictured as the traditional pyramid with a moral and economic elite at the peak. Morally and socially, society is a plateau, a mesa; with standing room for all at the top.

Public opinion is against pinning the label of deviant or inferior on individuals or groups. The label belongs to the "real" criminals who cause harm to other people. The life-style claims of everybody else should be accepted as valid. There are to be no special rights and special treatment, no privileged classes. The exceptions are only apparent; "affirmative action" is a device to overcome disadvantage, that is, unfair handicap; it is different from privilege which rests on a base of birth, breeding, natural superiority, higher moral status, or membership in the dominant majority. Except to a small group of radicals, the enormous real privileges of the rich and well-raised tend to be ignored; these things have become curiously invisible. At the fringes of the social sciences, a few extreme determinists huddle together for comfort, but the popular spirit of the times is unfriendly to determinism in its various shapes and guises. The average member of the middle class—politically and demographically the largest group—seems convinced that men (and women) can and should create their own conditions of self. They know, perhaps, that this is not literally possible; but it is a goal for society to aim toward. Above all, the law should put no barriers in the way of plural equality.

Taken to its logical extreme, plural equality implies that there *are* no minorities; there is no cultural and moral hegemony and hence no majority or dominating stratum of honor or prestige. Each person is a unique individual and selects his own affiliations. The "natural" groupings, like race, are all of equal dignity. Nobody should be handicapped because of membership in a natural group—or a voluntary group, for that matter—so long as these meet minimum standards of legality and worth.

This attitude spills over to include the physically handicapped, who have now become one more minority. They have not *chosen* to be blind or deaf, or to sit in a wheelchair; they have not elected their status, hence they must be treated as a "natural" grouping. Yet nothing in public discourse or public policy should suggest inferiority. Words like "crippled" or "retarded" are taboo; instead, decorum requires us to talk about handicapped people in neutral or even positive terms, as "different" or "special."

The physically handicapped are thus, on the one hand, "just like everybody else"; on the other hand, they have a legitimate claim to be treated specially, because they have special needs that are not of their choosing. They are, then, rather like celebrities who are different from the rest of us, yet essentially the same; or like the other minorities, who are also "special" and yet assert essentially the same claims for legitimacy and worth. Quite recently, law and policy have strikingly extended the rights of the handicapped. Yet the handicapped were never *blamed* for their afflictions; like minorities and women, they were simply expected to take what fate handed out.

A raft of laws in the United States now tries to put the handicapped on a par with the rest of us, with ramps in public buildings, specially built buses, and compensatory education.[51] These provisions are not defined as welfare or charity, handed down from on top; they take the form of entitlements. The point is to equalize life-chances; to give the handicapped the same access to options as other people. A ramp puts the wheelchair bound on the same plane of access as persons with two strong legs. In 1975, the United States Congress declared, as national policy, that "handicapped persons have the same right as other persons to utilize mass transportation."[52] Some commentators complain of the staggering cost of fitting up buses so that wheelchairs can get aboard; in some cases, it might be cheaper to hire taxis or chauffeurs for the handicapped. But this misses the point. The person in the wheelchair wants the option to ride the bus, to enter the building, to hold a job—like everybody else. A handicap, in racing, is meant to equalize chances; it is not charity given out to horses unable to run, or jockeys unwilling to ride. The policy message is a familiar one: the handicapped are equal human beings, different only in this one unchosen regard; they are entitled to the same options as other individuals; all they need, and must have, is a little push, which will get them to the starting line.

NINE

The Life-Style Society

A S CHOICE and the self gain paramount importance, matters fixed once and for all at birth, such as race and sex, either decline in significance or change their social meaning. In part, the change depends on how "biological" or inevitable these traits seem to members of society. As we saw, some aspects of status, such as race, strike people as inborn and immutable; others have a strong immutable element. Nonetheless, the social meanings or consequences of these traits have undergone dramatic change (see Chapter 5). In modern society certain immutable traits have lost all or almost all of their social significance—for example, birth order. Western law long ago shucked off primogeniture. In doing so, the law responded to usages and customs within families. Primogeniture made sense in the context of feudalism and in a society, like England's, dominated by the nobility and the landed gentry. It was quite out of place in a middle-class social order.

Gender and Society

Gender, of course, is a complicated issue. No one can eliminate the real physical differences between men and women, and no one wants to. Modern law, however, treats gender as irrelevant in many contexts where it was once of paramount significance. Laws against sex discrimination, in essence, are attempts to neutralize the consequences of those aspects of gender which *are* biological.[1] The law converts them, as much as possible, into matters of choice or lifestyle. Anatomical destiny is thus transmuted into a package of discrete, freely chosen options. Only women can get pregnant and have babies, but a woman should be free to cash in on this biological option or not. And ideally, the consequences of childbirth—in the home, on the job, in private lives—should be so handled as to make these consequences as gender-neutral as possible. (Obviously, there is a long, long way to go.)

Thus the critical feature is life-style—that is, the chosen pattern of behavior. A woman does not choose to be a woman, or a man a man; but each should be able to decide what conclusions follow from the basic premise: for a woman, whether to be a wife or not, or a mother or not; to cook and sew or to enroll in business school; to be a home-maker or to run for office; to be a nurse or to mine coal; or none of these. It is official policy in the West to get rid of restrictions on choice if they are rooted in gender. Many Western countries have elaborate legal structures geared to this end. Equal work should earn equal pay; women must have equal access to every kind of job; discrimination in education and in employment is against the law.

The women's movement reflects many ideologies; it is a branch of many trees of evolution. Fundamentally, however, it is imbedded in an individualistic social order. A member of the "Law Women Steering Committee" of New York University, in a letter to the *New York Times*, expressed the point well. Feminism, she wrote, is not merely a "subcategory of the civil rights movement." The "ultimate goal" is "self-determination"; "civil rights and legal equality" are simply "among the many prerequisites to achieving this ultimate goal." The feminist movement "began with the realization that women were prevented from understanding and actualizing their true individual selves." Feminists are working for "a society in which women may realize their true individual identities."[2]

Of course not everyone accepts this line, even within the feminist movement. Nor does everybody accept feminism itself. Equality is the official policy; but the gap between what formal law asserts or implies, and the real world of women and men, is simply enormous. Most women now work; they compete with men in the job market; they hold down exacting and demanding jobs, but at the end of the day millions of them confront men who still expect their wives to cook, clean house, take care of the kids, and serve the master's needs. Millions of women face dilemmas that men never face and do not think about.

Still, a great distance separates the status of women in the nineteenth century from the status of women today. There has been a women's movement at least since the early nineteenth century. Its underlying assumptions and aims have evolved over the years. Women formally achieved freedom of occupational choice, economic equality, and the right to vote and hold office long before they were in position to make full use of these rights; most women could not even try. To take one small example: women were allowed to run for political office in most Western countries by the early twentieth century (Switzerland excluded). Yet few women did so; even fewer were elected. Men who refused to vote for women bear much of the blame, but not all. The mentality of many women was still immersed in an older culture. The history of women at the bar is also significant. Women won the right to be lawyers in the United States by 1880. But again, few women were able to break out of role and claim this right until surprisingly recent times. The *new* women's movement has accomplished wonders because it probes far deeper and pushes harder; it is not satisfied with formal rights. Its strength is surely due in part to contemporary individualism, that is, the republic of choice. Not only are women *claiming* more; more men see the justice of these claims. They too are citizens of the republic.

Religion in the Republic of Choice

Gender is in some ways an extreme case, because its biological base in undeniable. Less extreme, but equally diagnostic, is the nature of religious affiliation in contemporary society. Religious heritage in the past was a crucial factor in fixing station in life. Most religions in most societies claimed there was one true faith—and of course it was theirs. All others were barbarities, heresies, and inventions of the devil. It was only right and proper to favor the true religion; if evil, stubborn, or ignorant people refused to accept the faith, they deserved persecution. It was a sacred duty to banish heretics or burn them at the stake. Lebanon, Northern Ireland, and Khomeini's Iran grimly remind us that religious strife and bigotry have been able to survive and flourish in the 1980s, even in countries which claim to belong to the advanced and developed world.

Western countries have generally abandoned the *idea* of an official religion—a religious establishment—except as a mere formality, as in England. In the United States the Supreme Court interprets the First Amendment to the Constitution as a ban on any religious establishment; in any event, the idea would now be inconceivable in this country. In American tradition religious tolerance is strong and has deep roots. Federal and state constitutions guarantee freedom of religion and the separation of church and state. The courts vigorously enforce this separation. They strike down laws which even vaguely hint of state involvement with religion or its preference for one religion over another. The goal is to treat all denominations, in public and official life, with studied neutrality and generalized respect. A creche on the lawn of city hall, Christmas symbols on public buildings, benedictions in Congress, silent meditations in the schools— these are considered difficult, borderline issues, and the high courts ponder and worry and divide over them.[3] Underlying the debate is this idea: all religions are legitimate; none can be ignored, derided, and downgraded. Each has the opportunity to try to sell its wares. The state must keep hands off; religion is an *individual* choice, a private not a public matter.

Historically this represents a major shift in policy in Western society. Religious tolerance in the West grew to legitimacy after epochs of rich, luxuriant bigotry. Tolerance replaced a system of established, exclusive, powerful churches. Persecution of minority religions was standard. Many settlers in colonial America arrived as refugees from religious hostility in England; they came to set up their own regimes of bigotry in the brave new world. English law discriminated against minority religions in innumerable ways. Catholics, Jews and dissenters did not sit in Parliament until the nineteenth century. Under English law a person who ridiculed the true faith committed the crime of blasphemy. It was never a crime to ridicule dissenters or minority religions. In the United States, too, blasphemy was a crime in some states well into the nineteenth century, though what was protected was not some branch of Christianity, but Christianity in general. Today blasphemy has disappeared from the corpus juris.[4] It is a moribund crime in England, too. In one case, decided in 1979, depiction of a gay Christ proved too much for the august House of Lords to stomach.[5] But this was the first prosecution in decades; it is not likely to be repeated. Blasphemy presupposes a single standard of legitimacy. It is not inconsistent with religious tolerance or even with religious pluralism. It coexisted with them well into the nineteenth century. It is out of place, however, in the republic of choice.

Disestablishment, too, has a deeper meaning in modern society than mere tolerance for diversity, mere pluralist neutrality. More and more, religion has become unstuck from birth or heritage. The ethnicity of religion survives (see Chapter 5) for certain smaller or minority religions—Jews, Buddhists, Moslems—in Western societies. But for a growing segment of the population, religion has now been detached from tradition and inheritance and has become a matter of personal choice. Modern religion takes what Thomas Luckmann has called a "consumer orientation." It is a "private affair"; the individual approaches it as a buyer, who "may choose from the assortment of 'ultimate' meanings as he sees fit."[6]

In the past it was not usual for people to convert or change religions; individual conversion was in fact slightly suspect. (Mass conversions, sometimes at the point of a sword, were another matter.) In the republic of choice, however, religion is much more mutable than before; Westerners are religiously mobile, just as they are occupationally, socially, and geographically mobile. Indeed, in practice, it is easier to slide from faith to faith, than to cross the invisible lines that separate classes and strata. Mixed marriages—marriages across religious lines—have become exceedingly common. More and more, then, religion is a matter of personal commitment, something a person has *chosen*. It is a matter of "affiliation," a choice made voluntarily—our contemporaries *join* religions; they also molt religions and take on new ones at will. Most people, of course, simply keep the religion they were born with. But even these people are aware of their window of choice; they are aware of religious mobility and the chance to switch if they wish.

"Old-time" religion has not by any means lost its magic. It has in fact made something of a come-back, in the United States most notably. A kind of religious revival has taken place—a modern version of the Great Awakening.[7] The people of the United States are, on the whole, quite religious—more so than people in most other Western countries, measured by such statistics as attendance at church.[8] Fundamentalism has incomparably greater power in the United States than elsewhere; a serious "creationist" movement would be unthinkable in Belgium or Sweden. But the more offbeat sects are by no means confined to America. One sees saffron robes and shaved heads on the streets of Berlin and London, as well as in San Francisco.

The revival of fundamentalism in the United States seems, at first glance, seriously out of place in the republic of choice. Old-time religion is not "pro-choice." Its values do not accord with expressive individualism. But American religiosity is not, at root, discordant with the general culture. Religious revival in the United States is canted heavily toward exciting, charismatic, emotional brands of religion. These religions stress dramatic *personal* choice. A "born-again" Christian has discarded her old, ascriptive religion; she has freely chosen a different religion, or a more vigorous and personal version of her parents' religion. The personal element shows up even more strongly in people who choose to follow eastern mysticism, Asian or African religions, or a guru here or there. The chase after the supernatural, the lust for the metaphysical, is widespread enough to worry the standard religions. To meet the competition they stress their own ties to intense, personal spirituality.

The United States is experiencing a good deal of religious ferment. There seems to be considerable switching of religions—not as much as the switching of husbands and wives, but considerable nonetheless. This religious mobility, to be sure, is in part a logical consequence of religious pluralism. The United States is a country of many religions; they tend, on the whole, to be scattered throughout the country. There are places where Baptists, Lutherans, or Catholics form the majority, but nowhere do they dominate completely. Even the Mormons in Salt Lake City must contend with a large minority of gentiles. The population is overwhelmingly Christian; but innumerable sizes, brands, and packages of Christianity are offered on the market.

Pluralism by itself neither encourages nor discourages the mixing and switching of religions. What has occurred in the United States, and elsewhere in the West, is more than a reflex of coexistence. In many countries, past and present, religious groups lived side by side, but in hermetically sealed and impermeable communities. In other places they live side by side in implacable hatred—Lebanon, or Northern Ireland. Different religions, within a single state, coexisted in the Ottoman Empire, each with its own laws; to some extent this is true of modern Israel. Few daring souls ever crossed the religious boundaries. American and European pluralism is different. A number of ingredients go into it: coexisting religions, geographic mobility, the mass media, and, very notably, the enthronement of choice. In modern pluralism many *models* of religion are presented, all of them treated as valid. The question is no longer which is the *true* or the official religion, but which one is meaningful to *you*. Tolerance, to be sure, is not unlimited; public opinion is wary of sects and cults; but, significantly, these are feared because they are defined as a kind of addiction. The sects are suspected of brainwashing, robbing people of their (true) wills, and turning them into robots.

In the republic of choice mass media bring messages of all faiths into the home; the process weakens the power of an ascriptive religious culture. In religion, as in other walks of life, horizontal messages and horizontal authority compete with vertical authority. Moreover, mobility opens the door for dissidents to escape from closed communities. Even isolated rural sects feel the pressures. Meanwhile, new sects form frequently, as they also did in the past. But even the more radical and utopian of these based their societies on consent, on free affiliation. The history of American utopian communities, as described by Carol Weisbrod, is "largely illuminated by the principles of voluntarism."[9] Members come, and members go.

Generally speaking, then, social factors of life in America and in the West generally tend to rob ascriptive or ethnic religions of their strength. The high rate of intermarriage—marriage of course is totally choice-centered—further breaks down barriers between religions. It is hard to cling to the view that only *your* faith leads to salvation, if this means that your brother-in-law, two nieces, and assorted relatives and friends face eternal damnation. But if your religion is not the route to *universal* salvation, then what is it? It is either no salvation at all, or it is a personal, custom-made, *individual* route to salvation, a route which differs from person to person.

This idea of salvation as *personal* allows pluralism, tolerance, and deep religious faith to coexist without emotional contradiction, which is precisely the situation in America. In general, modern culture fosters choice in religion; it exalts forms of spirituality which are chosen personally and cut to the needs of the chooser; it downgrades religion which is imposed from above, inherited from parents, or adhered to blindly out of tradition or habit. And church-state law, the tangle of First Amendment cases, for all their difficulties and asymmetries, follow the contours of the general legal culture.

What is true of religion has become true of many other aspects of a person's life. The various compartments and activities of life, personal habits, ways of eating and dressing, career, even sexual proclivities, have dissolved into matters of choice and personal commitment. Consider, to take one instance, the so-called gourmet revolution. At one time, food was an ingrained aspect of inherited culture. The Chinese ate Chinese food, the Italians ate Italian food; even the English were condemned to eat their own. The modern citizen feels no such barriers; she is not disqualified from cooking or eating Thai food or Russian food simply because she is not Russian or Thai herself. One eats what one likes; national cuisines are so many options to be chosen. To be sure, some national cultures are more tenacious than others. Young American professionals will eat absolutely anything, while their opposite numbers in Italy still adhere on the whole to pasta and other Italian delights. But, in general, cuisine has now entered the great market-place of option. A Frenchman can eat sushi, if he wishes, become a Buddhist, play *go*, and collect African art. The abandonment of ascription goes far beyond religion. For each aspect of life, so the theory goes, one makes (or can make) an intense, individual *personal* choice. We live in the born-again age.

The Life-Cycle

In recent years scholars have begun to explore the social history of the human life-cycle.[10] Every society defines the life-cycle differently. Of course all agree that it is biologically predestined; the human animal is born helpless, toothless, and squalling, sucks and kicks by instinct, grows slowly, develops locomotion and speech, gets bigger, goes through puberty, matures, matures still more, gets old, gets older, turns gray and toothless, sickens, dies. Biology sets bounds and attaches firm imperatives; neither a boy of five nor a woman of eighty are capable of reproducing; no customs and mores about marriage, sex, and family life can alter this brutal fact. But within broad biological limits, the social order decides and disposes. It attaches meanings and behavior to stages and phases of life. It gives names and labels to these stages, measures and fixes their social significance, and assigns age roles, just as it assigns varying sex roles to women and men.

The scholarship in this field has shown that conventional phases and stages of life are, on the whole, social inventions, which differ from culture to culture. Ideas about childhood and adolescence, for example, are not God-given, or even biologically given. Some of these ideas are relatively recent "discoveries."[11] Ideas about stages of adult life are on the whole less clear-cut than ideas about childhood or old age. Today we are in the midst of general redefinition. Swift currents of social change are influencing the concept of the life-cycle, blurring its boundaries and canceling the various phases as much as socially possible; in effect, dissolving the adult part of the cycle. The republic of choice reshuffles the relationship between age and role.

We live in a time of paradox: on the one hand, we show increased awareness and sensitivity to stages and phases of life, increased focus on old age and its meaning; and, on the other hand, there is a trend to cancel out phases of adult life (including old age) entirely.

In an important sense age is moving toward legal and social irrelevance, in the same way that race, sex, and religion have moved toward irrelevance. To begin with, medical technology smudges, to a degree, the distinction between the fixed (biological) and the variable (social and cultural). It has conquered *some* of the degeneracies that go with aging; in any event, the population is living longer. This no doubt has a certain influence on the point made here: the notion, widespread and spreading wider, that age must not interfere with choice; that a person's (social) age should, as much as possible, be what that person wants, neither more nor less. There is, of course, an unavoidable aspect of age, but legally and socially this unavoidable part should be kept as neutral as is earthly possible.

Nobody to be sure *chooses* to be thirty, or forty, or ninety; but people do choose patterns, habits, and styles of behavior, and these can often be divorced from chronological age. People speak loosely about the "youth culture" of modern society. From a certain point of view the culture does seem to glorify youth—young styles, young music, young habits. But in a basic sense the phrase is misleading. Young people do not hold political, economic, or social power. The term "youth culture" recognizes the power of peer groups among the young; in part it is a salute to mass media and their celebrities, who are mostly young and beautiful, but fundamentally the phrase has to do with behavioral choices made by people who are not themselves young at all. It means that older people are set free from classic age stereotypes; they may, if they wish, worship youth, behave like youth; they may (and do) adopt the styles and habits of the young. Thus the so-called youth culture is really a culture of nonyoung people who have decided to dissolve their adulthood and absorb it into patterns once considered appropriate only for children and adolescents.

To say that old age as a distinctive phase of life is heading for extinction would of course be exaggerated. Life expectancy is increasing throughout the West. People are living longer. A sizeable number live to be *very* old. There is a burst of scientific interest in aging and geriatric affairs. The elderly are also a powerful interest group. But in a curious way emphasis on the elderly and on the aging process only proves the irrelevance of age. The old need no longer *act* old; they need not retire to their porches and rocking chairs, their places of decay and irrelevance. They can join the Gray Panthers and lobby and make noise. They can decide not to dress old and act old; they are free to crack open the life-cycle, to start new hobbies, to act in the ways of the young. In this sense the stages of adult life have been defined away or welded together into a single, overarching phase of life, which is not young life nor old life but *life* pure and simple.

This dissolution of the life-cycle is an important social change; naturally enough, it has had an impact on law. In every Western country a vast array of benefits and rights fall to the middle-aged and the elderly. These benefits and rights did not appear overnight; and they had, at first, little or nothing to do with the vanishing life-cycle. On the contrary, old-age pensions, designed (among other things) to make it possible for workers to retire with bread and dignity, may have sharpened the line of division between younger and older adults. Young adults worked; old adults retired. Young adults of course benefited from pension laws: the job situation improved insofar as older workers were eased out of the labor market, and a system of pensions meant that young workers were less likely to be saddled with the burden of supporting their elderly parents.

For some of the elderly, pensions were a kind of Faustian bargain: they traded pensions for jobs; to gain security in old age they gave up meaningful work. For millions of older workers, of course, the bargain was well worth it; they had tough, menial, unrewarding jobs, or they were unable to compete in the job market because of failing health or strength. Pensions made it possible for more of the elderly to live independent lives—a goal some wanted desperately to achieve. The term "independent" is interesting, even curious in this context. Pensioners, after all, are dependent on the state. But pensions are impersonal checks that arrive in the mail. This is preferable to begging from snarling, frustrated kinfolk. The pensions, like many welfare and regulatory institutions, do not look like stigmata of dependence, but, on the contrary, like badges of independence. Moreover, people define their pensions as (social) insurance; they have "earned" the pension; and since the payments come in the form of money, pensioners are free to spend them as they wish.

More recently governments have expanded the rights and benefits of the elderly. The new provisions demonstrate, in part, how strong is the organized lobby of the elderly, and how successfully it battles for its interests. Laws against age discrimination are among the most interesting examples of the new wave of laws. These are almost exclusively North American (United States and Canada), without parallels elsewhere.

Age-discrimination law in the United States began, practically speaking, with the Age Discrimination in Employment Act (ADEA) passed by the United States Congress in 1967.[12] This act was primarily for the benefit of the middle-aged; it applied to workers over forty but under sixty-five. Employers were forbidden to discriminate against members of this age-group in hiring, firing, and in the conditions of work. Before this time, many companies refused to hire workers over forty. Under ADEA, it was even illegal to advertise for "young people" or "young workers." A later amendment to ADEA raised the ceiling age to seventy, and in 1986 the age ceiling was removed altogether for all but a handful of occupations. This in effect abolished forced retirement—a development which a number of states, including California, had anticipated. Since 1986, then, no company of any size can adopt a *rule* getting rid of employees who reach a certain age—sixty-five, seventy, or even ninety. Each person must be handled as a unique individual.

What lies behind these laws? The gray lobby is of course one factor in the story. But the original law (1967) did not benefit those older than sixty-five. The civil rights movement was undoubtedly a major influence. The great Civil Rights Act of 1964[13] swept away job discrimination on the basis of race, sex, religion, and national origin; it seemed logical to add age to this list, which happened in fact three years later. But it would be wrong to explain so important a development as if it were merely an attractive analogy that slipped into law almost casually. Underlying the law were changes in the social conception of old age. The new conception is neatly captured in one phrase: the fluid life-cycle. Society is no longer sure, as Bernice Neugarten puts it, "where to put the punctuation marks in the life line."[14] Should there be any marks at all? At one time, Western society, like most societies, rigidly defined age phases. The life-cycle was a one-way conveyor belt, a kind of assembly-line process, which started at birth and moved inexorably in a single direction from phase to phase, through adulthood to weakness, retirement and death. Each stage or station was firmly irreversible. There was little variation in the process and never any turning back.

To be sure, the facts of life make certain passages irreversible—a child is a child, an adult an adult. Death is the ultimate irreversibility. But little else on the assembly line is completely fixed by biology. The kind of behavior that is deemed suitable to each age and stage of life is socially determined. Most people are unaware of their attitudes and feelings about age-appropriate behavior; they simply take these for granted. If a child throws a tantrum, that is normal behavior; if an adult does the same, something is wrong. An adolescent who leaves home is deviant; a twenty-six-year-old is *expected* to move out.

The fluid life-cycle is a reaction against traditional ideas of age-appropriate behavior. In its most radical form, it denies the whole idea of age-roles across the adult life-span. No such utopia has actually arrived, of course. People are still acutely aware of phases and passages in adult life; there is a large popular and scientific literature about mid-life crises, golden years, transitions of this or that variety, and other cultural artifacts. Despite this, the line which separates the child from the grown-up is the only *clear* demarcation. In the sweep of time from, say, eighteen to death, fluidity has become a powerful if implicit concept. Indeed, the literature on crisis and transition presupposes it. After all, real changes do take place as we get older; the whole point of the literature is how to contain, neutralize, adjust to, or capitalize on these changes. The body goes into mild and then ominous decay; old parents die; children grow up; work situations mature and stabilize. Every developmental transition "involves termination and initiation: the termination of an existing life structure and the initiation of a new one." To handle this, "a person must reappraise and modify the existing life structure."[15]

In this quotation from a prominent book on adult development there is no hint that people should and must remain fixed in old, time-honored age slots; that they should ride serenely along on their conveyor belt. To the contrary, the language presupposes the fluid life-cycle and the conflicts, doubts, tensions, the miseries and raptures of choice. It is choice which *creates* the sense of passages and transitions. All would otherwise be securely fixed by nature and society. But the fluid life-cycle, and the irrelevance of age, means that it is no longer necessarily freakish or odd to get divorced at forty, start a new career at fifty, take French lessons at sixty, ride a motorcycle at seventy, or a bicycle at eighty if this is what a person wants to do, can do, and is an imperative of his self-development at any stage or phase of life. Indeed, what the books prescribe as a cure for mid-life and any-time-of-life crisis is to make a fresh start, to reexamine premises, to rethink one's personal life; often in ways that would once have been condemned as improper or inappropriate to that age or station in life. The literature on "passages" assumes the reality of *choice*: crises are to be expected, but we can *do* something about them. No one is required to go gentle into twilight or night unless he wants to.

The fluid life-cycle is obviously linked to dominant ideas about option and choice. The passage of time should not close doors and shut out opportunities; age should not impede the making and remaking of the self any more than race, sex, or religion. This is a corollary of the basic postulate of legal culture—freedom of choice—and of the general expectation of justice. It is no surprise, then, that the bias against irreversibility and in favor of "second chances" operates here too, that is, in the realm of the life-cycle. And this wave of social change has powerfully reinforced developments in family life. It is at least partly responsible, for example, for the eruption or epidemic of divorce among middle-aged couples. Why adhere to an old, dead marriage? Why not start over again? The mistake can be reversed. It is never too late.

Starting over is a deep-seated need in the culture. As one cliché has it: "Today is the first day of the rest of your life." In a cultural climate of this sort, the meaning of old age gets drastically redefined. Consider the recent articles and books which discuss the sex life of elderly people, how to foster it, how to keep it fresh and green. The subject was once almost taboo. Sex was meant for young reproducers. Old people had memories; and that was that. What was once unseemly is now actively encouraged. If the body can do it, and the heart is willing, why not?

As usual, legal arrangements are remolded to reflect the new social definitions. For the United States and Canada we have mentioned the age-discrimination laws, which have also generated an astonishing number of lawsuits and administrative actions. People over forty have a right to new jobs or old jobs, fresh starts or old ruts. These laws also essentially demand that each person be dealt with as an *individual*. Group stereotypes, in age no less than in race or sex, violate the most fundamental right: to be treated as a unique citizen in the republic of individuals and choice.

I do not mean to suggest a direct, causal connection between age-discrimination law and the fluid life-cycle. "Concepts" do not produce laws; social pressures do. The culture of fluidity affected the wish-list of the gray lobby and thus may have had an *indirect* influence on the law. Moreover, this branch of law is confined to North America so far.[16] In Europe one finds few traces of a ban on age discrimination. Rules against forced retirement are completely unheard of. Indeed, the trend in Europe runs strongly in the opposite direction: toward earlier and earlier retirement. In some countries—Holland, for example—this is encouraged by public and private schemes.[17] Unemployment has so traumatized the European welfare states since the 1970s that any policy which seems to add to the glut of workers is at present unthinkable. Early retirement is popular in the United States as well; companies in economic difficulty often buy out middle-aged employees to reduce their work force. But early retirement is not mandated by law; the law, as we have seen, forbids most employers to force retirement on unwilling workers.

Paradoxically, however, early retirement and late retirement may come to the same thing, socially speaking. A man or woman who retires from a job at fifty or fifty-five does not necessarily sit on the porch in a rocking chair. Early retirement brings with it the chance to try something else—a different career, new hobbies and activities, an altered line of work. Thus early retirement is itself a reflex of the fluid life-cycle; it springs up in modern welfare states whose unions have a strong grip on the labor market and are able to hold on to key jobs for younger members, despite a shrinking demand for their labor. Early retirement, in short, is itself the opportunity to make a fresh start. Retirement is no longer a semifinal act, a brief punctuation on the road to death. Instead, it can be a beginning; a vital, growing stage of life. A person who retires with a pension check every month, and is still curious and ambitious, can experiment with jobs and activities foreclosed to those who must work until the absolute end. The rocking chair is only one option out of many. Early retirement is thus a temporal form of the social safety net, an opportunity and a challenge to try out new styles, with the cushion and protection of an income for life.

Family Law and Family Life

Family life in the modern West has been as volatile as other aspects of the social order. One change, still controversial, is the high rate of marital breakup. Divorce is common in all Western societies (at least in those that allow it). It is often taken as a sign of social disorganization. Divorce is extremely common in the United States. For at least a century the divorce rate has evoked suspicion, fear, and dismay among clergymen, moral leaders, and respectable citizens in general.

What is ultimately responsible for the amazing career of divorce? Why is there so large a demand for a legal exit from marriage? William O'Neill, writing about divorce as it was at the turn of the century, points to a change in the social meaning of marriage. In traditional marriage husband and wife had clear, fixed roles. In marriage, and only in marriage, was sex proper and even commendable; marriage was also the framework for a stable family; it meant a home and children. The husband ran the family, lovingly or otherwise; he provided food and money; his wife was a servant, a housekeeper, a sexual partner, a social support. By the late nineteenth century traditional marriage had gotten into rougher waters. Both men and women were unsatisfied; they expected more out of marriage than before. They wanted marriages to carry much heavier freight. Husbands and wives were supposed to fill each other's needs in profound and pervasive ways. Marriage had a new task; it was becoming a mode of self-fulfillment. It was a freely chosen arrangement, a partnership. Each partner had to satisfy and enrich the life of the other. If a marriage failed to provide this kind of fulfillment, each partner had the moral right to break off and try again.[18]

In many older societies marriage customs and laws presupposed patriarchal or extended families. Families arranged marriages for their children—still a common practice in parts of the Third World. In the modern West arranged marriages seem heartless, barbaric, primitive. Anything but a freely chosen partnership is unthinkable. Marriage was once a status, a sacrament; by the early nineteenth century it had become a contract, legally and socially. Until fairly recent times, however, it was a rather deviant form of contract; for the most part, it was irreversible and indissoluble; it was a dead-end or one-way street. In the United States divorce was extremely rare before the Revolution. By the early ninteenth century most states allowed judicial divorce, but it was nowhere common. In England, practically speaking, there was no divorce at all until 1857.[19] In many other countries, particularly where the Catholic church was powerful, divorce was also not available, as is still true in Ireland and was true until recently in Argentina and Italy.

For Western Christianity the sanctity and permanence of marriage was a strong tradition and a dogma. Marriage in the nineteenth century lost some of this quality; by the end of the century, it was no longer indissoluble and irreversible. It was becoming, more and more, a contract in the full sense—in other words, an option, an agreement, a matter of choice. Like other choices and options in life, it began to be influenced by norms that disfavored the irreversible. A marriage, if it cannot be dissolved, can become a trap, a slavery, a burden; such a marriage interferes with individual growth and development; it stifles the unfolding of the self.

These attitudes are familiar ones; they were part of the developing legal culture; and they were reinforced by the mobility of the population, which made it much easier, physically, for men at least, to walk away from marriage. The law changed with the changing culture, though always in the teeth of furious opposition. Demand for divorce increased inexorably and corroded the formal law. But the formal law was tough and resistant, because the opposition was tough and resistant. Marriage had a special moral and religious status, and divorce was considered immoral in itself, or at best an open door to immorality. By the middle of the nineteenth century divorce was in fact available through regular courts. But only an innocent victim—of adultery, desertion, habitual drunkenness, or other legal "grounds"—had the privilege of suing for divorce. A few states loosened their laws much more, but they later retreated in the face of savage criticism. From roughly 1870 on, however, consensual divorce was one of the dirty little secrets of American law. Formal law recognized no such thing, but it was part of the living law in fact. Preachers railed at it from the pulpit; legislators denounced it; jurists sneered at it; but the parties demanded it, and judges winked at it. Collusion dominated the divorce courts and showed a remarkable ability to survive, despite repeated scandals and exposes.

Suddenly, after a century or so of life in the shadows, the idea of divorce at will burst out of its closet with amazing force. California enacted the first "no-fault" divorce law in the United States in 1970.[20] Today every state has its version and many other countries have enacted similar reforms. In Germany, under the Marriage Reform Act of 1976, divorce is based exclusively on "disruption of marriage" (Zerrüttung), although the law still contemplates a period of separation.[21] Even Italy has adopted a divorce law, over the vigorous protest of the Vatican. Thus divorce is no longer defined in the West as a privilege, something the innocent claim against a wicked or guilty spouse. It has become an absolute right, freely available to any married person who wants one.

The precise details differ from country to country. But the main line of development is the same outside of a few strongholds of Catholic power. *Either* party to a marriage has the right to end it; there is no need to allege or prove formal "grounds" for divorce; innocence and guilt no longer matter, at least with regard to the marriage itself. (They are still relevant in matters of child custody and division of property.) To stay married is a matter of individual choice; it cannot be forced on anyone; thus marriage is emphatically no longer a status, a permanent state.

In short, the revolution in legal culture has completely reshaped the law of marriage and divorce. Family law has come to reflect, as it must, the central postulates of the republic of choice and the growing influence of expressive individualism. The whole conception of the family has moved, as it were, from status to contract. Family formation begins with a contract of marriage; this is a continuing agreement, which presupposes perpetual renewal, a perpetual process of accommodation. When agreement fails, the alternative is no-fault divorce. Within family life, the decision to have children—thanks to sexual technology—is no longer solely in the hands of God. It is part of the package of agreements. Couples decide to have children or not; they are just another option, like a new refrigerator, a job-change, or a trip to the Canary Islands. Millions of couples, especially in the Federal Republic of Germany, find the trip to the islands more attractive.

In most contemporary families, then, children do not arrive unless parents want them. Nor are they an obvious or easy choice. Children are a miracle, a source of wonder and joy, but they are also a terrible responsibility. The birth of a baby is irreversible in a way that marriage is not, cohabitation is not, job-choice is not. Not everyone can handle a situation which *forecloses* so many options and interferes so radically with personal freedom. Childlessness, of course, has its own difficulties, most obviously when it is *not* a matter of choice. It then becomes a kind of handicap, and many couples search desperately for ways to overcome the physical barriers—including surrogacy and artificial insemination—or try to adopt children, as a contractual substitute for biological childbirth.

Adoption was unknown to the common law; there were no legal substitutes for the God-given blessing of children. Modern adoption law dates from the nineteenth century. In the United States the first major adoption law was passed in Massachusetts in 1851.[22] In the

1980s it has become difficult for childless couples to find adoptable babies. The main source, illegitimate children, has been drying up, partly because so many single mothers, even teen-agers, choose to hold on to their children. There are of course many reasons why this is so, but one of them is surely the transmuted *concept* of the family. The single, all-powerful model or image of the family, which monopolizes legitimacy and respectability, has been fragmented into a thousand possibilities. Single motherhood—unmarried motherhood—no longer carries so heavy a freight of disgrace. Thus, in a sense, single motherhood is now a chosen status, or can be; its social consequences are not quite so irreversible. Most unmarried mothers did not choose their status, but the culture does not isolate them, oppress them, as it did in the nineteenth century, and the welfare system grants them some sort of safety net. For a few women at the top of the social scale single motherhood is in fact a chosen option; some couples, too, choose to have children without marriage, while single parents and gay or lesbian couples occasionally succeed in adopting children on their own.

Under standard adoption law, the adopted child is assimilated to the status of a natural child. The child inherits from its adoptive parents only. Legally, it is as if the birth parents never were. But recently, in a startling turn of the wheel, adoptive children have questioned these standard propositions. Many American states have changed their law so that adopted children can discover their natural parents, at least under certain conditions. In England adopted children have the right to their original birth records.[23] Sealed records have become unsealed. By implication, adoptive children have the option to choose between two competing mothers (and sometimes fathers). In part this reflects the usual high value placed on options and choice. It also reflects the idea that one has the right to choose—or reject—one's ethnic and biological nature. The path to rejection has always been open to "natural" children; now the path to *acceptance* is open for children given away at their birth.

Privacy

In the contemporary world the concept of privacy has come to play a major role in society. In the United States, as in a number of countries, it is an important legal concept as well. In a striking line of cases, mostly concerning marriage and sex, the Supreme Court has read a right of privacy into the federal Constitution—a significant, controversial development.

The word "privacy" has subtle overtones and suggests various legal meanings, some of them in apparent conflict. In American law, a famous article by Samuel Warren and Louis Brandeis, published in the *Harvard Law Review* in the 1890s,[24] formally launched the right of privacy. Warren and Brandeis stressed the "right to be left alone," to keep one's personal life private and secret. Their prose had a faintly priggish flavor. Yellow journalism, scandal-sheet gossip, and that dangerous new device, the candid camera, threatened to disrupt the harmony and reticence that decent people had the right to expect in their homes and in their lives. These people needed the protection of law against intrusive strangers.

This conception of personal privacy is by no means obsolete: quite the contrary. It is connected to the sanctity of the home, the idea of the home as a "castle"—enclosed, inviolate, private. This idea is crucial to the modern, individualistic notion of personal liberty. It assumes that everyone needs a sanctuary, everyone needs "space." Every child needs privacy to grow up properly; if possible, a child should have a room of her own. Middle-class parents consider this a must. Adults too need a haven. These needs and wants, needless to say, would be totally foreign to communal and traditional societies; in such societies privacy was virtually impossible. Nor was any particular value placed upon it; the demand for privacy is distinctly modern.[25] To be sure, privacy is greatly treasured today; people believe that neither the state nor large organizations should have the right to pry into personal affairs; personal life should be sacrosanct. An exaggerated sensitivity on this point has complicated plans for a federal census in West Germany. Unlike the United States, the census there had no long constitutional tradition; arranging for one set off a firestorm of protest (1987).[26] There was and is a deep suspicion of state questionnaires.

But privacy in contemporary law goes beyond the elemental demand for personal space; it goes beyond the right to keep one's private life a secret. Indeed, in an important sense, the battle for *this* form of privacy is as good as lost. Modern technology has doomed it to extinction. Government, if it wishes, can literally hear a pin drop anywhere—not only in the Soviet embassy, but in the home of its citizens. It can spy from the sky, it can listen in on phone lines, it can peek through the walls. One argument raised with regard to the German census was that government already *had* all the data it claimed to need, stored in national computer banks. Perhaps this was true. Genuine secrecy is already untenable; it will become more so as time goes on. The facts of our lives, who we are, what we buy, how many parking tickets we have had, our job histories, marital status, education, can be gathered and stored electronically and shared rapidly, almost instantaneously, with other states and agencies all over the world. A secret lost in Maine can be trumpeted to the hills in California, or in Tokyo. The worst fears of Warren and Brandeis have become living reality.

Famous people are especially vulnerable. Neither law nor custom assign much value to the privacy rights of public figures; these people, after all, have been converted into "celebrities." Fame implies familiarity, not ineffable remoteness. There is no barrier to "news" about the President's underwear, about what rock stars like to eat or wear, or what image Reagan's Secretary of State, George Shultz, has tattooed on his bottom (a tiger).[27] Warren and Brandeis wanted to shield public figures, to keep all such "news" from prying eyes, except for facts that were directly relevant to policy. They meant privacy quite literally: a peaceful, invulnerable zone in one's personal life; freedom from idle gossip and unwelcome intrusion. And for the mere mortal, the private citizen, today, the eyes and ears of Big Brother are more of a threat than mass media.

To be sure, prying and snooping can be resisted, and are resisted; civil libertarians and ordinary citizens alike recognize the problem and the dangers. There is a good deal of discussion about how to control, limit, and suppress threats to privacy; there is a search for ways to counterbalance the power of government and large organizations that collect information about personal lives and amass data on habits, credit, buying and spending, political views, troubles in the family, and so on. But fundamentally the battle is not about *gathering* the information; it is about *using* it to a person's detriment. People in the computer age expect everything to be recorded, or are at least resigned to this turn of events. What privacy comes to mean, in essence, is noninterference, and this is more or less coextensive with the boundaries of the republic of choice. It is the right to exercise options in private behavior without adverse consequences. "Private" here means *personal*; it does not necessarily mean secret at all.

This is why people claim or desire what we might call the right to evanescence—the right to let memories die. Protesters on the march, with banners and flags, welcome the publicity of television. But the attention of the police, their cameras and notebooks, is extremely unwelcome. The protest behavior may have been open, public, and blatant; but the marchers do not want to be *officially* recorded; they do not want to end up in dossiers and protocols; they claim the right to forgetfulness, the right not to be haunted tomorrow by what they did yesterday; the right to express themselves and then perhaps to reverse themselves; the right to resist the corporate memory of state. They claim the right to what we have called "loser's justice," even before they lose. This is not privacy in any classic meaning of the word. It is privacy, however, in its distinctly modern sense.

This form of privacy reveals the same sharp asymmetry that we noted in labor law and the law of landlord and tenant. The rights of individuals differ sharply from those of corporations, government agencies, and other large institutions. Civil liberties groups fight to *reduce* the "privacy rights" of government. In the United States the Freedom of Information Act, for all its faults and loopholes, formalized the right of citizens to crack open the secret cabals of state.[28] British and continental law lag behind American law so far; the British Official Secrets Act is much tougher than its equivalents in the United States.[29] Even in Britain signs of change, or at least demands for change, are evident. Everywhere, individuals want to know what is in those awesome memory banks: their credit ratings, their personal files. Privacy thus is not so much the right to keep secret, as it is the right to live as one pleases—to conduct "private" affairs without interference. "None of your business" once meant "you have no right to know." Now it means, "you may know, I can't help that; but you may not interfere."

Meanwhile, in the United States, the "right to privacy," which began its career as a branch—a small twig—of private (tort) law has entered the exalted chambers of constitutional law. The key case was *Griswold v. Connecticut*,[30] decided in 1965. This case challenged an archaic and bedraggled Connecticut statute under which it was an offense to use "any drug, medicinal article or instrument for the purpose of preventing conception." Connecticut was alone in banning such devices; most other states allowed their sale and use. Even Connecticut made no serious attempt to stamp out birth control. But a dying statute, like a fresh-killed snake, can sometimes twitch and bite spasmodically. The statute made it awkward, to say the very least, to run birth-control clinics. In any event, *Griswold* was a test case, and the Supreme Court struck down the law.

The justices clearly looked on the statute as stupid and outmoded. This was no doubt the basic impulse behind their decision. They dimly felt that some constitutional principle was at stake; but it was hard if not impossible to find specific words or sentences in the text to support the decision. Justice Douglas, who wrote for the majority, invoked the *spirit* of the Bill of Rights; the text, he said, exuded "penumbras" and "emanations," and these implied certain "zones of privacy." He also spoke about the "sacred precincts of marital bed-rooms" and the "notions of privacy surrounding the marriage rela-tionship." Justice Goldberg, in a concurring opinion, mentioned a "right of marital privacy," which he described as "fundamental and basic"; he cited on behalf of this right the (little-used) Ninth Amend-ment, which stretched the limits of interpretation. Yet a line of later cases not only confirmed but strengthened this newfangled constitu-tional right; they extended privacy protection well beyond the "sacred precincts" of marriage.[31] The most notorious decision was *Roe v. Wade* (1973),[32] which has been enveloped in controversy since the day it was announced. In this case the Court, in essence, struck down all laws which limited a woman's right to abort her child in the early months of pregnancy. The majority opinion cited *Griswold*, stressed the "right to personal privacy," and spoke of a "guarantee" implicit in the Constitution, which covered "certain areas or zones of privacy."

Roe v. Wade began a troubled, conflicted line of cases on abortion: how far states and the federal government may go in controlling it, whether government is allowed to discourage abortion, whether it can refuse to pay for abortions among the poor, whether it can require young pregnant women to consult their parents before an abortion, and so on.[33] The decisions have rarely been unanimous; they have provoked endless debate; jurists and laymen alike have fiddled and worried about the underlying principles. Some justices of the Supreme Court have never accepted *Roe v. Wade* at all. They wonder, quite naturally, what abortion has to do with privacy, and what the Constitution has to do with privacy in the first place. The Court's privacy decisions, they say, have little in common with the right to be left alone, or the right to keep personal secrets. They are about marriage, sexual behavior, and procreation; and they deal with behavior that is often anything but secret.

In other words, the issue in these decisions turns on the right to make choices—choices about sexuality and life-style—personally, individually, without coercion, and without bad consequences in law or in fact. *Roe v. Wade* was not about *secret* abortion; quite the contrary. It was about *legal* abortion, open and above board, in hospitals or clinics. Similarly, gay liberation is not a struggle for life in secrecy, but for the right to be openly and legitimately gay; to live a gay or lesbian life. Cohabitation rights are not rights to have clandestine affairs, but to have relationships legitimately, openly, consequentially. These are demands for free choice in private affairs, untrammeled by persecution and prosecution, but also, and most significantly, without official or unofficial stigma.

This demand of course reflects the shift in the (inner) meaning of freedom that has taken place in law and society over the course of the last century or so, but most notably in the last two decades. In addition to market-place and electoral choices, contemporaries expect protection for private, life-style choices. The word "privacy" has become attached to this aspect of freedom, however awkwardly. These zones of life are not "private" because they are and must be hidden from view, but because they are wholly personal, based on the wishes, aims, hopes, and needs of the individual and leading to individual fulfillment. They concern the intimate as well as the workaday, humdrum spheres of life. Thus "privacy" implies the right to behave blatantly in public: to parade down Main Street in drag, to buy "dirty" books or contraceptives at the corner drugstore, to practice minority religions without loss of power or prestige, and to follow "alternative" life-styles. More prosaically, it includes choosing jobs, hobbies, consumer goods, friends, and modes and fashions of dress without discrimination, including discrimination based on what one does in one's private life. Privacy, then, does not refer exclusively to safety from the eyes of strangers; it is not merely the right to close the door to the bathroom; it means protection of life-choices from public control and social disgrace.

It is worth repeating that we are discussing trends, general tendencies, shifts at the margin, not opinions and actions that everybody shares. Substantial numbers of people bitterly resent and resist the trends we have mentioned, sometimes with considerable strength. The abortion decision was controversial from the day it was handed down, and the controversy has not abated one whit. At this writing (1989) its long-term survival is by no means assured. Only a bare majority on the Supreme Court seems to support *Roe v. Wade*; President Ronald Reagan was hostile to the decision throughout his eight years of office and would have killed it, had he had the chance, through the appointment power. President Bush may yet succeed in doing so. In West Germany, where social forces and cultural trends are presumably comparable to those in the United States, the Constitutional Court handed down a decision in 1975 almost the reverse of *Roe v. Wade*, though perhaps equally strained as a matter of interpretation. The Court read the *Grundgesetz* (fundamental law) to protect the rights of the fetus, rather than the rights of the mother.[34] The Spanish Constitutional Court, faced with a similar issue, waffled.[35] Some European countries allow abortion freely in the early months; others (Switzerland, for example) have tight laws in theory, but are loose in practice. In Ireland and Belgium abortion is hardly allowed at all.[36] In Canada the Supreme Court, flexing its new muscles, took a strong pro-choice position in January 1988.[37]

Thus privacy cases are not freaks and sports of American constitutionalism. They reflect a deep, pan-Western movement in which law is invoked on both sides of the issue. In the United States the language and rhetoric of the abortion controversy reflects (as it must) the dominant themes of legal culture. The "pro-choice" side argues from general feminist principles and asserts a woman's right to control her own body. It refuses to treat the mere fact of pregnancy, especially unwanted pregnancy, as legally irreversible; it is of course easily reversible *medically*. The "right to life" movement invokes traditional and religious values; but its main argument, legally and morally, rests on the assumption that the fetus is a person, a living being under the protection of law. This was the basis for the German decision. The text of the *Grundgesetz* guaranteed the "right to life" for "everyone." The claims of *another* human being, in other words, limit and constrain the mother's choice; the fetus is a potential individual, and its interests must be protected like those of all others. The tiny creature in the womb, like children and the incompetent, has no power to protect itself, but must be protected by others. It is not, in short, a consenting adult, and it thus has the right to live.

Informed Consent

In recent years the concept of "informed consent" has taken a central position in the law of medical malpractice. Of course it is nothing new to forbid unauthorized invasion of somebody else's body; a doctor must not operate on a patient without the patient's permission, except in dire emergency. The doctor is supposed to talk to the patient, explain what ought to be done (medically speaking) and why, and obtain the patient's consent. But until recent times, consent was simply not a major issue in the law of doctor and patient. In common-law countries medical malpractice was an insignificant appendage to the law of negligence in general. Few cases on the subject were reported before the twentieth century; lawsuits against doctors were apparently quite rare.[38]

The phrase "informed consent", it is said, first appeared in an American malpractice case in 1957.[39] Since then the concept has been widely discussed in legal literature and in the literature on medical ethics. The concept is also "well developed" in Europe, notably in Germany.[40] The phrase expresses an important ideal: the patient must be in ultimate control of all important choices. The doctor is obliged to tell everything: risks, alternatives, benefits. He must hide nothing, gloss over nothing.

This is more easily said than done. Some experts flatly assert that "informed consent in medicine is largely a failure." "Characteristics of the physician/patient relationship" are bound to frustrate the idea in practice.[41] Medical information is often technical, and the layman is hard put to understand it. Doctors are not particularly good at explaining, and some patients may even *prefer* to be passive and helpless; they want to put themselves in the doctor's hands and let her make the tough decisions.

Nonetheless, the very existence of the concept is (as it were) diagnostic. In a leading American case, *Natanson v. Kline*, the patient, Mrs. Natanson, had cobalt radiation therapy and suffered burns from the treatment. The doctor, she argued, never told her the risks. She won her case: the law, said the court, "starts with the premise of thorough-going self determination . . . [E]ach man is considered to be master of his own body." A doctor cannot "substitute his own judgment for that of the patient."[42]

"Informed consent" is thus connected with autonomy and choice; these are, along with consent itself, among the most highly favored legitimators in modern society. The emphasis on the concept grows out of, and blends with, the general consent and choice culture. Informed consent can be connected to other trends and movements as well. Martin Shapiro mentions one: the "revolt of the intellectuals against the establishment technocracy." Such a revolt is probably real and is by no means confined to "intellectuals." It is in every group and stratum, although as revolts go it is quite gingerly, piece-meal, and selective. Shapiro isolates certain "key premises" of the revolt. One is "that the lay consumer of technology, not the technician, must be the ultimate decision maker about how and where technology will be applied."[43] This of course captures the essence of "informed consent."

Choice and consent are relevant everywhere in life. They are certainly relevant to careers and to work life, but they are especially salient in matters of personal life—roughly, what we do with ourselves when our main occupation is not breadwinning but molding a viable self. Choice and consent are particularly important when the issue is control of bodies and emotions—for example, in health matters, where we shape ourselves in a literal, physical way. The popularity of body-building, the obsession with jogging, diets, and the rest, is not *merely* narcissism; it is a statement that we can and do control and *shape* our bodies, as well as our souls. The urge to maintain control is stronger than the authority of the doctor, which has somewhat declined relative to the authority of the patient. The decline took place in the teeth of the tremendous prestige of science and medicine and applies even to people not in "revolt" against technocracy, and who may have blind faith in their doctors. The doctor *knows*, but the patient *decides*.

Indeed, "patient" is no longer a status, meaningful only in *relation* to an authority, the doctor; the individual remains an individual even in the patient *role*; he must agree to each medical act explicitly and separately. Autonomy for the patient is also one of the ideological underpinnings of the deinstitutionalization movement, which has emptied many mental hospitals and made it difficult to commit people to hospitals and asylums "against their will." "Informed consent" then, like privacy, is an outgrowth of the culture of choice, which has permeated the whole legal system and affected the whole structure of authority.

TEN

A Stab at Assessment

THE DISCUSSION in this book has been pitched mostly at the level of description and explanation. I have made arguments about the nature of law and authority in the modern West, and where the contemporary concepts came from. The reader will decide whether I have made my case about the republic of choice. For those who are convinced (including myself), there is a further question: should we be pleased or displeased with this state of affairs? Are these developments good for society, or bad?

Benefits and Costs

In a society based on personalism, which has undergone the changes in law and authority described here, there are of course massive problems; society has run up enormous bills. There have also been enormous gains and benefits. It is an ill wind that blows no good; and most good winds blow considerable ill as well. It would take another book of this size to describe and assess the consequences, good and bad. Perhaps an example or two is in order. At the end of the last chapter, we mentioned deinstitutionalization of mentally ill patients—the movement which shook up the law of civil commitment and caused the population in mental institutions to shrink so drastically. Thousands were released from asylums and sent back into the community. Whatever its other causes, this movement was part and parcel of the culture of the republic of choice; it was a rejection of "paternalism," of forcing people into institutions against their will, except when absolutely necessary. But this movement, unfortunately, can also serve as a prime instance of mixed results and moral ambiguity. In principle, most people would agree that it is savage and barbaric to lock people up, unless their situation is truly desperate or they are dangerous. In the bad old days there were instances of monstrous evil. But easy commitment to mental hospitals has now been stunningly rejected—partly through the pressure of lawsuits. The criterion for commitment now is danger to the self or to others. No one capable of intelligent choice or consent, who has perpetrated no crime, should be confined to a public or private institution.[1]

This new approach strikes most of us as obviously correct; the other side seems as remote and obscure as arguments that the earth is flat or that the sun revolves around the earth. The old system was doomed by its shortcomings. There were real scandals, horror stories, and elementary violation of rights. There was also disillusionment with the "treatment" sick people were getting. Public mental health care was rotten to the core—starved for funds, callous, inhuman.[2] Hospitals were snake pits; patients were prisoners, locked up without due process. Liberals attacked the system as a violation of human rights. Conservatives hated the expense of public institutions; they also tended to be deeply suspicious of psychiatry and psychiatrists, whom they labeled as frauds, determinists, and enemies of traditional values. Both sides appealed to the concepts of choice and consent. Both agreed that people should be committed to asylums only as a last resort, and only under extraordinary circumstances.

Thus a large dose of reform and high-mindedness fed the movement to clean out the snake pits. The results were dramatic. The patient population of the United States dropped from almost 500,000 in 1964 to about 140,000 in 1980: the rest were mostly let go.[3] Yet today few people are happy about the results. In theory, the freed former patients would move to half-way houses, into warm loving families, or supportive institutions. No such support materialized. Instead, refugees from mental hospitals swelled the ranks of the homeless: the bag ladies on the streets of big cities; the ragged men with backpacks, sleeping on heating grates, sprawled on park benches and in railroad stations; the bearded men who push shopping carts down the streets, talking to themselves. These people are a living reproach to society, which has no idea what to do with them. They are, in a real sense, casualties of the republic of choice. Yet they are its citizens, too, as the vignette that opened this book makes abundantly clear; and they share its values willy-nilly. One of the homeless, a woman named Joyce Brown, even became a kind of celebrity when she fought back against the orders of the Mayor of New York, which interfered with her "right" to live on the sidewalk of New York's Second Avenue, next to a hot air vent.[4] The homeless, then, are victims; but some of them are also consumers of the modern legal culture.

The long-term trends in legal culture have increased the consciousness of right, the sense of entitlement. This creates new situations, new constellations of events, new trends and movements; and some of these are costly (in dollar terms), as well as socially problematic. One of the problematics is the liability crisis (so-called).[5] Personal injury damages, it is alleged, have increased tremendously, to the point where they are causing social damage. Juries have awarded huge sums of money, which thoroughly frightens some observers, some businessmen, and some insurance companies. A city bus crashes into pedestrians, a drug produces unexpected side-effects, a doctor bungles an operation, a lawyer blows a lawsuit—all of these can touch off litigation, perhaps more easily than before, and sometimes in areas of law where behavior was once immune to legal attack. Millions of dollars change hands, insurance rates skyrocket, business incentives (perhaps) are impaired. Litigation brings to a halt the whole asbestos industry. We also hear about defensive medicine, gynecologists shutting up shop, cities abandoning playgrounds, ski resorts going out of business, all because of the liability crisis.

There is, in short, a sense of unease, and a literature of invective and critique, over the ubiquitous legal effects flowing from the general expectation of justice, the idealization of choice and consent, and the removal of historic barriers to legal liability.[6] In newspapers, magazines, legal journals, and on television one reads and hears, over and over again, about an overlawyered, overlitigating, rights-mad, sick society. These criticisms are by no means confined to the United States,[7] though they are probably most virulent there, and the United States seems to be by far the worst example.

The problems are certainly real. Modern legal culture does have consequences, for good and for evil. Lawsuits—even civil rights cases—are a blunt instrument, often misused. When the courtroom opens its doors to the injured, to victims, to oppressed and subordinated groups, to underdogs in general, inevitably some of the people who make use of new rights are undeserving. Some plaintiffs are bound to be mistaken or misguided—cranks, blackmailers, paranoid schizophrenics, stubborn or obsessive nuisances. In San Francisco's federal district court (according to the *San Francisco Chronicle*), the judges compiled a "blacklist" of chronic litigators, whose persistent, groundless lawsuits were to be thrown out of court without further ado. One prize specimen on the list was a prison inmate who once "sued because he got a banana for dessert instead of fruit cocktail."[8]

Excesses—if they are excesses—are, of course, deplorable. Some of them may be nothing but newspaper exaggerations. The rest are inescapable side-effects of the revolution in legal culture. An open and expansive system of justice, in an age of expressive individualism, is a natural development; it is also a luxury good, precious but costly. Society, some think, cannot afford this luxury in a period of tight budgets and fierce, international competition for business. Something must be done about the liability system; it must be trimmed, chastened, curbed. Justice, like everything else, is a commodity which cannot be supplied in infinite amounts; there is a limit somewhere. Has the limit been reached? Some people say yes.

The criticism has had an impact; many American states, for example, have passed laws to reform or limit lawsuits against doctors, municipalities, or manufacturers. Other societies have avoided a good deal of the issue through a different style of control over products, or a different style of compensation. European countries tend to regulate harder and to pay more comprehensive benefits; tort recoveries, however, are much less generous. The American tort system is highly individualistic; and also more diffuse and decentralized. A tort system regulates business, in a way; but the "regulator" is a shifting, thousand-headed deity, one that can change into a mouse or a swan or an elephant at will, and be different things in different places.

The American system is therefore open to the charge that it is chaotic, inefficient, and produces annoying, harmful disincentives. This criticism has merit. But the critics focus exclusively on problems and costs; in their litany of complaints they ignore the *benefits* of litigation and liability. These benefits, to be sure, are subtle and do not easily translate into dollar terms; but they are unquestionably real.[9] There is, to begin with, the benefit of social justice itself, as people define it. If civil rights litigation produces a more just society in any respect, how can we put a price tag on this benefit? Members of a community with a sense of right, a sense of entitlement, who do not feel left out or oppressed, are less likely to be rebellious, disaffected, deviant; they have a stake in society. This is a good, whether or not we have factored it into our cost-benefit analysis. At the same time, the republic of choice does *not* make everyone happy, does not treat everyone fairly; in some ways, it is particularly cruel to its victims. Real deprivation, together with the gap between aspiration and achievement, fill up the camps of disaffected citizens. But critics of modern legal culture are more concerned with the excesses than with the shortfalls, which they tend to ignore.

These critics also generally lack a sense of context, of historical development. They rail against the culture without seriously trying to understand it. Expressive individualism, the general expectation of justice, claims-consciousness, the welfare state, the pervasiveness of law—these phenomena are linked; they have been a long time growing; they are not pathologies, errors, miscalculations, or random noise in the system; least of all are they the outcome of a lawyers' plot. Whatever their impact and side-effects, they are deeply anchored in public consciousness; they arise out of concrete social movements, reflect concrete historical trends, and cannot be dismissed with the wave of a hand. Nor will scolding and whining diminish them.

The core notion, the heart of the new legal culture, is the attitude that gives primacy to the concept of individual choice. I have argued that the primacy of choice—however crude, unformed, and internally inconsistent—is a ruling theme in modern society; many transformations in law and in authority systems can be read as glosses on this single basic text. For great multitudes of men and women, it is current scripture that human beings are or should be free agents. Each person deserves the right to choose whether to live or die, how to live, and how to die; the right to choose the roads to travel, the thoughts to hold or express, the jobs, ideas, and religions to pursue, the clothes to wear, the food to eat, the partners to have sex with, the family patterns to follow, and so on. All ought to be open to selection by individuals—as open as the choice of this or that brand of soup or soap in the supermarket just around the corner.

Indeed, members of the middle class in the West in the 1980s tend to think of themselves in ways that this homely metaphor rather neatly captures. They aim to go through life like shoppers in some cosmic department store, pushing a gigantic shopping cart, picking items at will off the endless shelves. The metaphor applies, as we have seen, even to choices in such crucial and personal matters as sex, religion, and mode of life; indeed, with special force in these areas. The supermarket is also a sex shop, a shopping center for religions, a fashion emporium, and a career fair, all at once. And, one might add, a kind of people's court.

In classical legal theory, the concept of "right" was always balanced by the concept of duty; one man's right was another man's duty; in theory, then, the creation of rights always implied the creation of fresh duties.[10] But "rights" and "duties" in *actual* legal systems are asymmetrically distributed; the trend, in modern law, is to impose duties on government and large institutions. The bearers of rights are individuals. To some observers, this asymmetry is not only illogical; it is downright harmful or unethical. The expansion of legal liability (in tort, for example), and the rise of programs of social insurance, whatever their virtues, produce moral laxity—a softness of soul, a flight from duty, an erosion of personal responsibility. "Rights" are expanded, but "duties" (of individuals) contract. Expressive individualism turns into selfishness and narcissism. Everybody looks out for number one; nobody cares for numbers two through *n*. One American citizen, writing an indignant letter to the newspaper, put the finger of blame on lawsuits. The litigation mania had converted the United States into a "place where one can never, ever, be responsible for one's actions . . . Everything bad that happens is always someone else's fault. And if the jury laughs your case right out of court, like it should, sue them, or your lawyer, or the judge."[11]

There is of course a grain of truth in this jeremiad. Choice and responsibility do not balance each other off logically or legally, as right and duty did in legal theory; nor do they stand in balance socially, that is, in the real world. More choice does not produce more responsibility on the *individual* level. On the level of larger entities, it does. Expanded liability in tort does reflect, as it must, modern legal culture, in particular individualism, the primacy of choice, and the general expectation of justice. But when bad things happen to us that are *not* our choice and cannot be laid at our door, it *is* necessary for some outside agency or institution to "take responsibility"; justice requires, in short, some recompense, some adjustment, some legal recourse.

In ordinary language, the word "responsible" has two quite different senses.[12] It refers both to causation and to consequence. If I do something that causes an accident, then I am "responsible" for that accident. I was the agency that brought it about. But "responsible" also refers to duties to pay or atone for an accident, whether I caused it or not. A parent may thus be "responsible" when a child accidentally breaks a vase in a china shop. Modern law in the welfare state tends to guarantee responsibility in the second sense; it elides or downgrades responsibility in the first, casual sense.

It is a common human failing (at any rate, a *modern* failing) to disclaim responsibility. When things go wrong we tend to "blame the other guy." But blaming has a vital social role, precisely because it deflects and avoids responsibility in the second sense of shouldering the consequences. Blaming does not deny the *idea* of responsibility (in either sense); it merely denies that some particular problem is my responsibility; often this is because some evil that occurred did not follow from my free-choice acts. Of course, I and I alone decided to walk on that street where I slipped on the ice. But I did not choose to fall; breaking a leg was certainly not my idea; I do not think of myself as "responsible." But some other person or institution *must* be, at least indirectly, responsible. "Responsibility" is a gapless whole. That is the heart of what I have called the general expectation of justice: modern society defines justice as the fulfillment of expectations, and these include recompense of some sort for calamities that were not my choice or my fault.

No doubt the thought patterns underlying these expectations are incoherent, inconsistent, and irrational. But irrational thought is as much a social reality as rational, systematic thought, and a lot more common. Popular culture is not a fine-tuned philosophical system. It has its logic, and it hangs together, but the chains of reason that link it do not meet professional standards. Its patterns and regularities do, however, leave their prints on every institution in society.

Right or Left? And Male or Female?

In this book I have tried to avoid flights into the normative or political. My general aim has been to *describe* social phenomena, not to evaluate them. Of course, pure neutrality is not really possible; moreover, an author's views of the world, the mental and cultural frame through which he looks, limit his awareness; it is impossible to wipe away all preconceptions and stereotypes. But objectivity is a decent goal, even if it is ultimately beyond our reach. No housecleaner can get at every speck of dust, every bit of dirt; "clean" and "dirty," then, are relative, not absolute terms, but does anyone think they are meaningless?

I have honestly tried to look at legal culture coolly, objectively. No doubt I have fallen short. Some of my earlier work on legal culture has been criticized as biased; the criticism came not from the right, where I expected it, but from the left, where I (perhaps naively) did not. One critic, for example, spoke of "complacency."[13] I admired the status quo (he felt), admired Western welfare states and what they have done, their freedom, tolerance, and wealth. And this was bad because it ignored the seamy underside of the West: racism, sexism, the hopelessness of the underclass, the disintegration of the cities, the collapse of family life, the mindless consumerism, and so on. I confused aspiration—for justice, for civil liberties, for individual autonomy—with actual achievement, and glossed over things that have gone totally awry.

No such sins were intended, and perhaps no such sins were committed. But I am aware the same line of criticism might be leveled at this book. My defense is quite simple. These pages deal with legal culture, among other things. They deal—speculatively, on the whole—with what some segments of the public think about law and authority, and how they respond to these. It is a book about consciousness and its behavioral consequences. The consciousness may be false; whether it is so in fact is by no means crucial to the argument. I leave this to the reader to judge. In all countries there is a depressing gap between aspiration and achievement—how large a gap is in dispute. This book has been about aspirations, their origins, their manifestations, and the legal forms they take; it has been less concerned with actual achievements or results. These are ignored not because they do not matter, but because they are not what the book is about.

My own assessment, I freely admit, tends to be guardedly positive. I confess I like many of the achievements, including legal achievements. Like most in the middle class, I like open societies and the republic of choice. I concede, as I must, the vast problems, the contradictions, the failures. Perhaps scholars who look at society historically or comparatively tend to be calmer, less militant, less relentless than those who look at society synchronically. *These* people see society's failures starkly, in all the dreadful clarity of here and now. Historians or comparativists see the failings, but consciously or unconsciously, they may measure their own times against societies which were or are worse; they may therefore end up too tolerant and appreciative of their own period and place. Furthermore, this book is an attempt to explain modern law and modern authority systems.

Explanation often sounds like forgiveness, and sometimes perhaps it *is*—either forgiveness or resignation. And in fact I do prefer the present (for all its deficiencies) to the past; we *live* in the present, and it is the only world we have.

I have an underlying bias which leads me to think that the world makes the mind, on the whole, not vice versa. I do not believe in disembodied consciousness. Modern society is in large part the result of real events, notably events of technology and discovery. The crucible of context forms the modern mind. The world is more than words, more than symbols, more than "interpretations of texts." The consciousness of mobility, for example, or of choice itself, cannot be *wholly* illusory. People may be sitting in caves watching shadows, but though shadows are not the same as *things*, neither are they wholly imaginary; they reflect, systematically, the objects that cast them. The interpretation of shadows cannot be divorced completely from the thing or text to be interpreted. And the *modes* of interpreting range within boundaries that are certainly not random, nor autonomous and self-contained. They are socially produced. These are assumptions, at least, on which this book rests, for better or for worse.

I want to add a word about gender issues. Discussions of gender are scattered about the book like raisins in a cake; they are not often at center stage. The core thesis is about legal culture and its relationship with modern individualism. Men have dominated every society discussed, past and present; they dominate still. Does legal culture vary systematically by gender? Almost certainly it does. Whose legal culture is expressive individualism? Is it predominantly the culture of *men*, rather than women? Possibly it is. A culture of rights, autonomy, privacy, and entitlement may be more of a male than a female culture, for one reason or another. Carol Gilligan has criticized the literature on character formation and moral development; it reflects (she says) male standpoints and values, emphasizing the "morality of rights and noninterference," and celebrating "separation, autonomy, individuation, and natural rights." If the literature paid more attention to women and girls, it would notice a different "voice," one that stresses "morality of responsibility" and "the continuing importance of attachment in the human life cycle."[14]

The Gilligan thesis, which has been much discussed, has intriguing implications for the themes of this book. Legal culture indeed varies along the lines of personality;[15] and personality, character structure, and culture in turn surely vary along gender lines—perhaps the very lines Gilligan suggests. But I suspect that the legal cultures of women and men have traveled along parallel tracks, though they may have started from different baselines. In other words, women today may be *more* expressively individual, *more* rights-conscious, *more* concerned with autonomy and choice than in the past, even if they speak in voices not quite the same as the dark-toned voices of men.

Indeed, feminism itself, in a number of its variants and in the very act of denouncing the republic of choice, pays tribute to it and reveals its inner allegiance; just as fundamentalism, while denouncing the modern world and all of its works, is inescapably its product. At the core of grass-roots feminism are two positions: a vigorous refusal to accept a subordinate position in society; and an insistence on the woman's right to choose her own path, whether it looks like a man's path or not. If a woman chooses woman's distinctive voice, role and sensibilities, then society must grant that voice, role, and sensibilities equal value, equal legitimacy, equal space. Nothing could be more consonant with themes of the republic of choice.

A Note on Theories and Methods

I began this book with a statement of broad, general theory: I put forward the assumption that legal systems are not autonomous but reflect social norms or dominant social opinion. This means, among other things, that general legal culture *makes* the law, at least in some ultimate sense. Almost on every page of this book I have argued, or assumed, that social configurations—including what people want and expect out of law—explain configurations of law.

It is easy to translate this assumption into the misleading assertion that the source of modern law is something called "public opinion." The assertion can be defended, but this is hardly worth doing, because the phrase "public opinion" is so easily distorted, so apt to be misunderstood. No one can deduce the shape of the law on, say, civil rights, or abortion, from the findings of the usual sort of opinion poll. Researchers constantly turn up "gaps" between lay values, expectations, and opinions, and the state of "the law."[16]

These gaps may also bedevil some of the arguments presented in this book. To take one example: criminal justice is full of second chances: many of its institutions—probation is one—go easy on first offenders; a number of states do not permit capital punishment, and the courts seem to disfavor it strongly. "The public" is not by any means so keen on second chances. Polls show huge majorities in favor of the death penalty, and people seem to want tougher policies with regard to crime: lock these evil people up and throw away the key.

Does a gap of this kind cast doubt on the general thesis of this book—first, about the nature of law; and second, about the relationship between (assumed) popular culture, and the legal arrangements that flow out of it? Not necessarily. In the first place, this book sets out an argument about movements and trends—a slipping and sliding in this direction, a creeping in that direction, tugs and bunches at the margins of measurements. As I have said a number of times, each example has a counterexample, each trend, a countertrend; yet these do not overthrow the general argument. Compared to a century ago, the death penalty may have weakened its grip on the system because of a drift in legal culture. Very likely this is so.

There is also the problem of method: how to ferret out legal culture. Survey research is *not* a reliable guide. The forces that make up living law are too subtle for that. Polls do not reflect real opinion, to begin with, but only expressed opinion; they leave out factors of power, social structure, and intensity of view. A half-hearted yes counts the same as a militant yes, in most polls. The yes of a rich and powerful banker counts the same as the yes of a welfare mother.[17] Moreover, the questions asked simply are not—and cannot be—situational enough. Most people believe in the death penalty, if you ask them point blank, but this does not necessarily predict how the *system* will deal with capital punishment—how juries, prosecutors, judges, and others will behave in concrete instances. If we knew everything about social norms, their meaning and their intensity, and about social structure, in theory we *could* predict the shape of the law; every last jot and tittle. As it is, I can only estimate, interpret, and infer.

The Wider World

American experience, American culture, have been at the center of my argument. But the *logic* of the argument extends to the whole Western world. Each country has its own special version, its peculiarities of culture and structure. It is easy to ignore the forest because there are too many different trees, vines, underbrush, air plants, shrubs. But above and beyond the jungle of idiosyncrasies there is, I believe, a general line or trend that holds good throughout the West.

Where possible, I have brought in examples from other Western countries. My own ignorance and parochialism have prevented full use of the treasure-house of European experience.

I have deliberately sidestepped the experience of Third-World countries, and countries of the Socialist bloc. Of course, these are important societies, and becoming more so. But to add them to the narrative would increase the complexity and strain the limits of the argument. The Socialist countries present special data problems, while the developing countries have their social, cultural, and historical peculiarities and call for skills and knowledge which few scholars in developed countries have at their fingertips. These countries are certainly not immune to global trends, but they need subtle, careful, full-length treatment on their own.

The West, and developed countries in general, exhibit many cross-cultural differences in law, legal culture, and authority systems. To take one specific point of comparison: Americans are much more likely than Australians to bring lawsuits for personal injury;[18] Australians are more likely to sue than the English, who in turn are more likely to sue than the Japanese. How much of this is pure culture, and how much should be ascribed to legal structures and rules of law that encourage or discourage lawsuits? It is hard to say. The Japanese system sets up obstacles to tort litigation; English law does not permit lawyers to work on the basis of contingent fees, and this rule may choke off lawsuits. But culture and structure are after all intertwined and interrelated; structure is the long-run bony residue of culture.

Moreover, cultural differences tend to reinforce themselves. A legal culture does not come out of thin air; it is the product of socialization and social learning. People in society take their institutions for granted; they think of them as natural and inevitable, when they think of them at all. Behavior and attitudes are molded by the context into which people are born, and which they accept for want of an alternative. To be sure, tremendous forces also pull in the opposite direction—television, for one, with its amazing capacity for leveling cultures and for unteaching and unlearning ethnicities. But structures and differences persist. This is not inconsistent with the existence of the republic of choice, at the level of conscious expectations. People are aware of choices they have, or could have; they tend to be unaware of the *limits* on choice, insofar as the limits are imposed by cultural and structural postulates which are below the conscious level, or which they take for granted.

A culture, including a legal culture, is always embedded in a mosaic of microcontexts; these affect legal behavior, as they do everything else. The study of national and community differences is a study of these microcontexts and their impact on attitudes and behaviors. Herbert Kritzer, for example, offers an intriguing suggestion about one striking disparity between American and British legal culture. Why are Americans much more eager and willing to sue than the British? In the British welfare system, he points out, those who use the National Health Service "never even see a bill, and seldom have to make direct payments, for medical treatment." In the United States most people have some health insurance plan, but under such plans "reimbursement is not automatic; one must submit claims." Consequently, "claiming" has come to be "a very routine part of everyday American life." This habit, perhaps, has "washed over" into the "adversarial context."[19]

The very notion of individualism, however, implies a certain amount of assertiveness. Modern individualism posits, as a goal, developing the self to its maximum potential. Success is important, but even success is an intensely personal state; it is not something that can be seen, felt, and measured objectively. Success is meeting individual goals. If you cannot win the race, you can aim at least for a "personal best." Witness, in recent years, the amazing proliferation of sports and athletic events in which there are no teams, where "winning" hardly matters. Thousands of people of all ages, sexes, and sizes, run in the Boston marathon. For all but a handful of them there is no question of winning; it is victory and success just to cross the finish line.

We can define success however we want to. We can choose to be monks, or nuns, or drop-outs; beachcombers, or high-school teachers; we can select our individual trajectories. Precisely this point distinguishes modern individualism from its nineteenth-century ancestor. "Success" in the nineteenth century was a monochrome, not a rainbow. General norms defined and described it, not individual choices. It is in *modern* society, in contrast, where people can march to their own private drummers. Modern society, as a result, is curiously ambivalent about success and its analogs. The social order is, on the one hand, intensely competitive; on the other hand, it is more liberal than most past societies in allowing people to craft and shape goals for themselves, to develop *private* definitions of success. And failure too, for that matter.

The themes discussed in this book do vary from culture to culture in significant ways. Claims-consciousness and assertiveness certainly do. They vary because of differences in legal structure, in national traditions, in the state of technology—in cultural, economic, and political factors. It is a scholarly task of enormous value to explore these differences, as Kritzer did in his essay. Another good example of such an exploration is Cohen-Tanugi's provocative book about the contrast between French legal culture—highly centralized, statist, and deeply suspicious of judges—and American legal culture, strongly decentralized and favoring the market, individual enterprise, and judge-made law.[20] Similarly, Mary Ann Glendon, in a recent book on abortion and divorce in Western law, finds American law on these subjects "extreme" and "unique" in the Western world.[21]

Undeniably, national cultures, if not national character, are social facts. American society has always struck European visitors as peculiarly different; arguably American exceptionalism goes back to the beginning of the Republic, or even earlier.[22] But there are also great differences within the European cluster of nations—England versus the Continent, Germany versus the Romance-speaking countries, north against south, and so on. Japanese exceptionalism is legendary. Nonetheless, the *similarities* among developed countries are many, persistent, and striking.[23] This book has been mainly concerned with similarities and convergences that exist above and beyond all peculiarities and localisms. What I have essayed is an explanation for some of the master trends in authority and law.

The argument—or suggestion—is that Western societies, though they leave from different ports and travel at different speeds, are ships sailing in one general direction. What may be true as to men and women, may be so for societies as well; the trends are the same, but the baselines are not. Suing or making claims of right—to take one example—is an extreme form of behavior. Most people, even when sorely provoked, do not rush to the nearest lawyer and insist on litigation to the death. Most people go to great lengths to avoid trouble, disputes, litigation. In this book, I tried to build a case about attitudes toward law and authority. Western legal culture, in comparison to others, has a highly expressive and individualistic baseline. Citizens are more conscious of rights and entitlements. But consciousness does not translate automatically into anything so drastic as suing. Many other factors are involved in such decisions: cultural, structural, economic. Suing is at one end or pole of a continuum of behaviors. Presumably, more Americans than Belgians or Japanese will cluster at that end, in some specific situation. Presumably, too, American legal culture is more supportive of litigation, and legal structures are supportive as well. But the Western societies seem to be traveling on parallel escalators, each rising to the next stage or floor, carried along by the same motive force, but starting on different levels or stages of the building.

Not everybody in society shares the behaviors and attitudes described. They are *tendencies* that need not be typical of the whole population. Modern individualism has not driven out other forms of individualism, but modern forms do seem widely diffused in American society; perhaps not *quite* so widely diffused in other Western countries. These matters are hard to pin down in survey research, and that research is skimpy at best.

Moreover, *small* differences in extreme personality traits, or their distribution, can have a major impact on society even when those traits are fairly rare. The way people raise children (or, perhaps, the way children raise themselves in the TV age) may result in more syndromes of nastiness, even criminal traits. But, as is obvious, most people escape these consequences: they do not murder, rob, and rape. Violent criminality is extreme behavior, based on extreme attitudes. These attitudes are probably uncommon in society, but as I pointed out earlier, an increase from 1 percent to 2 percent would double the crime rate, and society would surely notice. A handful of terrorists can produce a crisis; three handfuls can throw a whole society into turmoil, even though 99.9 percent of the population abhors terror and rejects all its uses.

Similarly, a society might seem claims-conscious, even though most citizens are meek and passive and accept their lot. If we double a (small) rate of claims, the results can easily look like an absolute epidemic of claims. The same is true, of course, of litigation, which is one form of asserting a claim. We need broad, careful research on both attitudes and conduct. Without it, it is impossible to know the distribution of traits and behaviors within the population, to compare societies, establish trends from the past, or extrapolate into the future.

Although the discussion has been largely confined to the Western world, I do not rule out the idea of global trends. Trends of this kind surely exist. One theme is globalism itself—the pervasive, growing universal culture. Every country is linked to every other country, directly or indirectly; there is a single world economy; when one country sneezes, the others catch cold; there are no hermit kingdoms any longer, or forbidden cities.[24] Traditional societies and native cultures are changing rapidly all over the world; many seem to be in the process of disintegration. Preliterate cultures are vanishing rapidly; anthropologists, as if fleeing a flood, have been driven to the high ground of the cities, in order to continue their work. The decay of the local, the native, the tribal, is often laid at the door of Western influence. But why is the West so influential? Is it simply the money and the power? Is it imperialism, or something more? Is it the toys of technology? Why is Western culture—the blue jeans, the rock music—so tremendously narcotic?

But first one may ask: how Western is modern Western culture? What we call the West is a motley collection of peoples and countries from Iceland to Israel. Each people of the West has a history, each comes out of some traditional past. The crowds on the streets of Rome, Paris, London, or Berlin rush blindly past the graves of their own indigenous experience. Western culture is a deathhouse of tradition. Quaint bits survive here and there—wooden shoes in Holland, kilts in Scotland, a few odd songs, poems, holidays; these remind us of departed tribalisms, old worlds ruthlessly extinguished by whatever it is we call the modernizing process.

What happened to these fossil cultures? What killed them off? Some strands in social science—in anthropology in particular—stress the tightness and persistence of culture. We are warned of the primacy of traditional norms. The human animal, and its behavior, cannot be fathomed, outside of the particular cultures or groups into which those animals are sorted. People are less atomistic, rational, self-made, less individualized than many of them think. The scholars stress durability, continuity—the cultural, the traditional, the non-rational, the symbolic, the web of inherited meanings. There is power and truth in these assertions. Some elements of culture (language is one) are indeed tough, autonomous, and resistant to change. Other elements of culture seem able to survive, to adapt, to remain compatible with modernization, like hardy plants that grow through cracks in the sidewalk. Alex Inkeles remarks that "industrialization and Westernization . . . drove the Japanese businessman out of his kimono into the Western business suit, but not out of the geisha house."[25] Still other elements of traditional culture live on as options, chosen, as we have seen, as free-standing elements of personality—

the Japanese still eat sushi, indeed, they have lent it to the rest of the world. But hamburgers are also popular in Tokyo.

This is one side of the story. There is another. Some elements of culture have proven quite fragile and mutable, as delicate as a butterfly's wings. "Modernization," as Inkeles and Smith have argued, is a powerful force which sweeps away rivals that get in its way.[26] A lot of inherited culture melts away like snowflakes in the sun. Coca-Cola, pizza, T-shirts, transistor radios, popular music, TV cop shows are somehow more seductive, more powerful, than the costumes, customs, and foods they supplant, and which disintegrate at the touch.

Certainly no single key solves the riddle of modernization, or explains the power of "Western" culture. In one sense perhaps there is less to the puzzle than meets the eye. It is not "the West" that is overpowering traditional cultures, but modernization itself—the tremendous force which first invaded the West, then conquered it; and whose armies are now enlarging their empire throughout the inhabited world. Technological imperatives and other forces of social change ultimately manufactured modern Swedes and Danes out of primitive Nordic tribes. Today the process of change occurs on a global scale and is undoubtedly more ruthless and rapid; this may be because the *instruments* are infinitely more powerful—technology sweeps on like a whirlwind; transport and communications bridge the whole world, and more, in seconds.

The mass media in particular have a lot to answer for in destroying cultural diversity and creating a kind of world system. The messages carried on radio and television reach into the home powerfully and directly. The media insidiously weaken and then destroy the local and the traditional. They undermine established authority, insofar as that authority depends on isolation, on the strength of primary groups. Television, radio, and movies wreak havoc among native cultures; they ravage societies like the measles, smallpox, and other diseases which Europeans brought to traditional societies.

Traditional societies are local societies. Power is defined within a small, bounded circle. Local and traditional cultures are face-to-face cultures. They depend on the primary group. What is remote and unseen is an enemy—or a God. Radio, television, and movies foster or create horizontal groups—groups far apart in space, with no face-to-face contact, but with similar interests and demands. Without the media, such groups could not organize themselves, at least not easily.

On the whole, such groups did not exist before modern times. Culture and ideas traveled slowly, spread by conquest, or did not travel at all.

Politically, central governments gain power when society reshapes itself horizontally; local governments, local power-centers lose. Horizontal groups do not necessarily vote or exert their pressure in compact groups and contiguous localities; they are geographically and socially diffuse; they gravitate, politically, toward the unifying core, the center from which messages radiate, the metropole. The President or Prime Minister is the natural leader, the orientation point, of horizontal groups. Not surprisingly, then, horizontal and peer cultures are compatible with dictatorship in Third World countries—one-party rule from the center. Tribalism remains a powerful force in these countries, but it is eroded by intermarriage, political centralization, Western culture, urbanization. The horizontal organization of personal life may be the force that, in the long run, does the most to weaken local authority and local culture. Television programs are broadcast in national languages; local dialects and speechways are reduced to mere patois without prestige or importance. The media flatten out and trivialize the decaying tribalisms; they proclaim, instead, a new hegemony, a new system of authority, culture, and law—the kingdom (if not the republic) of choice.

These kingdoms are not, of course, monolithic, nor do they necessarily achieve their centralizing goals. Cultural pluralism and ethnic diversity remain strong in the Third World, at least for now. Lipset has commented on how sociologists failed to predict the survival of ethnic, religious, and national conflict. These were supposed to wither away, under the leveling impact of modernization, and as the one-world culture spread. The giant engine of social change was expected to assimilate minorities, inexorably, into a "larger integrated whole."[27] Instead, all over the world, people bomb, murder, terrorize, and make war in the name of some faith, tribe, nation, or group.

There is no simple explanation for these depressing facts. The war between Iran and Iraq, the strife in Northern Ireland, the uprising in the Gaza strip, the tribal massacre in Burundi or in Sri Lanka—all have particular causes. A number of these conflicts have roots that go back centuries in time; some rest on ancient grievances, festering for generations. But why has modernization failed to mitigate these grievances?

No doubt it has, in some places. The Swiss, a model of peaceful pluralism, the very paragons of bourgeois success, were once quite willing to hack each other to death. But, more generally, modern culture does not imply a reign of world peace. "Tribalisms" will realign, but will not go extinct. In a kingdom or republic of choice, strong differences in personal identification do not or need not level out. Quite the opposite: choice and expressive individualism tend to destroy tribal *custom*, but tribal *identity* survives. (I use "tribe" here in an expanded sense, defined as ethnic identity; in this sense there are "tribes" in France and the United States, as well as in Botswana.) A person in our mobile world can erase most or even all of his tribal identity, through conscious choice,[28] but he can also choose to exalt it or rediscover it. He can raise it to a higher level of intensity, just as adherents of born-again religions—*chosen* religions—can burn with a flame more intense than adherents of casual, traditional, or inherited religion. Fundamentalist Islam, Palestinian nationality, or militant Afro-American identity are, in a real sense, deep passions that modernity makes possible, even though nationalists or fundamentalists reject modernity or limit its effects.

Modernism, including expressive individualism, is the natural breeding ground for all sorts of liberation movements. It has been a fairy godmother, blessing oppressed races and minorities, inviting them to throw off their chains; it has also been the wicked witch breeding violent, fanatical movements. Modern individualism, at its core, rejects passive acceptance of fate, a soft acquiescence in one's given life-station. It fosters pluralism, and at the same time, carried to extremes, it can destroy the ethical basis on which a plural society rests. Even at its best, it requires a delicate balance. That balance, alas, is not easily achieved or easily kept.

Appendix
Notes
Index

Appendix. Social Meanings of Key Terms

This appendix briefly touches on the social meanings of four key terms: law, authority, personality, and culture.

Law

Every society or community in human history has had hierarchy, structure, authority. This seems to be inherent in human groups, communities and societies, whether they are tiny ones (like the nuclear family), or enormous aggregations joined politically, like the United States of America. Every society, community, or group must have some way of governing itself, some way of making decisions, some organization (however vague) that can be described in terms of leadership and authority. Of course modes of governing differ tremendously from society to society, and the hand of "government" can be heavy or light—sometimes, in some small groups, and in some simple societies, so light and silky as not to seem like "government" at all.

Does every human society also have "law"? This question has touched off a certain debate among legal scholars. The answer seems to depend on how the word is defined. It is clear enough that large and complicated groupings—countries like Austria or France—have aspects of polity which are conventionally referred to as "law" or "the legal system." These features are not to be found in the ordinary small family, except in a kind of metaphorical sense ("Mother's word is law").

Arguably, too, there is no "law" in very simple societies, past and present—hunters and gatherers, nomadic tribesmen of various cultures, and the like. Some of these societies lack courts, judges, police, lawyers, or any of the obvious mechanisms for making and enforcing rules. Yet E. Adamson Hoebel has argued that Eskimos, and other stateless societies, nonetheless have "law."[1] By this he means that they have norms or rules, and ways of getting them enforced.

There are basically two ways to approach the definition of law. One way emphasizes rule-making and rule-applying, functions which are (at least theoretically) aspects of any known group. In this sense, there is "law" in every tribe or society and even inside a small family: father and mother make "rules" for their children, and enforce these rules.

There is nothing intrinsically wrong with this approach. For some purposes it can be very fruitful—for example, in studying group behavior. But for other purposes it is useful to distinguish between a public and a private sphere—between "the state" or "government," and the private sector.[2] Max Weber described the state as an institution that possesses the "monopoly" of use of force, that is, legitimate violence. [3] This "public," institutional aspect of law is the one which on the whole this book emphasizes—though not to the total exclusion of "law" in the broader sense.

Still another way to separate law from non-law is to focus on the level of *formality*. Rules inside a family tend to be informal. Nobody has ever written them down; there is no list of regulations, no code, no book of laws. Furthermore, "procedures" and "process" within the family will almost certainly be ad hoc and irregular. State law, on the whole, is more formal than "private" law: it has written rules, regular procedures, and a sense of fixity, permanence, and pattern.

Nonetheless, the distinction between formal and informal is blurred and difficult. A corporate personnel department—part of the "private" sphere—can be as formal as any government bureaucracy. Within any bureaucracy, too, state or private, informal practices abound—norms and patterns of behavior not covered or contemplated by official rule-books. Informal processes are pervasive in society. The sociology of legal and administrative systems takes the informal as a major theme—authority and rules which do not follow official lines; or which operate on the basis of broad discretion.[4]

Many legal systems—systems everybody thinks of as legal—are largely informal, or have highly informal elements. This is not true only of simple societies. In Western societies, too, local justice, justice at the bottom of the social ladder, tends to be informal, paternalistic.[5] Nonetheless, "law" in complex societies has a distinct and important formal element; this element distinguishes it from processes which, though they follow rules, lack any element of formality.

Authority

Law, however defined, is obviously a facet of authority. But law and authority are by no means identical. Many kinds of authority have no legal status, and do not work through law; indeed, some forms of authority stand in contrast to law, or in opposition to law—the authority of a religious leader, in modern secular societies; the authority of leaders of rebels, or gangs, or organized crime. The precise relationship between law and forms of authority in a given society is usually quite complicated. Only in very simple societies does it make sense to treat law and authority as basically the same.

A person in authority is a person in power. But authority (as people use the term) means more than power. Authority is *legitimate* power, at least in part. It is power that is institutionalized[6] and backed by a theory of rightness.[7] Indeed, the theory, very likely, is the actual source of the power. A man with a gun has power but no authority, even though he can make other people do what he wants. On the other hand, there are leaders who command great armies, who make thousands do their bidding, without guns, force, or any physical means of enforcing their will. Authority surrounds them and gives them strength. In point of fact, the permanence and survival of any society—or, at any rate, its governing structures—depend on some mix of force and authority. Authority is basic.

It is also, at times, somewhat mysterious. Authority, as we have described it, is obviously linked to the concept of legitimacy; it refers, essentially, to a mode of *entitlement* to power. One of the great themes of social theory, as one would expect, is authority, its types and its sources. Weber described three "ultimate principles" of justification or legitimacy.[8] Two of these rest on "personal authority." The authority of a tribal chief, for example, or of a hereditary king, is founded on "the sacredness of tradition," that is, "that which is customary and has always been so and prescribes obedience to some particular person." Secondly, there is authority which flows from "charisma"; Weber defined this as "actual revelation or grace resting in . . . a savior, a prophet, or a hero." Charismatic authority is in some ways the polar opposite of traditional authority: it is the authority of the unprecedented, the magical, the impact of some remarkable and unique personality. Charisma, in Weber's sense, is a rare and almost miraculous trait; it is nonetheless of great historical significance.

The third principle is legitimacy "expressed . . . in a system of consciously made *rational* rules." The subject obeys "the norms rather than . . . the person." This phrase of Weber's immediately brings to mind the slogan, "a government of laws and not of men," so often used to describe one of the ideals underlying modern democracy. This third, impersonal form of authority, rational-legal in nature, is the type which (relatively speaking) is dominant in modern times and the modern world. In Western democracies at least, this principle is built into the structure of government, replacing more personal forms of authority. Law has supplanted the prophets and the kings.

In some ways rational-legal authority is the most troublesome of the three Weberian types. To a certain extent, it is a catch-all, a residual category—that form of authority left over once the traditional and the charismatic are subtracted. Nonetheless, the idea captures at least one element of the modern state. Government today is formal, bureaucratic, legalistic; it is rational and instrumental, at least compared to most historical forms of government. It is committed to rules, to legal processes;[9] it rejects the personalism of its predecessors. Fundamentally, it rests on universal norms, rather than on the grace and favor of particular holders of power. It outlaws the arbitrary, the *ad hoc*—in theory. Reality, of course, is considerably more complex.

Authority, as Weber discussed it, was an aspect of what for want of a better term we might call government. But authority has a broader meaning as well. People obey or follow others, for a variety of reasons, and in a variety of contexts. They orient themselves toward various forms of authority—popular heroes, for example;. they want to dress, act, and sing like certain rock stars, they follow certain religious leaders, and so on.

Personality and Culture

To discuss law and authority in society implies concepts of personality and culture as well. If we claim that Americans are litigious, or that some people are passive and obedient, while others are fractious and unruly, we are talking about personality, or culture, or both.

This book assumes a common-sense view of these two subjects.

The word "personality" refers to individual variations.[10] "Culture" defines the range of these variations. For example, some people are short, others are tall. There is a great deal of variation, but it falls within a definite range. No grown-up is five inches tall or ten feet tall. "Personality" is like the degree of shortness or tallness; "culture" is like the range of possibilities. There are (to pursue the analogy) differences *between* populations as well as *within* populations; Americans are taller than Japanese, men are taller than women, on average. Modern people are taller, on average, than medieval people.

We are interested here in those aspects of personality and culture that influence attitudes and behavior with regard to authority and law. We are interested, in other words, in *legal* personality, and *legal* culture. *Legal culture* refers, as we have said, to ideas, attitudes, expectations and opinions about law, held by people in some given society.[11] It is the "network of values and attitudes . . . which determines when and why and where people turn to law or government or turn away." It is thus the "immediate source of legal change, whatever the ultimate source may be."[12] The term covers those thoughts and ideas which act as motives or incentives for "legal behavior"— behavior oriented toward or away from legal rules, legal institutions, or the uses or nonuses of law.

Similarly, one can talk about legal personalities, or legal character—that is, specific personality types or character types, defined in relationship to legal culture. After all, there is no single legal culture in our complex societies; there is instead a dizzying array of cultures. In the United States there is a legal culture of the rich and of the poor, of blacks, whites, or Asians; of steelworkers or accountants; of men, women, and children; and so on. Each society has a different mix of cultures. Corresponding to this range of cultures, there will be a range of personalities or character types. Some people are nonlitigious within a litigious culture; some are litigious within a nonlitigious culture; some are knowledgeable about law and some are ignorant, within any culture; but the median point will be differently placed in different societies. And so it goes.

Notes

1. Introduction

1. *New York Times*, Nov. 15, 1985, p. B1.

2. The literature is extensive. For representative treatments see, for example, Roger Cotterrell, *The Sociology of Law* (London: Butterworths, 1984), pp. 87–90; Richard Lempert and Joseph Sanders, *An Invitation to Law and Social Science* (White Plains, N.Y.: Longman, 1986), pp. 401–427; Gunther Teubner, "Auto-poiesis in Law and Society: A Rejoinder to Blankenburg," *Law & Society Review*, 18 (1984), 291; Niklas Luhmann, "The Self-Reproduction of Law and Its Limits," in Gunther Teubner, ed., *Dilemmas of Law in the Welfare State* (Berlin: de Gruyter, 1985), p. 111. Lempert and Sanders define an "autonomous legal system" as "one that is independent of other sources of power and authority in social life." Cotterrell, *Sociology of Law*, p. 50, distinguishes two aspects of legal autonomy. The first is its "capacity to function as an autonomous agency of social control not dependent on the support of morality or custom." In this regard, it is "merely an aspect of the apparent autonomy of the modern state," that is, the separation of state and society. The second, and primary, aspect is the extent to which legal institutions, legal systems, and legal doctrine "are autono-mous of other aspects of the state." An extreme argument for legal autonomy can be found in Alan Watson, *The Evolution of Law* (Baltimore: The Johns Hopkins University Press, 1985).

3. Lawrence M. Friedman, "Legal Culture and the Welfare State," in Teubner, ed., *Dilemmas of Law in the Welfare State*, pp. 13, 14–17.

4. On this point, see Robert W. Gordon, "Critical Legal Histories," *Stanford Law Review*, 36 (1984), 102–109.

5. For the concept of legal culture, see Lawrence M. Friedman, *The Legal System: A Social Science Perspective* (New York: Russell Sage Foundation, 1975), pp. 15–16. A related concept is "legal consciousness"; see Setsuo Miyazawa, "Taking Kawashima Seriously: A Review of Japanese Research on Japanese Legal Consciousness and Disputing Behavior," *Law & Society Review*, 21 (1987), 219.

2. Legalism and Individualism

1. The revolt of minorities might appear to be a group phenomenon, not an *individualistic* one. Of course, it has this aspect, but I will try to show, at various points in the argument, that the *individual* side is deeper and more primary.

2. On the meaning of religion in the republic of choice, see Chap. 9. The shift described in the text is, naturally, a matter of more or less. For reasons that will be later explored, the voluntarism of religion in the United States probably predates voluntarism in other countries.

3. The subject of litigation has stimulated much heated polemic, especially in the press. In addition, see Stephen D. Sugarman, "Doing Away with Tort Law," *California Law Review*, 73 (1985), 555, 581–586.

4. Richard L. Abel, "Comparative Sociology of Legal Professions: An Exploratory Essay," *American Bar Foundation Research Journal* (1985), 5, 21; on Germany, see Christoph Hommerich and Raymund Werle, "Anwaltschaft zwischen Expansionsdruck und Modernisierungszwang," *Zeitschrift für Rechtssoziologie*, 8 (June 1987), 1; on increases in the Canadian legal profession, see H. W. Arthurs, R. Weisman, and F. H. Zemans, "The Canadian Legal Profession," *American Bar Foundation Research Journal* (1986), 447, 458–459.

5. On the increase of judicial review in Germany see Brun-Otto Bryde, *Verfassungsentwicklung: Stabilität und Dynamik im Verfassungsrecht der Bundesrepublik Deutschland* (Baden-Baden: Nomos Verlagsgesellschaft, 1982).

6. See The Canada Act (chap. 11, 1982), officially terminating the rights of the British Parliament to legislate for Canada, and "patriating" the Canadian Constitution. Appended to the Act is the Canadian Charter of Rights and Freedoms; on judicial enforcement see §24(1).

7. On this general subject, see Mauro Cappelletti, *Judicial Review in the Contemporary World* (Indianapolis: Bobbs-Merrill, 1971).

8. On the problems and travails of the welfare state see, for example, Pierre Rosanvallon, *La Crise de L'etat-providence* (Paris: Seuil, 1981); Rüdiger Voigt, "Regulations Recht im Wohlfahrtsstaat," in Rüdiger Voigt, ed., *Abschied vom Recht?* (Frankfurt: Suhrkamp, 1983), p. 19. On the "crisis" of authority see Hannah Arendt, "What Was Authority?" in Carl Friedrich, ed., *Authority, Nomos,* 1 (1958), 81.

9. The law "absorbs" many more young people in America than "in any other industrialized nation; it attracts an unusually large proportion of the exceptionally gifted. Far too many of these rare individuals are becoming lawyers at a time when the country cries out for more talented business executives, more enlightened public servants, more inventive engineers, more able high school principals and teachers." Derek C. Bok, remarks to the Board of Overseers of Harvard College, reported in *Los Angeles Daily*, vol. 96 (April 27, 1983), p. 4, col. 3.

10. Ibid. For a more measured view of law and society in Japan, see Frank Upham, *Law and Social Change in Postwar Japan* (Cambridge, Mass.: Harvard University Press, 1987), esp. chap. 6.

11. On this point, see especially Lawrence M. Friedman, *Total Justice* (New York: Russell Sage Foundation, 1985), pp. 15–27; Marc Galanter, "Reading the

Landscape of Disputes: What We Know and Don't Know (and Think We Know) about Our Allegedly Contentious and Litigious Society," *UCLA Law Review*, 31 (1983), 4.

12. On Germany, see Hubert Rottleutner, "Aspekte der Rechtsentwicklung in Deutschland," *Zeitschrift für Rechtssoziologie*, 2 (Dec. 1985), 206; concerning a recent rise in litigation rates in Spain see José Juan Tohária, *¡Pleitos Tengas! Introducción a la Cultura Legal Española* (Madrid: Siglo Veintiuno de España Editores, 1987) pp. 67–96.

13. On the "colonization" point, see Jürgen Habermas, *The Theory of Communicative Action*, vol. 2, *Life World and System*, trans. Thomas McCarthy (Boston: Beacon Press, 1987), pp. 356–373; see also, for example, Axel Görlitz and Rüdiger Voigt, *Rechtspolitologie, eine Einführung* (Opladen: Westdeutscher Verlag, 1985), p. 120. The authors are speaking of "legalization," which includes the process whereby more and more areas of life are "subjected to legal regulation. The relationship between the regulated and unregulated spheres changes constantly, to the detriment of the latter." See also Gunther Teubner, "Juridification—Concepts, Aspects, Limits, Solutions," in Gunther Teubner, ed., *Juridification of Social Spheres* (Berlin: de Gruyter, 1987), pp. 3–4.

14. Kenneth I. Winston, ed., *The Principles of Social Order: Selected Essays of Lon L. Fuller* (Durham, N.C.: Duke University Press, 1981), pp. 111–113.

15. See Holt v. Sarver, 309 F.Supp. 362 (E.D. Ark. 1970). The court attacked the "entire penitentiary system" of Arkansas and held that "conditions and practices in the Penitentiary System are such that confinement therein amounts to a cruel and unusual punishment," in violation of the Constitution.

16. *New York Times*, July 26 and July 28, 1978.

17. On this point in general see Laurent Cohen-Tanugi, *Le Droit sans l'état: Sur la démocratie en France et en Amérique* (Paris: Presses Universitaires de France, 1985).

18. *London Times*, May 25, 1987, p. 13, col. 1; the editorial was headed "Empty Tables." It reported that a restaurateur, Frederick Bolingbroke, brought an action against two customers who booked for Christmas Eve and "failed to turn up." They settled out of court for £110 and £49 respectively, "following a separate case . . . in which a legal precedent was set."

3. Modernity and the Rise of the Individual

1. The literature is, of course, vast. See Alex Inkeles and David H. Smith, *Becoming Modern: Individual Change in Six Developing Countries* (Cambridge, Mass.: Harvard University Press, 1974); C. E. Black, *The Dynamics of Modernization: A Study in Comparative History* (New York: Harper and Row, 1966); Richard D. Brown, *Modernization: The Transformation of American Life, 1600–1865* (New York: Hill and Wang, 1976); see also Nathan Rosenberg and L. E. Birdzell, Jr., *How the West Grew Rich: The Economic Transformation of the Industrial World* (New York: Basic Books, 1986), which scrupulously avoids the word. On the specific meaning of "modern" in relationship to law, see Marc Galanter, "The Modernization of Law," in Myron Weiner, ed., *Modernization: The Dynamics of Growth* (New York: Basic Books, 1966), p. 153.

2. One striking example is Laurent Cohen-Tanugi, *Le Droit sans l'état* (Paris: Presses Universitaires de France, 1985), comparing France and the United States.

3. On the French view that "formal legislation . . . must suffice to yield all the rules social life may require," see Francois Gény, *Method of Interpretation and Sources of Private Positive Law*, 2d ed., trans. Jaro Mayda (St. Paul: West Publishing, 1963), p. 19.

4. For an overview of judicial review in the postwar period, see Mauro Cappelletti, *Judicial Review in the Contemporary World* (Indianapolis: Bobbs-Merrill, 1971).

5. Lawrence M. Friedman, "On Legal Development," *Rutgers Law Review*, 24 (1969), 11.

6. There is a large literature on the concept of individualism and its relation to modernization, the industrial revolution, and capitalism. See, for example, Nicholas Abercrombie, Stephen Hill, and Bryan S. Turner, *Sovereign Individuals of Capitalism* (London: Allen and Unwin, 1986).

7. Henry Maine, *Ancient Law* (1861; London: J. Murray, 1890), pp. 163–170.

8. Ferdinand Tönnies, *Community and Society (Gemeinschaft und Gesellschaft)*, ed. and trans. Charles P. Loomis (East Lansing: Michigan State University Press, 1957).

9. Émile Durkheim, *The Division of Labor in Society* (New York: Free Press, 1964).

10. The sections on law have been separately published in English. Max Weber, *Max Weber on Law in Economy and Society*, Max Rheinstein, ed. and trans. (Cambridge, Mass.: Harvard University Press, 1954).

11. See, in general, Patrick S. Atiyah, *The Rise and Fall of Freedom of Contract* (Oxford: Oxford University Press, 1979); Lawrence M. Friedman, *Contract Law in America* (Madison: University of Wisconsin Press, 1965).

12. J. Willard Hurst, *Law and the Conditions of Freedom in the Nineteenth-Century United States* (Madison: University of Wisconsin Press, 1964), p. 9. On liberty as the "enlargement of options," see p. 37.

13. Alexis de Tocqueville, *Democracy in America*, ed. J. P. Mayer, trans. George Lawrence (NewYork: Doubleday, 1969), p. 19; Frances Trollope, *Domestic Manners of the Americans*, ed. Richard Mullen (1832; New York: Oxford University Press, 1984), pp. 272–273.

14. Atiyah, *Rise and Fall*, p. 273.

15. Robert W. Gordon (private communication, June 5, 1988) points out that there were "expressive forms of nineteenth century individualism," including the "romantic" ideal of "self-realization as bringing out one's true authentic nature," which by the end of the century verged on "the development of individual character, idiosyncrasy, etc." and, in its "extreme" form, "dandyism." These strains, including romanticism in general, no doubt existed, but those mentioned in the text strike me as more central and pervasive.

16. Tocqueville, *Democracy in America*, pp. 510–511.

17. J. R. Pole, *The Pursuit of Equality in American History* (Berkeley: University of California Press, 1978), p. 5.

18. See Robert W. Malcolmson, *Popular Recreations in English Society, 1700–1850* (Cambridge: Cambridge University Press, 1973), chap. 6; Douglas A.

Reid, "Interpreting the Festival Calendar: Wakes and Fairs as Carnivals," in Robert D. Storch, ed., *Popular Culture and Custom in Nineteenth-Century England* (London: Croom Helm, 1982), pp. 125, 141–147.

19. The argument was that "distress and poverty multiply in proportion to the funds created to relieve them"; relief was thus counterproductive because it tended to "relax individual exertion by unnerving the arm of industry." *Report of the Secretary of State on the Relief and Settlement of the Poor*, New York Assembly Journal, Feb. 9, 1824.

20. Gustave de Beaumont and Alexis de Tocqueville, *On the Penitentiary System in the United States and Its Application in France* (1833; Carbondale: Southern Illinois University Press, 1964), p. 79.

21. Stephen Nissenbaum, *Sex, Diet and Debility in Jacksonian America: Sylvester Graham and Health Reform* (Westport, Conn.: Greenwood Press, 1980), p. 113.

22. J. Richardson Parke, *Human Sexuality: A Medico-Literary Treatise*, 4th rev. ed. (Philadelphia: Professional Publishing Company, 1909), p. 375. Men who masturbate fail in business because their sexual practices engender "a love of solitude and a shrinking from . . . healthy human contact," and because "there is an atmosphere of repulsion about the victim of the habit," which makes the man "a moral leper."

23. Carroll Smith-Rosenberg, *Disorderly Conduct: Visions of Gender in Victorian America* (New York: Knopf, 1985), p. 258.

24. Sigmund Freud, *Civilization and Its Discontents*, ed. James Strachey (1930; New York: Norton, 1961), p. 49. Civilization, according to Freud, obeys "the laws of economic necessity, since a large amount of the physical energy which it uses for its own purpose has to be withdrawn from sexuality. In this respect civilization behaves towards sexuality as a people or a stratum of its population does which has subjected another one to its exploitation." Ibid., p. 57.

25. Roger Lane, "Urbanization and Criminal Violence in the 19th Century: Massachusetts as a Test Case," in Hugh D. Graham and Ted R. Gurr, eds., *The History of Violence in America* (New York: Praeger, 1969), pp. 468, 477. Joseph R. Gusfield makes a similar point, stressing factory discipline: "Frugality, punctual appearance, scheduled activities are all part of an institutional structure in which loose, erratic, and spontaneous behavior threaten the coordination of parts and whole." Thus the emergence of strong norms against drinking and drunkenness. *The Culture of Public Problems* (Chicago: University of Chicago Press, 1981), p. 149; see also, Atiyah, *Rise and Fall*, pp. 273–274.

26. Nissenbaum, *Sex, Diet and Debility*, p. 136.

27. Similarly, Article 3 of the Italian Constitution of 1948 asserts it is the "task of the Republic" to remove "obstacles" to the "freedom and equality of citizens" which "impede the full development of the human personality." Quoted in Appendix A, Mauro Cappelletti, John Henry Merryman, and Joseph M. Perillo, *The Italian Legal System: An Introduction* (Stanford: Stanford University Press, 1967).

28. Quoted in Roy Porter, *English Society in the Eighteenth Century* (New York: Penguin Books, 1982), p. 181. Education was also, of course, useless for women. Indeed, it was dangerous to their health; see Barbara Ehrenreich and Deirdre

English, *For Her Own Good: 150 Years of the Experts' Advice to Women* (Garden City, N.Y.: Anchor Press, 1979), pp. 125–131.

29. David Tyack and Elisabeth Hansot, *Managers of Virtue: Public School Leadership in America, 1820–1890* (New York: Basic Books, 1982), pp. 54, 55.

30. David Tyack, Thomas James, Aaron Benavot, *Law and the Shaping of Public Education, 1785–1954* (Madison: University of Wisconsin Press, 1987), p. 156.

31. "The aim of the enterprise is to influence students to become thinking, autonomous, sensitive people"; see Joseph Featherstone, *What Schools Can Do* (New York: Liveright, 1976), p. 11.

32. Max Weber, *Max Weber on Law in Economy and Society*, Max Rheinstein, ed. (Cambridge, Mass.: Harvard University Press, 1954).

33. See, for example, Anthony T. Kronman, *Max Weber* (Stanford: Stanford University Press, 1983); David M. Trubek, "Max Weber's Tragic Modernism and the Study of Law and Society," *Law & Society Review*, 20 (1986), 573; Manfred Rehbinder and Klaus-Peter Tieck, eds., *Max Weber als Rechtssoziologe* (Berlin: Duncker und Humblot, 1987).

34. Edward L. Ayers, *Vengeance and Justice: Crime and Punishment in the 19th Century American South* (New York: Oxford University Press, 1984), chap. 1, esp. p. 25; see also, Bertram Wyatt-Brown, *Southern Honor: Ethics and Behavior in the Old South* (New York: Oxford University Press, 1982).

35. There are, of course, other meanings of dignity, stressing the giving and receiving of respect; for an interesting discussion of honor and dignity in the modern American law of defamation, see Robert C. Post, "The Social Foundations of Defamation Law: Reputation and the Constitution," *California Law Review*, 74 (1986), 691.

36. Robert Bellah and others, *Habits of the Heart: Individualism and Commitment in American Life* (Berkeley: University of California Press, 1985), pp. 334, 336.

37. Ibid., p. 82.

38. David Riesman, *The Lonely Crowd: A Study of the Changing American Character* (New Haven: Yale University Press, 1950), p. 11.

39. Ibid., p. 14.

40. Ronald Inglehart, "Post-Materialism in an Environment of Insecurity," *American Political Science Review*, 75 (1981), 880, 881.

41. David M. Engel, "The Oven Bird's Song: Insiders, Outsiders, and Personal Injuries in an American Community," *Law & Society Review*, 18 (1984) 551, 558–559.

42. Warren I. Susman, *Culture as History: The Transformation of American Society in the Twentieth Century* (New York: Pantheon Books, 1985), chap. 14.

43. Daniel Bell, *The Cultural Contradictions of Capitalism* (New York: Basic Books, 1976), p. 37.

44. Joseph Raz, *The Morality of Freedom* (New York: Oxford University Press, 1986), p. 369.

45. Herbert Marcuse, *One-Dimensional Man* (Boston: Beacon Press, 1964), p. 7.

46. Michel Foucault, *Discipline and Punish: The Birth of the Prison* (New York: Vintage Books, 1979), p. 304.

47. See, for example, Victor Barnouw, *Culture and Personality* (Homewood, Ill.: Dorsey Press, 4th ed., 1985), p. 6.

48. Walter Mischel, *Introduction to Personality*, 3d ed. (New York: Holt, Rinehart, and Winston, 1981), p. 64.

49. See, for instance, Wolfgang Seibel, " 'Gesetzesflut,' konservative Staatsrechtslehre und kritische Sozialwissenschaft," *Demokratie und Recht* (1980), p. 123.

50. See Brun-Otto Bryde, *Verfassungsentwicklung: Stabilität und Dynamik im Verfassungsrecht der Bundesrepublik Deutschland*, (Baden-Baden: Nomos Verlagsgesellschaft, 1982); the sixth edition of Bruno Schmidt-Bleibtreu and Franz Klein, *Kommentar zum Grundgesetz für die Bundesrepublik Deutschland* (Neuwied: Luchterhand, 1983) runs to almost 1,500 pages.

51. See Arthur Zilversmit, *The First Emancipation: The Abolition of Slavery in the North* (Chicago: University of Chicago Press, 1967). The schools of Boston were segregated long before the Civil War, and this segregation was upheld in 1849 in Roberts v. City of Boston, 59 Mass. (5 Cush.) 198. Of course, the problem did not arise in the southern states, which made little or no provision for educating blacks at all in this period.

4. Technology and Change

1. The phrase, of course, is from Christopher Lasch, who used it to refer to the family, in *Haven in a Heartless World: The Family Besieged* (New York: Basic Books, 1977).

2. Alex Inkeles and David H. Smith, *Becoming Modern: Individual Change in Six Developing Countries* (Cambridge, Mass.: Harvard University Press, 1974), p. 290.

3. This is not to say that modern society is necessarily a "youth culture," as that term is ordinarily used; on this point, see the discussion in Chapter 9.

4. John H. Goldthorpe, *Social Mobility and Class Structure in Modern Britain*, 2d. ed. (New York: Oxford University Press, 1987), pp. 327–328. "The fact that the chances of men of all social origins gaining entry into the expanding higher levels of the occupational and class structures steadily increased served effectively to distract attention away from the issue of whether at the same time any equalization of relative mobility chances was being achieved." Ibid., pp. 328–329.

5. Lawrence M. Friedman, *Total Justice* (New York: Russell Sage Foundation, 1985).

6. Infant mortality rates among blacks in slum areas of American cities are much larger than the rates among middle-class whites (and blacks); but even these rates are of course much lower than the rates for upper-class children two centuries ago. Moreover, these relatively high rates are considered a reproach to a society that ought to be able to avoid them; they are certainly not accepted fatalistically.

7. Some observers—Ulrich Beck, for one, in *Risikogesellschaft, auf dem Wege in eine andere Moderne* (Frankfurt: Suhrkamp, 1986)—have argued that the "risk

society" (a society in which the most salient social fact is the pervasiveness of environmental and other risks) is already upon us.

8. Friedman, *Total Justice*.

5. On Modern Legal Culture

1. Brown v. Board of Education, 347 U.S. 483 (1954). The literature on this case, and what happened afterwards, is of course staggering in its bulk. The background of the case is beautifully told in Richard Kluger's book, *Simple Justice* (New York: Knopf, 1976).

2. For example: Turkish guest-workers in West Germany; Pakistanis and West Indians in Great Britain; East Indians in the Netherlands.

3. Thus the European Convention on Human Rights proclaims a right to "respect for . . . private and family life," see Arthur Henry Robertson, *Human Rights in Europe*, 2d ed. (Manchester: Manchester University Press, 1977), p. 86. On privacy, see below, chap. 9.

4. 26 Stats. 209 (Act of July 2, 1890); on its background and early history, see William Letwin, *Law and Economic Policy in America: The Evolution of the Sherman Antitrust Act* (New York: Random House, 1965).

5. 15 U.S.C.A. § 13, § 13a.

6. Quoted in Carl Fulda, "Food Distribution in the United States, The Struggle Between Independents and Chains," *University of Pennsylvania Law Review*, 99 (1951), 1051, 1079–80; see also Thomas W. Ross, "Store Wars: The Chain Tax Movement," *Journal of Law and Economics*, 29 (1986), 125.

7. There is a large literature on railroad regulation in the United States; see, for example, George H. Miller, *Railroads and the Granger Laws* (Madison: University of Wisconsin Press, 1971); Gabriel Kolko, *Railroads and Regulation, 1877–1916* (Princeton: Princeton University Press, 1965); Stephen Skowronek, *Building a New American State: The Expansion of National Administrative Capacities, 1877–1920* (Cambridge: Cambridge University Press, 1982), pp. 138–160.

8. Private communication from Robert A. Kagan, July 11, 1988.

9. Tenn. Code, Sec. 63-18-103. Under the "Massage Registration Act of 1979," counties could choose to license masseurs.

10. For occupational licensing and similar laws in Germany, see Ingo von Münch, ed., *Besonderes Verwaltungsrecht*, 6th ed. (Berlin: de Gruyter, 1982), pp. 351–355.

11. There is also the notion that one's "private" life should not count against one on the job—this is a core idea in the law of job discrimination.

12. See Lawrence M. Friedman, "Freedom of Contract and Occupational Licensing 1890–1910: A Legal and Social Study," *California Law Review*, 53 (1965), 487.

13. See Peter Temin, "The Origin of Compulsory Drug Prescriptions," *Journal of Law and Economics*, 22 (1979), 92; compare the situation in U.S. v. Rutherford, 442 U.S. 544 (1979), where desperate cancer patients lost their battle to get Laetrile legally (Laetrile was a drug made out of peach pits, which they believed could cure them). The Food and Drug Administration (and virtually all doctors) considered Laetrile a useless quack medicine and refused to license it.

14. Moreover, taking the wrong drug may have irreversible, catastrophic consequences, and thus preclude further choice; on the norm against irreversibility, see chap. 6.

15. 15 U.S.C. § 1601, first enacted in 1968.

16. The subject is complicated by any number of factors, including the alliance of one wing of the feminist movement with the anti-pornography movement. On this, see Robin West, "The Feminist-Conservative Anti-Pornography Alliance and the 1986 Attorney General's Commission on Pornography Report," *American Bar Foundation Research Journal* (1987), 681.

17. See, for example, Peter A. Köhler and Hans F. Zacher, eds., *The Evolution of Social Insurance, 1881–1981* (London: Pinter, 1982).

18. For a discussion, see Manfred Rehbinder, "Status, Contract and the Welfare State," *Stanford Law Review*, 23 (1971), 941.

19. Indeed, this may be true because of the very definition of "contract" in nineteenth-century legal theory. On this point see Lawrence M. Friedman, *Contract Law in America* (Madison: University of Wisconsin Press, 1965), chap. 1.

20. Grant Gilmore, *The Death of Contract* (Columbus: Ohio State University Press, 1974). Gilmore remarks that the "decline and fall of the general theory of contract and, in most quarters, of laissez-faire economics may be taken as remote reflections on the transition from nineteenth-century individualism to the welfare state and beyond." In the present era, we are "all cogs in a machine, each dependent on the other." Ibid., pp. 95–96. What Gilmore perhaps failed to see is that mutual dependence is not necessarily inconsistent with freedom of choice; that freedom of choice is not the same as "freedom of contract" as the nineteenth century understood it; and, for these reasons, it can be argued that individualism is not only not dead, but in fact much more vital and alive than it was in the nineteenth-century heyday of "freedom of contract."

21. Patrick S. Atiyah, *The Rise and Fall of Freedom of Contract* (Oxford: Oxford University Press, 1979), pp. 726–727. Atiyah sees generally in the law a "decline in the importance attached to the element of consent or free choice," p. 729; but his examples do not really show this. He mentions, as one instance, that the excuse of assumption of risk has vanished from tort law, p. 730. A coal miner's acceptance of a job used to be treated as "consent" to run the risks of mining coal; this is no longer good law. Was it ever really "consent"?

22. On this point, see Lawrence M. Friedman and Stewart Macaulay, "Contract Law and Contract Teaching: Past, Present, and Future," *Wisconsin Law Review* (1967), 805; on the reality, see Stewart Macaulay, "Non-Contractual Relations in Business: A Preliminary Study," *American Sociological Review*, 28 (1963), 55.

23. See Robert W. Gordon, "Unfreezing Legal Reality: Critical Approaches to Law," *Florida State University Law Review*, 15 (1987), 195.

24. See Friedrich Kessler, "Contracts of Adhesion—Some Thoughts about Freedom of Contract," *Columbia Law Review*, 43 (1943), 629; for an assessment of the impact of this article, and the adhesion doctrine, on the actual course of decision-making in American courts, see Walter Schmid, *Zur sozialen Wirklichkeit des Vertrages* (Berlin: Duncker und Humblot, 1983).

25. Kessler, "Contracts of Adhesion," p. 640.

26. Thus, in the well-known case of Williams v. Walker-Thomas Furniture Company, 350 F.2d 445 (C.A. D.C. 1965), a poor woman signed a complex and tricky form contract under which she bought goods on the installment plan. Judge Skelly Wright struck down the contract as "unconscionable." He said: "when a party of little bargaining power, and hence little real choice, signs a commercially unreasonable contract with little or no knowledge of its terms, it is hardly likely that his consent, or even an objective manifestation of his consent, was ever given to all the terms."

27. The right of the worker to quit a job was, both legally and practically, subject to severe limitations in older agricultural societies; if the worker quit in the middle of the growing season, he was apt to forfeit all of his pay. See Morton Horwitz, *The Transformation of American Law, 1780–1860* (Cambridge, Mass.: Harvard University Press, 1977), p. 186. There were, of course, even sharper limitations on black farm workers in the late nineteenth-century; see William Cohen, "Negro Involuntary Servitude in the South, 1865–1940: A Preliminary Analysis," *Journal of Southern History*, 42 (1976), 31.

28. On England, see, for example, Henry Pelling, *A History of British Trade Unionism*, 4th ed. (London: Macmillan, 1987), pp. 107–110, 121–122.

29. In Allgeyer v. Louisiana, 165 U.S. 578 (1897), the Supreme Court read the word "liberty" in the due process clause to include "the right of the citizen to be free . . . to live and work where he will; to earn his livelihood by any lawful calling . . . and for that purpose to enter into all contracts which may be proper . . . to . . . carrying out . . . the purposes . . . mentioned." There is a large literature on the work of the court in this period; see, for example, Michael Les Benedict, "Laissez-Faire Constitutionalism," *Law and History Review*, 3 (1985), 293.

30. Lochner v. New York, 198 U.S. 45 (1905). The dissent by Holmes contains his famous line, "The 14th Amendment does not enact Mr. Herbert Spencer's *Social Statics*."

31. Godcharles v. Wigeman, 113 Pa. St. 431 (1886); see Arnold Paul, *Conservative Crisis and the Rule of Law: Attitudes of Bar and Bench, 1887–1895* (New York: Harper and Row, 1969), pp. 15–18.

32. See, for example, the discussion of the subject in West Coast Hotel v. Parrish, 300 U.S. 379, 391 (1937) sustaining a minimum wage law for women and minors: "The Constitution does not speak of freedom of contract. It speaks of liberty . . . But the liberty safeguarded is liberty in a social organization which requires the protection of law."

33. See Lawrence M. Friedman, "Comments on Edward H. Rabin, 'The Revolution in Residential Landlord-Tenant Law, Causes and Consequences,'" *Cornell Law Review*, 69 (1984), 585.

34. Adair v. U.S., 208 U.S. 161 (1908).

35. The Court continued in *Adair* along these lines: "The right of the employe to quit . . . is the same as the right of the employer, for whatever reason to dispense with the services of such employe . . . In all such particulars the employer and employe have equality of right."

36. Of course, there are borderline situations—small businesses and private clubs—where the line between the individual and the entity blurs.

37. Milton Friedman, *Capitalism and Freedom* (Chicago: University of Chicago Press, 1962), pp. 110, 112. The book was written before the passage of the Civil Rights Act, but Friedman disapproved of the work of existing State Fair Employment Commissions, which he labeled as "interference with the freedom of individuals to enter into voluntary contracts with each other," p. 111.

38. This does not mean, of course, that private businesses, large and small, should not be free to set prices, or to lay off workers if the economy contracts. The sphere of behavior of a steel company or of the corporate owners of a huge housing development should be determined on the basis of efficiency and social equity, that is, as matters of public policy, not as matters of "rights" and "freedoms" in the sense individuals possess these. At least this is how I read current legal culture, and judicial culture as well.

39. See, for example, Philippe C. Schmitter, "Interest Intermediation and Regime Governability in Contemporary Western Europe and North America," in S. Berger, ed., *Organizing Interests in Western Europe: Pluralism, Corporatism and the Transformation of Politics* (Cambridge: Cambridge University Press, 1981), p. 285.

40. The reference is to Erving Goffman's *Asylums: Essays on the Social Situation of Mental Patients and Other Inmates* (New York: Anchor Books, 1961), chap. 2, "On the Characteristics of Total Institutions."

41. Richard M. Merelman, *Making Something of Ourselves: On Culture and Politics in the United States* (Berkeley: University of California Press, 1984), p. 30, describes American culture as "loosely bounded"; large numbers of Americans have been "released" from "comprehensive group identifications and from firm cultural moorings. The liberated individual, not the social group, must therefore become the basic cultural unit . . . Group membership thus becomes voluntary, contingent, and fluid."

42. Frontiero v. Richardson, 411 U.S. 677 (1973).

43. Article 119 of the Treaty Establishing the European Common Market requires each member state "to maintain . . . the principle that men and women should receive equal pay for equal work." On Japan, see Frank Upham, *Law and Social Change in Postwar Japan* (Cambridge, Mass.: Harvard University Press, 1987), chap. 4.

44. For a general exposition of American law on discrimination, see Laurence H. Tribe, *American Constitutional Law*, 2nd ed. (Mineola, N.Y.: Foundation Press, 1988), chap. 16.

45. 372 U.S. 335 (1963). The background of the case is described in Anthony Lewis, *Gideon's Trumpet* (New York: Random House, 1964).

46. Harper v. Virginia Board of Elections, 383 U.S. 663 (1966). The state, said Justice Douglas, violates constitutional principle when it "makes the affluence of the voter or payment of any fee an electoral standard."

47. As Justice Powell remarked in San Antonio Independent School District v. Rodriguez, 411 U.S. 1 (1973), the Court "has never . . . held that wealth discrimination alone provides an adequate basis for strict scrutiny."

48. On this point generally, see Jennifer L. Hochschild, *What's Fair? American Beliefs About Distributive Justice* (Cambridge, Mass.: Harvard University Press, 1981).

49. Carole Shammas, Marylynn Salmon, and Michel Dahlin, *Inheritance in America: From Colonial Times to the Present* (New Brunswick, N.J.: Rutgers University Press, 1987), p. 3.

50. Herbert McClosky and John Zaller, *The American Ethos: Public Attitudes toward Capitalism and Democracy* (Cambridge, Mass.: Harvard University Press, 1984), p. 125. It should be added, though, that the majority of the respondents took no position on these issues at all, so that the authors feel that "the Protestant ethic no longer functions as strongly as it once did to legitimate the great material inequalities associated with capitalism."

6. The Chosen Republic

1. The culture does, however, accept *advantages* which come about because of inherited, immutable traits—athletic ability, musical gifts, great intelligence.

2. On the liability explosion, see Lawrence M. Friedman, *Total Justice* (New York: Russell Sage Foundation, 1985), pp. 52–63; Jethro Lieberman, *The Litigious Society* (New York: Basic Books, 1981); on the doctrinal underpinnings, see G. Edward White, *Tort Law in America: An Intellectual History* (New York: Oxford University Press, 1980). Parallel developments have occurred in European law, though with greater emphasis on recompense through social insurance than through tort law. The underlying principles may be much the same, however. See Hein Kötz, *Sozialer Wandel in Unfallrecht* (Karlsruhe: Müller juristischer Verlag, 1976).

3. Medical malpractice, in a sense, is nothing new. The law has always accepted the notion that a doctor is liable for negligence. Actual cases of medical malpractice were not common before the twentieth century, however, and the modern burst of cases is best treated as a new development, even though some of the doctrines are respectably old. See Friedman, *Total Justice*, pp. 89–91.

4. Robert A. Kagan, in a private communication (July 11, 1988), remarked on the disparity between the willingness of society to equip buses to aid the handicapped, and the unwillingness to do anything for "inner city black youths" who "can't afford cars to get to factory jobs in the suburbs." Why, he asks, is it not "injustice" for these unemployed blacks to be barred from access to jobs? The situation certainly is not "their fault," yet it does not give rise to a claim for "free cars or at least free bus service." The point is (ethically) well taken; but the white middle class, whose legal culture predominates, simply has less sympathy and understanding for the problems of urban blacks, whose plight is thoughtlessly regarded as indeed their fault. The unsympathetic white (or black) points to those who "made it" to the top or the middle, despite a childhood spent in the slums. Poverty as such does not always evoke sympathy in this country; paralyzed legs seem so much more final and decisive, so much less dependent on will, choice, and character.

5. John Kaplan, "Taking Drugs Seriously," *The Public Interest*, 92 (Summer 1988), 32, 36.

6. On the rise of contributory negligence, see Wex S. Malone, "The Formative Era of Contributory Negligence," *Illinois Law Review*, 41 (1946), 151; on the operation of the nineteenth-century tort system, Lawrence M. Friedman, "Civil

Wrongs: Personal Injury Law in the Late 19th Century," *American Bar Foundation Research Journal* (1987), 351.

7. 10 M. & W. 546 (1842).

8. See, for example, Li v. Yellow Cab Co., 13 Cal.3d 804, 534 P.2d 1226 (1975).

9. See Lawrence M. Friedman and Thaddeus T. Niemira, "The Concept of the 'Trader' in Early Bankruptcy Law," *St. Louis University Law Journal*, 5 (1958), 223.

10. On the history of bankruptcy law in the United States, see Charles Warren, *Bankruptcy in United States History* (Cambridge Mass.: Harvard University Press, 1935); Peter Coleman, *Debtors and Creditors in America: Insolvency, Imprisonment for Debt, and Bankruptcy, 1607–1900* (Madison: State Historical Society of Wisconsin, 1974).

11. See, for example, Cal. Penal Code sec. 851.7. Note also that in a criminal trial the prosecution cannot bring in evidence of past convictions.

12. Lawrence M. Friedman, *A History of American Law*, 2nd ed. (New York: Simon and Schuster, 1985), p. 596; Cal. Penal Code sec. 1203, as amended.

13. On the rise of the juvenile courts, see David J. Rothman, *Conscience and Convenience: The Asylum and Its Alternatives in Progressive America* (Boston: Little, Brown, 1980), chap. 6; Peter D. Garlock " 'Wayward' Children and the Law, 1820–1900: The Genesis of the Status Offense Jurisdiction of the Juvenile Court," *Georgia Law Review*, 13 (1979), 341.

14. For a general overview see W. F. Connell, *A History of Education in the Twentieth Century World* (New York: Teachers College Press, 1980), chap. 12.

15. For the U.S. see Friedman, "Civil Wrongs"; for England, see Patrick Atiyah, *The Rise and Fall of Freedom of Contract* (Oxford: Oxford University Press, 1979), p. 275.

16. Compare the norm that "the beneficial retention of a status quo is considered a right where removal is considered unjust." Edward E. Zajac, "Perceived Economic Justice: The Example of Public Utility Regulation," in H. Peyton Young, ed., *Cost Allocation: Methods, Principles, Allocations* (New York: North-Holland, 1985) pp. 119, 141.

17. See, for example, Lenore J. Weitzman, *The Divorce Revolution: The Unexpected Social and Economic Consequences for Women and Children in America* (New York: Free Press, 1985), chap. 6, on alimony, California law, Civil Code sec. 4801, specifically authorizes the judge to consider "the duration of the marriage" in deciding issues of support payments.

18. On the law of "redundancy" and "unfair dismissal" and its equivalents in England, France, and Germany, see Tony Honoré, *The Quest for Security: Employees, Tenants, Wives* (London: Stevens, 1982), chap. 1. On the increasing use of the right to complain of such dismissals, and the relationship of these complaints to legal and economic factors, see Jörn Diekmann "Kündigungsschutz und Konjunktur," *Zeitschrift für Rechtssoziologie* 6:1, (1984), 79, 96–98.

19. See, for example, Donald H. J. Hermann and Yvonne S. Sor, "Property Rights in One's Job: The Case for Limiting Employment-at-Will," *Arizona Law Review*, 24 (1982), 763; William L. Mauk, "Wrongful Discharge: The Erosion of One Hundred Years of Employer Privilege," *Idaho Law Review*, 21 (1985), 201.

20. The terms are from Albert O. Hirschman, *Exit, Voice, and Loyalty* (Cambridge, Mass.: Harvard University Press, 1970).

21. Mary Ann Glendon, "The Transformation of American Landlord-Tenant Law," *Boston College Law Review*, 23 (1982), 503; Lawrence M. Friedman, "Comments on Edward H. Rabin 'The Revolution in Residential Landlord-Tenant Law, Causes and Consequences,' " *Cornell Law Review*, 69 (1984), 585. Of course, this is a matter of more or less; a tenant who misses rent payments consistently will have to go, although eviction here too is harder and takes longer than before.

22. Honoré, *Quest for Security*, chap. 2. The British have gone furthest of the three countries surveyed in protecting tenants; their rights are "such a serious inroad on the right of the landlord that it runs close to expropriation," p. 59.

23. Of course, it is also the case that the welfare state sucks up a huge amount of money in the form of taxes and redistributes it. Money taken away in taxes is money which cannot be used as the earner of the money would choose. It shifts these choices to the collectivity. But for most people there is a *felt* net gain in the realm of choice—at least I suspect as much—for the reasons mentioned in the text.

7. Gods, Kings, and Movie Stars

1. See the discussion of David Riesman's book, *The Lonely Crowd*, in Chapter 3 above.

2. "No, but I Saw His Show." *New York Times*, November 6, 1985, p. 23.

3. The line is from a story, "The Rich Boy," published in 1926. See *The Stories of F. Scott Fitzgerald: A Selection of 28 Stories* (New York: Scribner, 1951), p. 177. On the famous response of Ernest Hemingway, "Yes they have more money," see Matthew J. Bruccoli, *Scott and Ernest: The Authority of Failure and the Authority of Success* (New York: Random House, 1978), p. 4.

4. In the middle of the nineteenth century, when another Queen (Victoria) was on the throne, Walter Bagehot wrote: "The best reason why Monarchy is a strong government is, that it is an intelligible government." He described the monarchy as a *"family* on the throne," a fact which "brings down the pride of sovereignty to the level of petty life." Walter Bagehot, *The English Constitution* (1867; London: Collins, 1963), pp. 82, 85.

5. Baby M—for Melissa—was the child born to a surrogate mother who refused to go through with her agreement to give the baby up. The case was a sensation of 1988. See In re Baby M, 109 N.J. 396 (1988).

6. Leo Braudy, *The Frenzy of Renown: Fame and Its History* (New York: Oxford University Press, 1986), p. 504. Braudy also remarks that Barnum "brilliantly exploited the desire of a democratic audience to become involved in the show . . . This was not an audience that expected nothing more than to look passively upon aristocratic display . . . This was an audience . . . that wanted to be 'in the know,' privy to the backstage, aware of the finances of programs, and up to the minute in matters of con-man sleight of hand and trickery," p. 500.

7. On this point, see Douglass Adair, *Fame and the Founding Fathers* (New York: Norton, 1974), pp. 3–26. The quote is from p. 11.

8. On Cleveland's operation, see Allan Nevins, *Grover Cleveland: A Study in Courage* (New York: Dodd, Mead, 1932), pp. 528–533; on Wilson's condition, see Edwin A. Weinstein, *Woodrow Wilson: A Medical and Psychological Biography* (Princeton: Princeton University Press, 1981), chap. 21; on Roosevelt, see Hugh G. Gallagher, *FDR's Splendid Deception* (New York: Dodd, Mead, 1985). Gallagher reports that although there are over 35,000 still photographs of Roosevelt at the Presidential Library, only two show him seated in his wheelchair; no newsreels "show him being lifted, carried, or pushed in his chair." This was "the result of a careful strategy . . . to minimize the extent of his handicap," p. xiv.

9. The Senator went on to say: "We can't have all Brandeises and Frankfurters and Cardozos . . . here." *Washington Post,* Mar. 17, 1970. p. A2.

10. James Bryce, *The American Commonwealth*, 2nd ed. (London: Macmillan, 1891), vol. I, p. 75. The voters in America, Bryce observed, had a "lower conception" of the qualities needed by a head of government than did the people who "direct public opinion in Europe."

11. Terence H. Qualter, *Opinion Control in the Democracies* (New York: St. Martin's Press, 1985), p. 124.

12. One exception, of course, is national security, where the public has been persuaded that it needs to know nothing, and does know nothing, often with disastrous results. Courts, too, are on the whole quite secretive and avoid "public relations." A book about the Supreme Court by Bob Woodward and Scott Armstrong, *The Brethren* (New York: Simon and Schuster, 1979), had the subtitle "Inside the Supreme Court," and delivered, in breathless tones, tidbits of gossip and "inside dope" about this very dignified and close-mouthed institution. Somewhat surprisingly, the book was a huge bestseller. Perhaps it filled a gap: it was an attempt to reduce or raise the Court to its proper celebrity status, which the Court refused to do for itself.

13. See, for example, Edwin Emery, *The Press and America: An Interpretive History of Journalism*, 2d ed. (Englewood Cliffs, N.J.: Prentice-Hall, 1962), chap. 19.

14. See, in general, the very perceptive study by Joshua Meyrowitz, *No Sense of Place: The Impact of Electronic Media on Social Behavior* (New York: Oxford University Press, 1985); see also, on the rise of the media, S. Robert Lichter, Stanley Rothman, and Linda S. Lichter, *The Media Elite: America's New Powerbrokers* (Bethesda, Md.: Adler and Adler, 1986), chap. 1.

15. Anthony Trollope, *North America*, ed. Donald Smalley and Bradford Booth (1862; New York: Knopf, 1951), p. 267; his mother's comments are in Frances Trollope, *Domestic Manners of the Americans*, ed. Richard Mullen (1832; New York: Oxford University Press, 1984), chap. 10. The traits mentioned go back as far as the colonial period; see J. R. Pole, *The Pursuit of Equality in American History* (Berkeley: University of California Press, 1978), pp. 28–30.

16. In other senses, of course, proximity remains important. A car accident that kills two people in one's town gets as much television coverage as the death of hundreds in a far-off country.

17. In some parliamentary systems the head of state has ceremonial powers only—is, in short, almost purely a celebrity—and the head of government has more power but is less of a celebrity. The English case is quite pronounced. But

heads of government have everywhere gained status; and the Prime Minister of Sweden by now may be more of a celebrity in his country, for example, than the King.

18. President Calvin Coolidge, in a speech to newspaper editors on January 17, 1925, stated that "the chief business of the American people is business." *New York Times*, January 18, 1925, p. 1, col. 5; p. 19, col. 2.

19. The phrase is from a speech by President Theodore Roosevelt, August 20, 1907; see Theodore Roosevelt, *Presidential Addresses and State Papers*, vol. 7 (New York: Review of Reviews Company, 1910), pp. 1358–59.

20. See Lawrence M. Friedman, "Litigation and Its Discontents," forthcoming, *Mercer University Law Review*, 40 (1989), 973.

21. See, in general, Joel F. Handler, *Social Movements and the Legal System: A Theory of Law Reform and Social Change* (New York: Academic Press, 1978); Lawrence M. Friedman, *The Legal System: A Social Science Perspective* (New York: Russell Sage Foundation, 1975), pp. 148–165.

22. Ulrich Beck, *Risikogesellschaft: Auf dem Weg in eine andere Moderne* (Frankfurt: Suhrkamp, 1986), p. 213.

23. Jeffrey K. Tulis, *The Rhetorical Presidency* (Princeton, N.J.: Princeton University Press, 1987), p. 4.

24. Ibid., pp. 186–187: "the press has emerged as an autonomous institution, as much a rival and impediment to as facilitator of presidential initiatives." Presidents now "need to attend to the entire set of expected news stories when constructing a speech or announcement."

25. Compare the point made in Roland Marchand, *Advertising the American Dream: Making Way for Modernity, 1920–1940* (Berkeley: University of California Press, 1985), p. 339. Marchand argues that Americans responded to modernization by splitting their lives into "two distinct spheres: the hard, rational, competitive, and impersonal realm of work and economic transactions; and the soft, sentimental, intimate world of home, family, and warm personal friendships." But this "rigid" compartmentalization did not prove wholly satisfactory; "desires for psychological gratification and personal interaction spilled messily over from the world of private intimacy into the public realm of economic transactions." This "spilling over," I would argue, is characteristic of the replacement of nineteenth-century individualism by its twentieth-century counterpart.

A dichotomy similar to Marchand's is found in some feminist literature, which contrasts women's special "voice" or "sphere," with that of men; see the discussion of Carol Gilligan's point in Chapter 10.

8. Crime, Sexuality, and Social Disorganization

1. On this point, see Ted R. Gurr, Peter N. Grabosky, and Richard C. Hula, *The Politics of Crime and Conflict: A Comparative History of Four Cities* (Beverly Hills: Sage Publications, 1977); Roger Lane, "Urbanization and Criminal Violence in the 20th Century: Massachusetts as a Test Case," in H. D. Graham and Ted R. Gurr, eds., *Violence in America: Historical and Comparative Perspectives* (Washington: U.S. Government Printing Office, 1969); James Q. Wilson and

Richard J. Herrnstein, *Crime and Human Nature* (New York: Simon and Schuster, 1985), chap. 16.

2. Gwynn Nettler, *Explaining Crime* (New York: McGraw Hill, 1974), p. 195.

3. On this point see Ysabel Rennie, *The Search for Criminal Man: A Conceptual History of the Dangerous Offender* (Lexington, Mass.: Lexington Books, 1978).

4. These examples are drawn from the Old Bailey Sessions Papers (1830), Cases No. 909 and 1014. Mary Ann Ward was convicted, and sentenced to seven years transportation; Isabella Fell was sentenced to three months in jail.

5. Wilson and Herrnstein, *Crime and Human Nature*, pp. 420, 435; on the shift from "character" to "personality" see also Warren Susman, *Culture as History* (New York: Pantheon Books, 1984), chaps. 13 and 14.

6. On cultural shifts in education, see Chapter 3.

7. Wilson and Herrnstein, *Crime and Human Nature*, p. 437.

8. Jonathan D. Casper, *American Criminal Justice: The Defendant's Perspective* (Englewood Cliffs, N.J.: Prentice Hall, 1972), p. 156.

9. On this point, and for a general critique of the more conservative theories of crime, see Elliott Currie, *Confronting Crime* (New York: Pantheon Books, 1985), pp. 186–210.

10. Frank G. Carrington writes: "Pursuit of the criminals' rights, to the exclusion of the rights of the law-abiding, has caused a deep and abiding frustration . . . It becomes more and more clear that the criminal justice system has broken down and is either unable or unwilling to protect the law-abiding." *The Victims* (New Rochelle, N.Y.: Arlington House, 1975), p. 29.

The distinction Herbert L. Packer draws between the "due process" model and the "crime control" model of criminal process is in *The Limits of the Criminal Sanction* (Stanford: Stanford University Press, 1968), pp. 153–173.

11. Hans Zeisel, for example, argues that the problem of street crime "*cannot be solved solely through the institutional mechanisms of the police, the courts, or the prisons*"; rather, society must focus on the "underlying causes of crime." Hans Zeisel, "The Limits of Law Enforcement," *Vanderbilt Law Review*, 35 (1982), 527, 528.

12. John P. Reid, *Law for the Elephant: Property and Social Behavior on the Overland Trail* (San Marino, Calif.: Huntington Library, 1980); see Johannes Andenaes, "The General Preventive Effects of Punishment," *University of Pennsylvania Law Review*, 114 (1964), 949, 961–962 (police strike in Liverpool; situation in Denmark when German occupation forces arrested the local police force).

13. James Eisenstein, Roy B. Flemming, Peter F. Nardulli, *The Contours of Justice: Communities and Their Courts* (Boston: Little, Brown, 1988), pp. 287, 288.

14. On plea bargaining see, for example, Milton Heumann, *Plea Bargaining: The Experiences of Prosecutors, Judges and Defense Attorneys* (Chicago: University of Chicago Press, 1978); on its history in the United States, Lawrence M. Friedman, "Plea Bargaining in Historical Perspective," *Law & Society Review*, 13 (1979), 247.

15. John Baldwin and Michael McConville, "Plea Bargaining and Plea Negotiation in England," *Law & Society Review*, 13 (1979), 287.

16. Eisenstein et al., *The Contours of Justice*, p. 231.

17. William L. F. Felstiner, "Plea Contracts in West Germany," *Law & Society Review*, 13 (1979), 309, 310.

18. See John H. Langbein's account in *Torture and the Law of Proof* (Chicago: University of Chicago Press, 1977).

19. See Ashcraft v. Tennessee, 322 U.S. 143 (1944).

20. Douglas Hay, "Property, Authority and the Criminal Law," in Douglas Hay et al., *Albion's Fatal Tree: Crime and Society in Eighteenth Century England* (New York: Pantheon Books, 1975), p. 17.

21. William E. Nelson, *Americanization of the Common Law: The Impact of Legal Change on Massachusetts Society, 1760–1830* (Cambridge, Mass.: Harvard University Press, 1975), p. 39.

22. Ibid., p. 37; Lawrence M. Friedman, *A History of American Law*, 2d ed. (New York: Simon and Schuster, 1985), pp. 72–74.

23. Hendrik Hartog, "The Public Law of a County Court: Judicial Government in Eighteenth-Century Massachusetts," *American Journal of Legal History*, 10 (1966), 282, 299–308.

24. For example, *all* sexual offenses accounted for a mere 2.4 percent of the crimes prosecuted in one Indiana county between 1823 and 1860. David J. Bodenhamer, *The Pursuit of Justice: Crime and Law in Antebellum Indiana* (New York: Garland, 1986), p. 140.

25. Illinois Crim. Code 1874, chap. 38, sec. 11.

26. On the rise of the penitentiary see, in particular, David J. Rothman, *The Discovery of the Asylum: Social Order and Disorder in the New Republic* (Boston: Little, Brown, 1971), chap. 4; Michel Foucault, *Discipline and Punish: The Birth of the Prison* (New York: Vintage Books, 1979); Adam J. Hirsch, "From Pillory to Penitentiary: The Rise of Penal Incarceration in Early Massachusetts," *Michigan Law Review*, 80 (1982), 1179.

27. Michael Ignatieff, *A Just Measure of Pain, the Penitentiary in the Industrial Revolution, 1750–1850* (New York: Pantheon Books, 1978).

28. Gustave de Beaumont and Alexis de Tocqueville, *On the Penitentiary System in the United States and Its Application in France* (1833; Carbondale, Ill.: Southern Illinois University Press, 1964), p. 79.

29. Rothman, *The Discovery of the Asylum*, p. 107.

30. Hay, *Albion's Fatal Tree*.

31. Rennie, *The Search for Criminal Man*, pp. 86–87; see Johannes Lange, *Crime as Destiny: A Study of Criminal Twins* (London: Allen and Unwin, 1931), a German study which argued, on the basis of research on twins, that heredity "does play a role of paramount importance in making the criminal," p. 173; see also Marc Haller, *Eugenics* (Rutgers, N.J.: Rutgers University Press, 1963); Charles E. Rosenberg, "The Bitter Fruit: Heredity, Disease and Social Thought in Nineteenth-Century America," in *Perspectives in American History*, eds. Donald Fleming and Bernard Bailyn, Charles Warren Center for Studies in American History, vol. 8 (Cambridge, Mass.: Harvard University Press, 1974), p. 189.

32. Rennie, *The Search for Criminal Man*, chap. 31.

33. In general, see Lawrence M. Friedman, "History, Social Policy and Criminal Justice," in *Social History and Social Policy*, ed. David J. Rothman and Stanton Wheeler (New York: Academic Press, 1981), pp. 203, 223–231.

34. See Martin Killias, *Jugend und Sexualstrafrecht* (Bern: P. Haupt, 1979), especially pp. 114–117.

35. Thomas C. Mackey, *Red Lights Out: A Legal History of Prostitution, Disorderly Houses and Vice Districts, 1870–1917* (New York: Garland, 1987); Mark Thomas Connelly, *The Response to Prostitution in the Progressive Era* (Chapel Hill: University of North Carolina Press, 1980).

36. Act of June 25, 1910, 36 Stat. 825 (section 8 of the act directed that it "shall be known and referred to as the 'White Slave Traffic Act' ").

37. Susan Edwards, *Female Sexuality and the Law* (Oxford: Robertson, 1981), p. 23.

38. See Werner Sollors, *Beyond Ethnicity, Consent and Descent in American Culture* (New York: Oxford University Press, 1986), especially chap. 3.

39. Reynolds v. U.S., 98 U.S. 145 (1878).

40. Of course, within the Welsh or Basque communities, there may be a great deal of pressure to conform; but there is always the option of leaving for the big city and assimilating into the larger society.

41. Andrew J. Cesare, "Updating California's Sex Code: The Consenting Adults Law," *Criminal Justice Journal,* 1 (1976), 65. California, in its law, adopted a suggestion from the draftsmen of the Model Penal Code to "exclude from the criminal law all sex practices not involving force, adult corruption of minors, or public offense," p. 66.

42. Massachusetts upheld a law making adultery a crime in Commonwealth v. Stowell, 389 Mass. 171, 449 N.E. 2d 357 (1983); and the Supreme Court upheld the Georgia sodomy statute in Bowers v. Hardwick, 106 S.Ct. 2841 (1986). Until 1974, Texas defined homicide as "justifiable when committed by the husband upon one taken in the act of adultery with the wife"; and there was a similar statute in Georgia until 1977. Jeremy D. Weinstein, "Adultery, Law and the State," *Hastings Law Journal,* 38 (1986), 195, 230–236.

43. See Susan Estrich, *Real Rape* (Cambridge, Mass.: Harvard University Press, 1987); Ronald J. Berger, Patricia Searles, and W. Lawrence Neuman, "The Dimensions of Rape Reform Legislation," *Law & Society Review,* 22 (1988), 329.

44. Daniel Scott Smith and Michael Hindus, "Premarital Pregnancy in America, 1640–1971: An Overview and an Interpretation," *Journal of Interdisciplinary History,* 5 (1975), 537.

45. See John D'Emilio and Estelle Freedman, *Intimate Matters: A History of Sexuality in America* (New York: Harper and Row, 1988), p. 324.

46. Of course, the opposite of repression is not promiscuity, especially if promiscuity leads to other problems and dangers. For example, gays in the 1980s certainly reject "repression" in the sense of denial of the value and nature of their own sexuality; but the terrible problem of AIDS has led many of them to think twice about exactly what kind of sex life they ought to lead. Similarly, a lot of married people (mostly men) once found the idea of "open marriage" or "swinging" attractive, but later discovered that for them at least this behavior led to unhappiness and divorce. Rejecting repression is not the same as license.

47. David A. J. Richards, *Toleration and the Constitution* (New York: Oxford University Press, 1986), pp. 270, 280.

48. See Rainer Frank, "The Status of Cohabitation in the Legal Systems of

West Germany and Other West European Countries," *American Journal of Comparative Law,* 33 (1985), 185.

49. 18 Cal.3d 660, 134 Cal.R. 815 (1976).

50. Inheritance Act, Ch. 63, § 1(1)(e). The amount is such as would be "reasonable in all the circumstances"; see § 1(2)(b).

51. See Robert A. Katzmann, *Institutional Disability: The Saga of Transportation Policy for the Disabled* (Washington, D.C.: Brookings Institution, 1986), p. 2.

52. 88 Stat. 2282 (Jan. 4, 1975).

9. The Life-style Society

1. On "immutability" and sex discrimination law, see Chapter 5.

2. Laura Ann Silverstein, *New York Times,* November 24, 1987, p. 22, col. 5.

3. See, for example, Lynch v. Donnelly, 465 U.S. 668 (1984); Christmas display run by city of Pawtucket, Rhode Island.

4. On blasphemy law in the United States, see Lawrence M. Friedman, *Total Justice* (New York: Russell Sage Foundation, 1985), pp. 113–115; Robert C. Post, "Cultural Heterogeneity and Law: Pornography, Blasphemy and the First Amendment," *California Law Review,* 76 (1988), 297.

5. R. v. Lemon [1979], A.C. 517.

6. Thomas Luckmann, *The Invisible Religion* (New York: Macmillan, 1967), p. 99. The "autonomous" consumer "selects . . . certain religious themes from the available assortment and builds them into a somewhat precarious private system of 'ultimate' significance. Individual religiosity is thus no longer a replica or approximation of an 'official' model," p. 102.

7. The Great Awakening was a religious revival that swept the American colonies around 1740. See Alan Heimert, *Religion and the American Mind: From the Great Awakening to the Revolution* (Cambridge, Mass.: Harvard University Press, 1966).

8. Richard F. Tomasson reported in 1971 that only 4 or 5 percent of the Swedish population attended church; the figure for weekly attendance at church in Great Britain at the time was 15 percent. "Religion Is Irrelevant in Sweden," in *Religion in Radical Transition,* ed. Jeffrey K. Hadden (New York: Aldine, 1971), pp. 111, 112. But in 1975, 40 percent of all Americans attended church; 94 percent of the population believed in God, and 75 percent in an afterlife. John Wilson, *Religion in American Society: The Effective Presence* (Englewood Cliffs, N.J.: Prentice-Hall, 1978), pp. 397, 399.

9. Carol Weisbrod, *The Boundaries of Utopia* (New York: Pantheon Books, 1980), p. 209. Weisbrod goes on to comment that the principle of voluntarism had its limits. "Perhaps one can choose for oneself, but not for one's children." Moreover, the contract cannot be irreversible: it cannot "deny the individual the right to rejoin the larger community."

On the somewhat divergent ways the Mormons were treated, see chap. 2 of Weisbrod's study.

10. See, for example, W. Andrew Achenbaum, *Old Age in the New Land: The American Experience since 1790* (Baltimore: The Johns Hopkins University Press,

1978); Tamara K. Hareven, "Historical Changes in the Timing of Family Transitions: Their Impact on Generational Relations," in *Aging: Stability and Change in the Family,* ed. Robert W. Fogel et al. (New York: Academic Press, 1981), p 143.

11. See, for example, the treatment of childhood by Philippe Ariès, in his well-known book, *Centuries of Childhood: A Social History of Family Life* (New York: Knopf, 1962), which has a chapter entitled "The Discovery of Childhood," and which claims, indeed, that the very concept of the (nuclear) family was an innovation of relatively recent times (p. 363).

12. This branch of law is discussed in Lawrence M. Friedman, *Your Time Will Come: The Law of Age Discrimination and Mandatory Retirement* (New York: Russell Sage Foundation, 1984). A few states had provisions against age discrimination before ADEA; New York, for example, as early as 1958.

13. 42 U.S.C. sec. 2000 e-2(a).

14. Bérnice L. Neugarten and Dail A. Neugarten, "Changing Meanings of Age in the Aging Society," in *Our Aging Society,* ed. Alan Pifer and Lydia Bronte (New York: Norton, 1986), pp. 33, 36. "Adults of all ages are experiencing changes in the traditional rhythm and timing of events of the life cycle."

15. Daniel J. Levinson et al., *The Seasons of a Man's Life* (New York: Knopf, 1978), pp. 194, 195.

16. The Canadian Human Rights Act also barred age discrimination; for a popular account, see *Maclean's,* March 1, 1982, p. 50. Codes of individual provinces may also prohibit age discrimination; and, judging by annual reports of the relevant agencies, these laws are active at the provincial level in Canada.

17. On early retirement in Holland and several European countries, see Bernard Casey and Gert Bruche, *Work or Retirement?* (Aldershot, England: Gower, 1983), chap. 6.

18. William L. O'Neill, *Divorce in the Progressive Era* (New Haven: Yale University Press, 1967).

19. Before 1857, English divorce was available only through acts of Parliament, which effectively eliminated any possibility of divorce except for members of the upper class. See Allen Horstman, *Victorian Divorce* (New York: St. Martin's Press, 1985). On developments in the United States, see Lawrence M. Friedman, "Rights of Passage: Divorce Law in Historical Perspective," *Oregon Law Review,* 63 (1984), 649; Nelson Blake, *The Road to Reno: A History of Divorce in the United States* (New York: Macmillan, 1962).

20. Cal. Civil Code, sec. 4056, allows a "dissolution" of marriage on the grounds of "irreconcilable differences" that have "caused the irremediable breakdown of the marriage." In practice, this means divorce at will.

21. BGB, section 1565; if the parties have not been separated for a year, divorce can be granted only if it would work a hardship on the petitioner, and for reasons that "lie in the person of the other marriage partner." After a year (BGB section 1566), consensual divorce is available; after three years, the breakdown of the marriage is conclusively presumed (and thus consent is not needed).

22. See Jamil Zainaldin, "The Emergence of a Modern American Family Law: Child Custody, Adoption and the Courts, 1796–1851," *Northwestern Law Review,* 73 (1979), 1038.

23. For the relevant English law see the Adoption Act 1976 (chap. 36), part V,

sec. 51. Interestingly enough, in both the old system (of secrecy and sealed records) and the new system (open access to the facts) "privacy" has been an argument. "Confidentiality preserves the privacy of biological parents and their families when they relinquish parental responsibility." Diano Dinverno, "The Michigan Adoption Code's Response to the Sealed Record Controversy," *University of Detroit Law Review*, 62 (1985), 295. At a time when having an illegitimate child meant a huge scandal, quiet adoption was one way of avoiding irreversible harm; it was a way of burying the past. But the climate of opinion has changed, and this is no longer so powerful an argument. Adopted children now have "sought to establish that knowing one's own identity is a fundamental privacy right . . . Sealed record statutes have been said to impinge upon the fundamental right to know personal intimate information about ancestors and the ability to make decisions involving other fundamental rights." Ibid., p. 311. The courts have not embraced this particular argument, as it happens; but legislatures have responded by somewhat relaxing the seals.

24. Samuel D. Warren and Louis D. Brandeis, "The Right to Privacy," *Harvard Law Review*, 4 (1890), 193. For a perceptive history of the concept in American life and law, see Richard F. Hixson, *Privacy in a Public Society* (New York: Oxford University Press, 1987); see also the treatment by Ruth Gavison, "Privacy and the Limits of Law," *Yale Law Journal*, 89 (1980), 421.

25. Philippe Ariès writes: "until the end of the seventeenth century, nobody was ever left alone. The density of social life made isolation virtually impossible . . . Everyday relations never left a man by himself." It was in the eighteenth century that "the family began to hold society at a distance, to push it back beyond a steadily extending zone of private life." Ariès, *Centuries of Childhood*, p. 398.

26. *New York Times*, May 10, 1987, p. 3, col. 2. On the underlying issue, see Erhard Denninger, "Das Recht auf informationelle Selbstbestimmung und innere Sicherheit," *Kritische Justiz*, 18 (1985), 215; Verena F. Rottmann, "Volkszählung 1987—wieder Verfassungswidrig?", *Kritische Justiz*, 20 (1987), 77.

27. For this momentous fact, see *New York Times*, March 11, 1987, p. B6, col. 4.

28. The Freedom of Information Act is 5 U.S.C.A. sec. 552. It is of course subject to numerous exceptions, and has produced a great deal of litigation on scope and limits.

29. The Official Secrets Act of 1911, 1 and 2 Geo. 5, c. 28; section 2 makes it a crime to communicate secret information to *any* unauthorized person. On French law, see Pierre Péan, *Secret d'état: La France du secret, les secrets de la France* (Paris: Fayard, 1986).

30. Griswold v. Connecticut, 381 U.S. 479 (1965). For an insightful discussion of the Supreme Court's privacy cases, see Thomas C. Grey, "Eros, Civilization and the Burger Court," *Law and Contemporary Problems*, 43 (1980), 83.

31. In Eisenstadt v. Baird, 405 U.S. 438 (1972), the court struck down a law which made it a crime for anyone but doctors or druggists to distribute contraceptives; and only to married people. If the right to privacy means "anything," said Justice Brennan, "it is the right of the *individual*, married or single, to be free from unwarranted governmental intrusion into matters so fundamentally affecting a person as the decision whether to bear or beget a child."

32. Roe v. Wade, 410 U.S. 113 (1973).

33. See, for example, Planned Parenthood v. Danforth, 428 U.S. 52 (1976), on parental consent; Bellotti v. Baird, 443 U.S. 622 (1979); Maher v. Roe, 432 U.S. 464 (1977), on funding.

34. 39 B.Verf.G.E. 1 (Feb. 25, 1975); an English translation by Robert E. Jones and John D. Gorby is in *John Marshall Journal of Practice and Procedure*, 9 (1976), 605; the decision quoted provisions of the *Grundgesetz* protecting the "right to life" and the "inviolability of the person." An attempt to get around this decision, on the level of the European community, failed; but the European Commission did recognize a "privacy" right in a well-known case from Northern Ireland which protected adult homosexuals; see Pierre Kayser, *La Protection de la vie privée* (Paris: Economica, 1984), pp. 26–28.

35. Walter Perron, "Das Grundsatzurteil des Spanischen Verfassungsgerichts vom 11.4.1985 zur strafrechtlichen Regelung des Schwangerschaftsabbruch," *Zeitschrift für die gesamte Strafrechtswissenschaft*, 98:1 (1986), 187.

36. On this point, see Mary Ann Glendon, *Abortion and Divorce in Western Law* (Cambridge, Mass.: Harvard University Press, 1987), pp. 13–24, 145–154.

37. Morgentaler v. R., 1 S.C.R.P. (decision dated January 24, 1988).

38. See Lawrence M. Friedman, "Civil Wrongs: Personal Injury Law in the Late 19th Century," *American Bar Association Research Journal* (1987), 351.

39. Joel F. Handler, *The Conditions of Discretion: Autonomy, Community, Bureaucracy* (New York: Russell Sage Foundation, 1986), p. 273. See, in general, Ruth R. Faden and Tom L. Beauchamp, *A History and Theory of Informed Consent* (New York: Oxford University Press, 1986), especially chap. 4.

40. Josephine Shaw, "Informed Consent: a German Lesson," *International and Comparative Law Quarterly*, 35 (1986), 864; for England, see Margaret Brazier, "Patient Autonomy and Consent to Treatment: The Role of the Law?" *Legal Studies*, 7 (1987), 169.

41. Handler, *The Conditions of Discretion*, pp. 277–278.

42. Natanson v. Kline, 186 Kan. 393, 350 P.2d 1093, 1104 (1960).

43. Martin Shapiro, "Judicial Activism," in *The Third Century: America as a Post-Industrial Society*, ed. Seymour Martin Lipset (Stanford, Calif.: Hoover Institution Press, 1979), pp. 109–125.

10. A Stab at Assessment

1. See Roger Peters et al., "The Effects of Statutory Change on the Civil Commitment of the Mentally Ill," *Law and Human Behavior*, 11 (1987), 73.

2. The attack on the conditions of the mentally ill included also lawsuits demanding reforms in the institutions where the mentally ill were housed. The most famous of these cases was Wyatt v. Stickney, 344 F.Supp. 373 (M.D. Ala. 1972); here the court held that mental patients who were civilly committed had a consitutional right to treatment and could not be simply warehoused.

3. Peters et al., "Civil Commitment of the Mentally Ill," p. 75.

4. For the court cases, see Matter of Boggs, 522 N.Y. Supp.2d 407 (1987); reversed in Boggs v. N.Y.C. Health & Hosp. Corp., 523 N.Y. Supp.2d 71 (1987). ("Billie Boggs" was a name assumed by Joyce Brown.)

5. For a measured evaluation of the "crisis" see Robert L. Rabin, "Some Reflections on the Process of Tort Reform," *San Diego Law Review,* 25 (1988), 13; and for a dissenting view, Richard L. Abel, "The Real Tort Crisis—Too *Few* Claims," *Ohio State Law Journal,* 48 (1987), 443.

6. Lawrence M. Friedman, *Total Justice* (New York: Russell Sage Foundation, 1985), chap. 2.

7. See Chapter 2.

8. *San Francisco Examiner,* August 9, 1987, p. 2, col. 2; p. 9, col. 4.

9. Marc Galanter, "The Day After the Litigation Explosion," *Maryland Law Review,* 46 (1986), 3, 28–37.

10. The classic formulation is in Wesley N. Hohfeld's, "Some Fundamental Legal Conceptions as Applied in Judicial Reasoning," *Yale Law Journal,* 23 (1913), 16; see Julius Stone, *Legal System and Lawyer's Reasonings* (Stanford, Calif.: Standford University Press, 1964), pp. 137–161.

11. *San Francisco Chronicle,* December 22, 1986, p. 50, col. 5.

12. On the various legal senses of "responsibility" see Richard Lempert and Joseph Sanders, *An Invitation to Law and Social Science* (New York: Longman, 1986), pp. 20–22.

13. See Mark C. Rahdert, "Of Impressionists and Rorschach Blots," *Columbia Law Review,* 86 (1986), 1283, 1286 (review of *Total Justice*).

14. Carol Gilligan, *In a Different Voice: Psychological Theory and Women's Development* (Cambridge, Mass.: Harvard University Press, 1982), pp. 22–23. Mary Ann Glendon turns the argument to a different end, when she suggests that the majority opinion in *Roe v. Wade* is "masculine" because of its "emphasis on the separateness, the rights, and the self-determination of individual women"; while the West German decision, which struck down easy abortion laws, "with its emphasis on responsibility for others, and on the social bonds of the community as well as individual rights, seems more reflective of what Gilligan and others have identified as feminine values." Mary Ann Glendon, *Abortion and Divorce in Western Law* (Cambridge, Mass.: Harvard University Press, 1987), p. 51. Few feminists, probably, would see the issue in these terms.

15. On this point, see Neil Vidmar and Regina A. Schuller, "Individual Differences and the Pursuit of Legal Rights: A Preliminary Inquiry," *Law and Human Behavior,* 11 (1987), 299.

16. See, for example, Julius Cohen, Reginald A. Robson, and Alan P. Bates, *Parental Authority: The Community and the Law* (Rutgers, N.J.: Rutgers University Press, 1958); Herbert McClosky and Alida Brill, *Dimensions of Tolerance: What Americans Believe about Civil Liberties* (New York: Russell Sage Foundation, 1983); William M. O'Barr and John M. Conley, "Lay Expectations of the Civil Justice System," *Law & Society Review,* 22 (1988), 137.

17. On this point see Lawrence M. Friedman, *The Legal System: A Social Science Perspective* (New York: Russell Sage Foundation, 1975), pp. 162–165.

18. On the situation in Australia see Jeffrey Fitzgerald, "Grievance, Disputes and Outcomes: A Comparison of Australia and the United States," *Law in Context,* 1 (1983), 15.

19. Herbert Kritzer, "Political Culture and the 'Propensity to Sue,' " paper

presented at a Conference on Theory and Methods of Longitudinal Court Studies, Buffalo, New York, August 23–27, 1987.

20. Laurent Cohen-Tanugi, *Le Droit sans l'état: Sur la démocratie en France et en Amérique* (Paris: Presses Universitaires de France, 1985); see also Robert A. Kagan, "What Makes Uncle Sammy Sue?", *Law & Society Review*, 21 (1988), 717, on the subject of differences in regulatory styles between the United States and England (and, to a degree, Europe); see also Keith Hawkins, "Law in a Secular Society," in *European Yearbook in the Sociology of Law* (1988), 263.

21. Glendon, *Abortion and Divorce*, p. 112.

22. See the perceptive essay by Alex Inkeles, "Continuity and Change in the American National Character," in *The Third Century: America as a Post-Industrial Society*, ed. Seymour Martin Lipset (Stanford, Calif.: Hoover Institution Press, 1979), p. 389.

23. Although Glendon's main thrust is on the differences between American and European abortion and divorce law, she notes that these fields of law have undergone "profound and rapid change in Western countries" since the late 1960s, and that "the direction of change was broadly similar everywhere: divorce and legal abortions became more readily available." Glendon, *Abortion and Divorce*, p. 112.

24. Even Albania and North Korea, probably as isolated as any countries today, are more exposed to world economic and social trends than, say, Nepal was a century ago, or for that matter most tribal societies at least until recently.

25. Alex Inkeles, *Exploring Individual Modernity* (New York: Columbia University Press, 1983), p. 321.

26. Alex Inkeles and David H. Smith, *Becoming Modern: Individual Change in Six Developing Countries* (Cambridge, Mass.: Harvard University Press, 1974).

27. Seymour Martin Lipset, "Predicting the Future of Post-Industrial Society: Can We Do It?", in *The Third Century*, pp. 2, 9–11.

28. Some "tribal identities" are more easily dropped than others, of course; racial identity is especially difficult because it is visible. But it is possible even for racial minorities, if suitably middle-class, to assimilate culturally and "pass" for culturally white in terms of behavior, speech, dress, and general outlook.

Appendix

1. E. Adamson Hoebel, *The Law of Primitive Man, A Study in Comparative Legal Dynamics* (Cambridge, Mass.: Harvard University Press, 1954), p. 28. Another noteworthy attempt at a universal, cross-culturally valid definition of law can be found in Leopold Pospisil's book, *Anthropology of Law: A Comparative Theory* (New York: Harper and Row, 1971).

Hoebel tells, for example, how the Eskimos handle the problem of a killer who threatens the safety of the community. Some "public-spirited" man makes up his mind to act; he talks to other "adult males of the community." If they agree that the killer should die, the "public-spirited" man then kills him. The dead man's relatives have no right to take revenge. This process, according to Hoebel's reasoning, is close enough to count as legal process or law.

2. The line between "law" and "society" is criticized as misleading by Robert

W. Gordon, "Critical Legal Histories," *Stanford Law Review*, 36 (1984), 57. But it is an important line in common consciousness.

3. Max Weber, *Economy and Society*, ed. G. Roth and C. Wittich (New York: Bedminster Press, 1968), vol. 1, pp. 56, 65; see also Donald Black, *The Behavior of Law* (New York: Academic Press, 1976), p. 2, defining law as "governmental social control," which means that "many societies have been anarchic, that is, without law."

4. The literature on informal behavior and discretion in administrative agencies is large. See Kenneth C. Davis, ed., *Discretionary Justice in Europe and America* (Urbana, Ill.: University of Illinois Press, 1976), for a cross-cultural sampling on the issue of discretion.

5. For studies of informal police practice, see Jerome Skolnick, *Justice without Trial: Law Enforcement in Democratic Society* (New York: J. Wiley, 1966); and Johannes Feest and Erhard Blankenburg, *Die Definitionsmacht der Polizei: Strategien der Strafverfolgung und soziale Selektion* (Düsseldorf: Bertelsmann Universitätsverlag, 1972). On informal systems of justice in general, see the essays collected in Richard L. Abel, ed., *The Politics of Informal Justice*, 2 vols. (New York: Academic Press, 1982).

6. Ann Swidler, *Organization without Authority* (Cambridge, Mass.: Harvard University Press, 1979), pp. 15–16.

7. "Power based on authority has two essential elements: a rightful or legitimate effort to exercise control on the one hand and an inner, moral compulsion to obey, by those who are to be controlled, on the other," Gresham Sykes, *The Society of Captives: A Study of a Maximum Security Prison* (Princeton, N.J.: Princeton University Press, 1958), p. 46.

8. Max Weber, *Max Weber on Law in Economy and Society*, ed. Max Rheinstein (Cambridge, Mass.: Harvard University Press, 1954), p. 336.

9. See Niklas Luhmann, *Legitimation durch Verfahren*, 2nd ed. (Darmstadt: H. Luchterhand, 1975); see also Klaus F. Röhl, *Rechtssoziologie, ein Lehrbuch* (Köln: Heymann, 1987), pp. 409–420.

10. A popular textbook by Rita L. Atkinson, Richard C. Atkinson, and Ernest Hilgard, *Introduction to Psychology*, 8th ed. (New York: Harcourt, Brace, Jovanovich, 1983), defines personality in terms of "individual differences"—"characteristic patterns of behavior and modes of thinking that determine a person's adjustment to the environment," p. 383.

11. Lawrence M. Friedman, *Total Justice* (New York: Russell Sage Foundation, 1985), p. 31.

12. Ibid., p. 32.

Index